Changing Britain,
Changing Lives

The Bedford Way Papers Series

Changing Britain,
Changing Lives

Three generations at the turn of the century

Edited by
Elsa Ferri, John Bynner and Michael Wadsworth

Bedford Way Papers

INSTITUTE OF
EDUCATION
UNIVERSITY OF LONDON

First published in 2003 by the Institute of Education, University of London,
20 Bedford Way, London WC1H 0AL
www.ioe.ac.uk

Pursuing Excellence in Education

British Library Cataloguing in Publication Data:
A catalogue record for this publication is available from the British Library

ISBN 0 85473 650 6

Design and typography by Joan Rose
Cover design by Andrew Chapman
Page make-up by Cambridge Photosetting Services, Cambridge

Production services by
Book Production Consultants plc, Cambridge

Printed by Watkiss Studios, Biggleswade, Beds

Contents

List of contributors

Mel Bartley
Department of Epidemiology and Public Health, Royal Free & University College London Medical School

Suzie Butterworth
MRC National Survey of Health and Development, Department of Epidemiology and Public Health, Royal Free & University College London Medical School

John Bynner
Centre for Longitudinal Studies, Bedford Group, Institute of Education, London

Lorraine Dearden
Institute for Fiscal Studies

Peter Dolton
Centre for Longitudinal Studies, Bedford Group, Institute of Education, London

Anna Ehlin
Enheten for Klinisk Epidemiologi, Stockholm

Elsa Ferri
Centre for Longitudinal Studies, Bedford Group, Institute of Education, London

Fernando Galinda-Rueda
Centre for Economics of Education, London School of Economics

Alissa Goodman
Institute for Fiscal Studies

Heather Joshi
Centre for Longitudinal Studies, Bedford Group, Institute of Education, London

Gerry Makepeace
Cardiff Business School

Scott Montgomery
Enheten for Klinisk Epidemiologi, Stockholm

List of contributors

Samantha Parsons
Centre for Longitudinal Studies, Bedford Group, Institute of Education, London

Phillippa Saunders
Institute for Fiscal Studies

Ingrid Schoon
Department of Psychology, City University

Kate Smith
Centre for Longitudinal Studies, Bedford Group, Institute of Education, London

Michael Wadsworth
MRC National Survey of Health and Development, Department of Epidemiology and Public Health, Royal Free & University College London Medical School

Laura Woods
Centre for Longitudinal Studies, Bedford Group, Institute of Education, London

Preface

In 1999–2000, for the first time ever, simultaneous follow-up surveys took place involving three of Britain's world-renowned national birth cohort studies. These are tracking the lives of large, representative samples of individuals born in 1946, 1958 and 1970, and the information amassed over the years forms an unrivalled data source for longitudinal research in the health and social sciences.

Our aim in producing this volume is to use the data collected at comparable ages to provide a commentary on the major changes that have occurred in British lives across the second half of the last century. The book will also serve as a prime sourcebook to publicise the new information resource created by the recent surveys, and to promote the use by the research community worldwide of these new sets of unique longitudinal data. The main target audience for the book is thus a broad academic community of policy makers, researchers, teachers and students, and general readers with an interest in social change.

Covering all the major life domains addressed by the cohort studies, the book reports on similarities and differences in the experiences of the birth cohorts as they reached their 30s and 40s. Comparisons *between* the different cohorts represent an increasingly interesting and important use of these datasets for both scientific and policy-related research. *Changing Britain, Changing Lives* is the first sourcebook to compare all three cohorts across the whole spectrum of the multidisciplinary information collected, and highlights some of the key longitudinal research issues which future research using the data can seek to address.

Acknowledgements

This book is a celebration of the many thousands of members of the British birth cohort studies who have supplied the information on which the book is based. Their patience and commitment in participating in the studies throughout their lives is greatly appreciated. Their life histories comprise the scientific treasure trove that the birth cohort studies represent.

The research we report would also not have been possible without the continuing support of funders, particularly the Economic and Social Research Council and the Medical Research Council and numerous government departments and agencies and charitable foundations. We are grateful to them, and to those involved in the book's production including on the editorial side Deborah Spring and Brigid Hamilton-Jones and in producing the text and graphics, Gina Clements, Jessica Henniker-Major, Kara Smith, and Jackie Goossens.

1 Changing Britain

Michael Wadsworth, Elsa Ferri and John Bynner

Almost every aspect of British society has changed greatly since the end of the Second World War. This book describes the effects of those changes during the last 50 years through the experience of individuals growing up at different times in this period. It provides a 'living history' of the last half of the twentieth century, and some indicators of the ways adult lives are developing as the new century begins.

In this chapter we outline the historical changes in the second half of the twentieth century that affected people's lives, and then give an overview of the three longitudinal studies that are the subject of this book. They are the first three British national birth cohort studies, which began at the birth of their subjects in 1946, 1958 and 1970 and continued into their adult lives. The studies provide a unique picture of how postwar changes affected the lives of the population. By concentrating on early adulthood, we show the different outcomes of childhood and adolescence begun at these three times, in terms of education, training and preparation for work, occupation, family life, income and living standards, housing, health, and sense of community and social participation.

Half a century of change

At the end of the Second World War, there was a prevailing optimism in Britain, not only because of victory and the return of peace, but also because of the hope for fundamental social change (Thomson 1981). Although the immediate postwar period was one of food and fuel shortages, during that time the newly elected Labour government laid the foundation for great social change, by implementing the 1944 Education Act, setting up the National Health Service in 1948, and introducing a wide range of other legislation aimed at bringing greater equity and opportunity (Marwick 1982). The rationale for these radical changes had been prepared during the war, particularly in the Beveridge report of 1942, which recommended a national social security system to cover all citizens, and to deal with what were described as the five giants of postwar reconstruction: want, sickness, squalor, ignorance and idleness, the latter two referring to the need for education and employment.

During the second half of the twentieth century, great changes occurred in the structure of the British population. The proportion of those in the UK aged 65 and over rose from 11 per cent in 1951 to 20 per cent in 2000. One-person households in England and Wales increased from 11 per cent in 1951 to 29 per cent in 2000. Two peaks of fertility, or 'baby booms', occurred: the first in 1946–8, and the second in the 1960s, reaching its peak in 1964. There were also two troughs in the birth rate, in 1977 and at the turn of the century. After the trickle of migrants arriving from the Caribbean, India, Pakistan and Bangladesh before the early 1950s, there was an increased flow, which peaked in the years 1965–74, before gradually declining. In the 1991 census, the total minority ethnic proportion of the population of Great Britain was 5.5 per cent (Peach *et al.* 2000).

Profound changes also took place in the way in which the country made and maintained its wealth. In 1951, most work was manual (64 per cent) and most workers were men (71 per cent); by 1991, only 38 per cent of the labour force was occupied in manual work and 43 per cent of those in work were women. These changes were brought about by the demands first of automation and then of computerisation and the growth of service industries. Those changes required new policies in education and training (Gallie 1988). The need for educational change had been recognised in the 1944 Education Act, which introduced selective entry to secondary schools as a way to identify children of high IQ, who were thought most capable of continuing their education up to university level. The increased demand for a labour force that had been educated for longer, and the rise in numbers of young people born in the 'baby boom' years, brought a period of great university expansion, with numbers of full-time students rising from 82,000 in 1954/5 to 1,182,000 in 1994/5 (Halsey 2000). In 1954,

6 per cent of the population of student age were in full-time higher education; by 1997 the forecast was 'that more than half of today's school leavers will experience higher education' (ibid.: 227).

Preparation for work

In the years after the Second World War, work was predominantly manual, and preparation to take up skilled manual occupations was often by apprenticeship. University places were few by comparison with today, and the majority of people simply began work and acquired skills 'on the job'. However the introduction first of automation at work, and then, in the 1970s, of information technology, required a smaller work force, and new kinds of preparation for work. In effect a de-skilling of the work force took place throughout this period, as the old craft skills were replaced by new, more readily learned and, in some respects, more transferable skills associated with the new methods of production and management (Ainley 1988; Coles and McDonald 1990). Manufacturing industry that did not invest in new production methods closed down, and apprenticeships were no longer offered, with a consequent loss of opportunity for young school leavers who had traditionally begun work in this way (Ashton and Maguire 1983; Banks *et al.* 1992).

Successive governments tried to manage these fundamental changes by expanding higher education (Halsey 2000), and by setting up initiatives to supply vocational preparation. For example, the Labour government of the 1970s established the Manpower Services Commission, and the Youth Opportunities Programme, largely to keep young people off the streets. This was transformed by the following Conservative administration, elected in 1979, into the New Training Initiative, which became the national Youth Training Scheme (YTS) in 1983. This was the first comprehensive programme targeted at early school leavers that combined education and work-based training for all (Department of Education and Science 1981).

The intention of the Youth Training Scheme was to keep young unemployed people occupied and to provide the means of re-skilling the labour force (CBI 1989). The Youth Training Scheme was expanded from one to two years (Department of Employment 1986) and was intended to replace apprenticeship entirely, but by the end of the 1980s was in decline. Ironically apprenticeship then re-emerged as the three year 'Modern Apprenticeship' (Department of Employment 1988). Now, all young people who leave school at 16 years and enter government-supported training do so via an apprenticeship.

Despite the initiatives to engage all young people in vocational preparation to acquire skills for employment, a proportion either failed to take advantage of these opportunities or soon dropped out of any scheme when a job was offered. This is part of a particularly British aspect of transition into the labour market, where the idea of vocational preparation as a preliminary to work, instead of full-time work itself, is not easily accepted or understood (Bynner and Roberts 1991; Evans and Heinz 1994). It is notable, for example, that it took ten years through the 1980s before the rates of staying on at school beyond 16 extended to 70 per cent, where they have remained ever since. In other words, even through the 1990s, almost one-third of young people were leaving school at the minimum age, and nearly half of those were leaving without qualifications. In the modern world of increasingly high-tech employment requiring multi-skilled individuals, this bottom 30 per cent became increasingly marginalised (Hutton 1995). It is this aspect of labour market change, more than anything else, that has fuelled current concerns about social exclusion (Atkinson and Hills 1998).

Family life
The changes in the labour market and their impact on employment and employability are paralleled by those in domestic life. One of the most striking changes across the period was in attitudes and behaviour relating to relationships and the postponement of the commitments involved in marriage and parenthood. At the beginning of the period, marriage was the norm. In 1941–5, 71 per cent of men and 68 per cent of women aged over 15 years were married. The comparable figures in 1991–5 were 36 per cent and 44 per cent (Coleman 2000). By the end of the century, cohabitation rather than marriage had become the most common form of

first partnership (Ermisch and Francesconi 2000). Relationships became increasingly fragile and impermanent, with divorce rates rising more than tenfold between 1941 and 1995, and especially steeply after the 1970 Divorce Law Reform Act. Linked to these trends, lone parents formed just 8 per cent of families in 1971, compared with 25 per cent in 1998 (Coleman and Schofield 2001). Re-partnership also became increasingly common. By the last decade of the twentieth century, it was estimated that one child in eight in Britain would experience life in a stepfamily by age 16 years (Haskey 1992).

Well into the 1980s, the typical age of marriage and having a first child was in the early 20s, but by the end of the century first births were typically to women in their late 20s. However, this shift in mean ages was concentrated in the more highly educated sections of the population, and therefore to a large extent was brought about by educational expansion. First births to the 1946 cohort were at youngest ages among those with no or low qualifications, and at progressively later ages as level of educational attainment rose (Kiernan and Diamond 1983). In the 1958 cohort study 47 per cent of women graduates had not had a first child by the time they reached 33 years (Bynner and Egerton 2001).

At the other end of the educational scale, the traditional patterns still held, with young women leaving school with minimum qualifications tending to settle early into partnerships and parenting (Hakim 1996). Such partnerships, in a context of rising expectations and occupational aspirations among women, make this group appear increasingly isolated (Kiernan 1995; Hobcraft 1998; Social Exclusion Unit 1999a, 1999b). While marriage and parenting are being postponed in all European countries, Britain is still exceptional in having one of the highest levels of teenage pregnancy in Western Europe (Utting 1995; Coleman and Schofield 2001).

Affluence and poverty
There is evidence of increasing polarisation of those with and those without qualifications in the later parts of the twentieth century. The higher premium based on qualifications for employment placed increasing pressure on young people to extend their education and to postpone

personal commitment. Those without the educational attainment became increasingly marginalised into low-level employment and early parenthood.

These effects on the most poorly educated were, in many respects, accentuated by the growing affluence of the majority of the population. During this same period, personal income, purchasing power, individual ownership of financial capital, and standards of living all rose. The proportion of owner-occupied housing increased from 31 per cent in 1951 to 67 per cent in 1991. The proportion of consumer expenditure spent on food for the household fell from 25 per cent in 1960 to 11 per cent in 1995 (Dilnot and Emmerson 2000). All the indicators of housing circumstances show improvements throughout the period (Holmans 2000). Health statistics also point to remarkable advances in the nation's health.

Set against these positive changes, the labour market problems referred to earlier greatly affected the lives of individuals. A long period of high unemployment began in the mid-1970s, rising to over three million out of work in the mid-1980s (higher even than the 2.5 million peak of the prewar Depression years), and not falling below 1.5 million until 1994. As Coleman (2000) notes, the problem of unemployment 'was not helped by the increase of 30 per cent in the annual supply of young people seeking jobs each year compared with the 1960s'. It was further exacerbated by the fact that in 2001 people from minority ethnic backgrounds were 'around twice as likely not to be in work as the white population' (Rowntree 2001).

The proportion of those in poverty due to unemployment and all other causes was therefore also remarkably high (Kumar 1993). Poverty was initially defined using National Assistance rates, which showed that, in the period of relatively low risk of unemployment after the Second World War and before the 1970s, only 3.8 per cent received the benefit (Abel-Smith and Townsend 1965). Later an index of *relative* poverty was used (Piachaud 1988), set in this instance as below 50 per cent of the mean of equivalent disposable household income. The proportion in poverty estimated in that way rose from 8 per cent in 1979 to about 20 per cent by the end of the 1990s (Atkinson 2000).

Such overall figures disguise the raised risk of poverty in particular groups in the population. It was estimated that during the 1990s approximately a third of children lived in poverty (Gregg *et al.* 1999). The risk of poverty among families of Pakistani and Bangladeshi origin was four times higher than the rate among whites (Berthoud 1998). The proportion of lone parents receiving social security benefits for two or more years rose from 41 per cent in 1970 to 67 per cent in 1997.

Health

Changes in physical health during the last half of the twentieth century were extensive. Better nutrition and housing contributed to these, as did improvements in health care. These changes may be exemplified by two sensitive indicators of health: infant mortality rates and life expectancy at birth. Infant mortality in England and Wales per 1000 live births declined from 56.0 in males and 44.0 in females in 1941–5, to 7.1 in males and 6.0 in females in 1991–5. Expected years of life at birth rose from 66.4 in males and 71.5 in females in 1950–2 to 74.1 in males and 79.4 in females in 1993–5 (Fitzpatrick and Chandola 2000). However, these improvements have not been equally accessible to all members of the population. The infant mortality rate per 1000 live births for babies born to married couples in England and Wales in 1994 was 4.6 in social class I compared with 6.3 in social class V. For babies born outside marriage the difference in the infant mortality rate was even greater, at 3.6 in social class I and 8.2 in social class V (Office of Population Censuses and Surveys 1995). The interpretation of changes in rates of mental and physical ill-health is more difficult, because definitions have changed, diagnostic tests have become more sensitive, and new methods of care and medication have been introduced.

Nevertheless, the risk of poor growth in childhood, the likelihood of illness at any age, and of premature death in adulthood all rise as socioeconomic circumstances decline (Marmot and Wilkinson 1999).

Health was also adversely affected during the second half of the twentieth century by the change in the nature of work from predominantly manual to predominantly sedentary, the perceived rise in demands on time, particularly among women who were mothers and workers outside the home, the increase in choice of foods, and the rise in intakes of sugar, alcohol and fat (Thurman and Witheridge 1994; Wald and Nicolaides-Bouman 1991). These adverse effects have been strongest among those in the most socially disadvantaged circumstances (Marmot and Wilkinson 1999). Health policies have had to be sensitive to the problems of providing free access to health care, and to the question of how to initiate effective programmes to promote self-care of health, through dietary awareness, exercise, not smoking, and not over-indulging in alcohol. Policy on recreational drug use proves equally difficult to develop.

Social participation and social exclusion
Thus, despite the generally increasing health, prosperity and freedoms, there were still signs in the 1990s of the old problems associated with unequal distribution of opportunity and good health. There was a continuing feeling of social divide between those who were socially integrated and able to participate in, and thrive on, the changes described above, and those who were socially excluded, through relatively poor socio-economic circumstances, insecurity of employment, and lack of access to opportunities in education and its consequent benefits (Atkinson and Hills 1998; Atkinson 2000). Such evidence of increasing polarisation was increased by another phenomenon attracting concern across the western world, that of declining support for political institutions and withdrawal from civic engagement (Bruhn and Wolf 1979; Putnam 2000; Baron *et al.* 2000). There has been universal decline during the last 50 years in such things as voting, church attendance, community activity, and trades union membership.

These signs of breakdown in social cohesion are most evident in the least advantaged and most socially excluded groups. One of the first actions the incoming Labour Government took in 1997 was to establish the Social Exclusion Unit, with the task of galvanising government departments into transforming what was often disparate and uncoordinated provision into a comprehensive strategy for social cohesion (Social Exclusion Unit 2001).

The targeting of poor neighbourhoods, as one of the major lines of this new strategy, underlined the point that social exclusion in the 1990s seemed a much more lonely circumstance than at earlier times. Solidarity in family, neighbourhood and class had declined (Stacey *et al.* 1975). Social cohesion and social capital seemed greatly reduced, not only in Britain but in many western urbanised countries. Hobsbawm (1995) describes how

> conscious working-class cohesiveness reached its peak, in older developed countries, at the end of the Second World War. During the golden decades [described in the same volume as 'the period of astonishing economic explosion' from 1947 to 1953] almost all elements of it were undermined. The combination of secular boom, full employment and a society of genuine mass consumption utterly transformed the lives of working-class people, and continued to transform them. ... Prosperity and privatization broke up what poverty and collectivity in the public place had welded together. (Hobsbawm 1995: 306–7)

The impact of such extensive change ripples through the population, affecting each age group differently, and its effect on the future lives of those it touches may well continue for many years.

A dominant theme in the work of social analysts in Britain and elsewhere in Europe has been that of risk. Beck (1986) coined the term 'Risk Society' to capture a world in which adult destinies, determined largely by family background, were giving way to individualised pathways to and through adulthood, characterised by uncertainty and risk.

For example, the increased risk of unemployment in the 1980s brought forward retirement for workers then in middle life. This changed the life chances and, no doubt, expectations of those in their 20s, and brought reduced socio-economic circumstances to children whose parent(s) experienced loss of employment. The resources that each age group brought to this crisis in their lives had been in many respects shaped by their educational experience and their opportunities to acquire income, wealth and health. Those opportunities were products of their time. In the 'late modern' world described by Giddens (1991), such eventualities are faced not only at the time of retirement, but throughout working life, requiring the development of new more flexible and 'reflexive' adult identities (Beck *et al.* 1994). The restructuring of industry driven by technological change, the globalisation of commerce and the labour market, and the modern industrial strategies of 'downsizing' and 'outsourcing' could face employees at any level in the occupational structure with continual uncertainty about their occupational futures. Nevertheless, the resources to cope with the new challenges are still unevenly distributed, with such social structural features of people's lives as gender, social class, ethnicity and geographical location, still exercising a remarkably strong influence. They not only set the boundaries for the pathways taken during the transition from school to work but through the course of adult life (Roberts *et al.* 1994; Furlong and Cartmel 1996; Bynner *et al.* 2000).

The British birth cohort studies

Our review of these great changes makes it clear that each generation growing up in the postwar years has a different legacy from the times of their formative years. Understanding of the ways these changes have impacted on adult life is still, however, remarkably sparse. We aim to go some of the way in this book to making good the deficiency, by drawing on the unique research resource of the British birth cohort studies.

Britain has four national birth cohort studies, which began at, or in one instance before, the birth of their participants. Each has continued to study the same people as they grow up. The first, the Medical Research Council (MRC) National Survey of Health and Development, began in 1946; the second, the National Child Development Study, in 1958; and the third, the 1970 British Cohort Study, another 12 years later, in 1970. There was then a 30-year gap until a fourth national cohort study was launched to mark the new Millennium (Smith and Joshi 2002).

This book is concerned with the first three studies. They each cover England, Wales and Scotland, and their populations represent the national population of the same age, being based on one week's births in the year in question. The first study followed up a third of the births in the selected week (5,362 children), and the two later studies followed up all the births in their chosen week, a total of 17,414 in the 1958 cohort and 17,198 in the 1970 cohort. Figure 1.1 shows the ages, from birth onwards, at which

Figure 1.1 *Birth cohort studies: age of members at surveys*

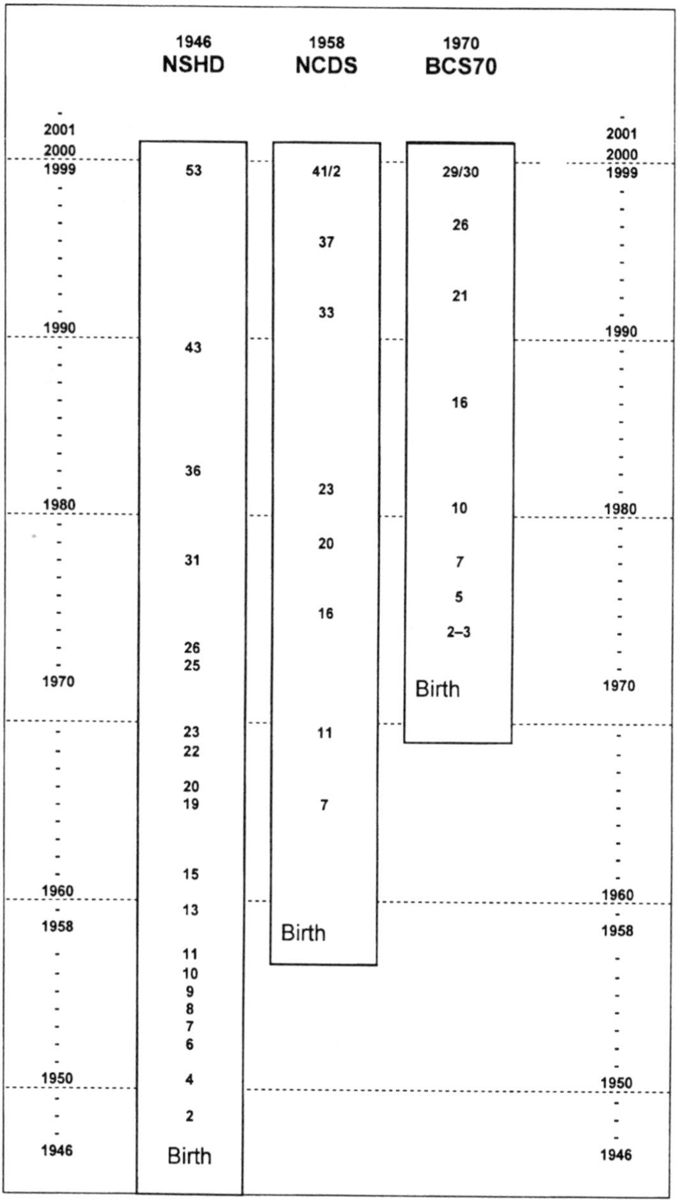

	1946 NSHD	1958 NCDS	1970 BCS70	
- 2001				- 2001
2000				2000
1999	53	41/2	29/30	1999
-			26	-
-		37		-
-				-
-			21	-
-		33		-
1990	43			1990
-				-
-			16	-
-				-
-	36			-
-		23		-
1980			10	1980
-	31	20	7	-
-			5	-
-		16	2–3	-
-	26			-
-	25			-
1970			Birth	1970
-	23	11		-
-	22			-
-	20			-
-	19	7		-
-				-
-	15			-
1960	13			1960
1958		Birth		1958
-	11			-
-	10			-
-	9			-
-	8			-
-	7			-
-	6			-
1950	4			1950
-				-
-	2			-
1946	Birth			1946

each cohort was surveyed. Details of each study's design and coverage are given in Appendix 1.

These investigations have incomparable value for the study of change over time in individuals. Each survey has collected detailed information in all the major life domains, including physical and mental health, intelligence and cognitive function, educational attainment, family and socio-economic circumstances, occupational history, parenting, and social attitudes.

Having these measures throughout childhood, adolescence and adult life provides an invaluable scientific resource:

- the study populations are large and representative, being selected solely by date of birth, which means that they have a high likelihood of providing a true prevalence of the factors measured

- information is collected currently, prospectively, or with a minimum degree of recollection, so that the chronological sequence of development, ageing and experience is known

- by beginning at birth, the studies provide the opportunity for research into how early life influences adulthood.

As the preceding pages have shown, these three studies represent populations born into very different British societies in terms of opportunities and policies in health, education and occupation, and in terms of social attitudes and values. The following chapters describe and compare findings from the three cohorts at approximately the same ages in early adulthood, and address questions about the differential impact of the changing social environment and policy context.

Table 1.1 shows the periods and corresponding life stages in each study during which data were collected and can be used for comparison. Three types of effects are highlighted; cohort effects, age effects, and period effects.

By comparing the three cohorts at the same or similar age we are able to show whether lives have differed at that age for people born at different times. This is called a *cohort effect*, and it gives the best picture of the

Table 1.1 *Periods and ages for data collection*

Age at data collection	1946 (N=5,362)	1958 (N= 17,414)	1970 (N=17,198)
birth	1946	1958	1970
1<5 years	1946–1951	1958–1963	1970–1975
6–16 years	1952–1962	1964–1974	1976–1986
early adulthood 17–30 years	1963–1976	1975–1988	1987–2000
early and middle adulthood 31–50 years	1977–1996	1989–2008	2001–2020
later middle adulthood 51–65 years	1997–2011	2009–2023	2021–2035
later life 66+	2012–	2024–	2036–

•————• Period covered by each study to date

impact of social change on the lives of cohort members. In Table 1.1 such a comparison (entering parenthood, for example) can be made for all three cohorts up to the early 30s, and for the two earlier cohorts up to the early 40s.

Age effects are of value in showing developmental changes with age that are common across cohorts or that differ between them. For example, we can compare the heights and weights of the 1958 cohort at ages 23, 33 and 42 years, and the same variables in the 1946 cohort at ages 26, 36 and 43 years.

The data for both these kinds of comparison were, of course, collected at different times, reflecting the third factor used in comparing cohorts born at different historical times, or periods, namely *period effects*. Here, the interest lies in whether the cohort members, at the different ages they have reached by the time of the survey, are showing similar responses compared with an earlier time. In other words the question is, is there evidence of a change impacting in much the same way on all of them?

Each of the following chapters focuses on one of the major life domains and compares the findings for all three cohorts at or around age 30, and for the two older cohorts (1946 and 1958) when they were in their early 40s.

The remainder of this chapter describes the origins and achievements of the studies, and illustrates their value, past, present and future, as resources for the investigation of human development, ageing, and social change.

How the cohort studies began

Each of the three British birth cohort studies was initially designed to address a policy question.

The first task of the 1946 study was to provide facts about the cost of childbearing, the care of mothers and babies at the time of birth, and the availability of specialist care at that time. The information was needed by the Royal Commission on Population, which sought to explain why national fertility rates had fallen consistently since the mid-nineteenth century. Planners of the National Health Service, which began two years later in 1948, also needed this data. The information was collected in a study of all the births that took place in one week in England, Wales and Scotland. It showed the high cost to manual workers' families of having a baby, the low likelihood of mothers receiving pain relief during labour and birth, and the wide social-class and regional differences in care, health and survival (Joint Committee 1948; Wadsworth 1991).

After a few years of the National Health Service, there was concern that the expected improvements in health were slow to become apparent, and that the cost was not, as expected, declining as the backlog of ill health in the poor was cleared up, but rather increasing. It was decided, therefore, to evaluate maternity care after ten years of the Health Service by undertaking, in 1958, a study of mothers and babies at birth that would be comparable with the 1946 study. The population was, again, all the births in one week in England, Wales and Scotland. The study showed that the social-class and regional differences in care, health and survival were still evident, despite the then free health care (Butler and Bonham 1963;

Butler and Alberman 1969). This finding had a profound effect on the subsequent care of mothers and babies.

The 1970 study was set up to measure the progress achieved by these changes in care, and was thus also designed as a study of all English, Welsh and Scottish births in one week. Findings showed that considerable improvements had taken place in health and survival over the period of 24 years covered by the three studies. Chamberlain *et al.* (1975) observed that in the 1946 investigation, 50 babies per 1000 mothers studied had been stillborn or had died in the first month of life; the comparable figures for the 1958 study were 39, and 25 in the 1970 cohort. However, the report of the 1970 study also concluded that 'There is nothing to contradict and everything to support the theory that social class differences (in perinatal mortality) are widening rather than diminishing' (Chamberlain *et al.* 1978).

How the studies continued: science and policy

The birth cohort studies became follow-up, or longitudinal, investigations because there were further national policy questions to be addressed and large-scale changes in society and in health to be understood. Findings from the cohort studies have contributed to debates and enquiries in a number of major policy areas that were dominant in the period between the end of the Second World War and the end of the twentieth century. These include education and equality of opportunity; poverty and social exclusion; gender differences in pay and employment; social class differences in health; changing family structure; and anti-social behaviour. In fact, if it had not been for the requirement of the influential Plowden Committee for evidence on children passing through primary school in the early 1960s, it is doubtful whether the 1958 Perinatal Mortality Survey would ever have transformed into a longitudinal study (Bynner *et al.* 1998). The cohort had reached the age of 7 at exactly the right time for the committee and a first follow-up survey of them was funded.

The three studies have also been concerned with new scientific approaches to the understanding of human development. The 57 years since the first study began has been a fast-changing time in all aspects of science. In the human sciences there has been continuing interest in how early life relates to adulthood, and how social context influences those relationships, and behaviour and attitudes. In health sciences, since the mid-1980s, there has been a rapid development of ideas about the relevance of health in early life to adult health. In a fortuitous fashion, not foreseen at the outset of these surveys, much of the information collected in early life for policy-related studies of health and education has become a source of robust data for testing hypotheses and for the development of new ideas in human biology.

The following sections of this chapter summarise contributions by these three national birth cohort studies to policy and science.

Educational policy and equality of opportunity
The 1944 Education Act introduced a means to raise the proportion of highly trained people in the country, in order to meet the changing needs of the economy for greater intellectual skill levels in an increasingly technological world. That requirement was to be satisfied by identifying the children most likely to benefit from further and higher education. Children were selected, by their scores in cognitive tests, for entry to academically inclined grammar schools at the age of 11 years; those not selected went to secondary modern or technical schools specialising in practical skills. The planned three-tier system was established only in a handful of Local Education Authority areas. There was much concern about whether such selection was fair and effective. Particularly, it was argued, there were differences in maturation rates, which disadvantaged slow maturing children; there was also the problem of equity arising through the dominance of family background factors in explaining the distribution of test scores. The Plowden Committee was therefore set up by the government to investigate the work of primary schools, for children aged 5 to 11 years, and the transition from primary to secondary school. It was hoped that this would show how the 'wastage of talent' could be stopped.

The first two cohorts were deeply involved in evaluating the practice of the 1944 Act's selection process. By measuring cognitive function at ages 8, 11 and 15, the 1946 study showed that by no means all the children with high scores on the tests went to grammar schools. Douglas (1964) showed that the origins of the problem were to be found in the pre-school and early primary school years, and highlighted the importance of parents' interest and involvement in their child's education. The 1946 study gave evidence to the Plowden Committee, and the 1958 study team (based in the newly established National Children's Bureau) undertook a survey that was published as part of the report (Plowden Report 1967). The findings from the 1958 study also showed the importance of the pre-school period in educational attainment in the primary school, and the power of parental interest and involvement (Pringle *et al.* 1966). The 1970 study, 17 years after the publication of the Plowden Report, also concluded that family life and pre-school experience were strongly influential in children's development (Osborn *et al.* 1984).

The experience of secondary school, and of higher and further education and training, were quite different for members of each cohort. The number of comprehensive schools increased, and the 1958 cohort provided an ideal source for the definitive study of their impact, since, by age 16, half were attending such schools and the other half were experiencing the old selective system (Steedman 1980).

Increased opportunities in post-school education (Halsey and Webb 2000) and the disappearance of traditional apprenticeship schemes meant that members of the 1970 cohort were more likely to stay on longer in education than their predecessors, and to have a much greater likelihood of qualification at university level (Bynner and Parsons 1997a). But, despite these changes in educational experience, the cohort studies have also shown that the adverse impact of poor attainment on adult life remains considerable. The effects on adults of inequality in terms of gender and of socio-economic circumstances in the family of origin were evident in all three studies. These effects were associated with highest qualifications attained, with the social class of cohort members' own occupation, with their earnings, and with the risk of unemployment (Wadsworth 1991; Kuh and Wadsworth 1991; Joshi and Hinde 1993; Joshi *et al.* 1995; Kuh *et al.* 1997; Bynner and Parsons 1997b; Joshi and Paci 1997; Bynner *et al.* 2000; Montgomery *et al.* 1996; Wadsworth *et al.* 1999; Schoon *et al.* 2002).

Cognitive and psychological development

The birth cohort studies have been greatly concerned with cognitive outcomes, originally in educational terms, as already described, but more
recently cognition has been studied in biological terms. Rodgers (1978)
showed in the 1946 study a positive effect on cognitive function at 8 and
15 years of exclusive breast-feeding for three months or more, and that
effect has been repeatedly shown elsewhere. Richards *et al.* (2001) showed
that birth weight was associated with cognitive test score at 8 years, such
that the higher the birth weight the higher the cognitive score, therefore
raising the possibility that lower birth weight may indicate less complete
cerebral development. Current studies in the 1946 cohort seek links between
these developmental aspects of cognition and adult measures of cognitive
function, particularly memory and its change with age. In the 1946 study,
the association of high cognitive scores with later experience of the
menopause suggests the influence of a biological factor common to both,
such as ovarian steroids (Richards *et al.* 1999).

The concepts of risk and protective processes for behavioural outcomes, and the notion of developmental vulnerability (Rutter 1991) have
been explored in the birth cohorts in relation to psychological outcomes.
Vulnerability to depression was shown in the 1946 study in women who
had childhood experience of parental separation and who had not themselves married, or who had married and then separated (Rodgers 1994).
On the other hand, marriage following childhood experience of separation had a protective effect (Rodgers 1994).

Researchers have also sought to find out whether there were critical
periods in childhood when children might be particularly vulnerable to
emotional disturbance, with greater likelihood of long-term or permanent
consequences. Some support for this notion of a high-risk period was
provided by studies in the 1946 cohort that showed childhood experience
of emotional disturbance (associated in this instance with hospital admissions of seven days or more, or repeated admissions, between the age of
6 months and 4 years) to increase the risk of poorer school performance
(Douglas 1975). Similarly, support for a vulnerable period hypothesis is
provided by the associations of parental separation with lower than expected

educational attainment (Wadsworth and Maclean 1986), and with a raised risk of delinquency and probable psychosomatic illness in early adulthood (Wadsworth 1979). It is not clear to what extent this apparent vulnerability may be the result of the emotional upheaval prior to the parental separation, or the separation itself. The socio-economic changes that usually happen at the same time, the consequent change of schools that many experience, or familial similarities in coping styles may all also be implicated. The power of emotional upheaval in the family was made clear in a study of the 1958 cohort, which showed that poor parental relationships among those who did not separate were also associated with a similar range of adverse outcomes (Kiernan 1997a).

Health and growth

A particular strength of the three cohorts lies in their unique ability to show links between early growth and development, and adult health and ill health.

All three studies focused in their early years on health and growth in childhood. In their analysis of 1946 cohort data, Douglas and Blomfield (1958) found that growth and physical development were slower in children in poor home circumstances. Their study of infant health showed that health visitors (community nurses) had a vital role to play in educating parents about health and nutrition, particularly breast-feeding, especially so among the most disadvantaged families, whose children were least likely to be taken to infant welfare clinics. These findings helped to make the case for continuing health visitor care of infants, which some had argued was no longer necessary (Wadsworth 1991). The 1958 study also found that children living in poor socio-economic circumstances and in large families were least often seen at preventive health clinics, and they were found at age 7 years to be at greater risk of poor speech, physical coordination and bladder control (Davie *et al.* 1972). Each cohort has published studies of the use of health services (Calnan *et al.* 1978; Wadsworth *et al.* 1993; Kuh *et al.* 2000), and of the incidence and care of disability (Pearson and Peckham 1977; Walker 1980; Kuh *et al.* 1994).

Comparisons between the birth cohorts have provided a source of information on changing prevalence of health conditions, for example of childhood obesity (Peckham *et al.* 1982), diabetes (Stewart-Brown *et al.* 1983), eczema (Taylor *et al.* 1984), undescended testis (Chilvers *et al.* 1984), and changes in height (Kuh *et al.* 1991). The studies have also been useful in the development of ideas about what may impede growth, and about how that process affects health. For example, the adverse effect of smoking during pregnancy on birth weight was first shown in the 1958 cohort (Butler *et al.* 1971), and the experience of stress associated with illness and with parental separation has been shown to be associated with slow growth in childhood in both the 1946 and the 1958 studies (Wadsworth 1986; Montgomery *et al.* 1997; Wadsworth *et al.* 2002).

The studies measured behavioural and psychological problems in childhood and adolescence, and those measures have been explored as possible precursors of adult mental health (van Os and Jones 1999; Maughan and Taylor 2001; Paykel *et al.* 2001), accidental death and suicide (Neeleman *et al.* 1998), and physical symptoms with no apparent cause (Hotopf *et al.* 1999; Hotopf *et al.* 2000).

The long reach of poor home circumstances in childhood has been evident among all three cohorts, in terms of the risk of adult morbidity and mortality (Wadsworth 1991; Power and Bartley 1993; Wadsworth 1997; Power and Hertzman 1997; Montgomery and Schoon 1997). There is also an indication that depression in young adulthood was of higher prevalence in the 1970 cohort than among those born in 1958 (Montgomery and Schoon 1997).

Data from these three national birth cohort studies have provided a test bed for the biological programming hypotheses (Barker 1991; Barker 1998), which suggest that many key aspects of physical development take place in the prenatal and early postnatal period of life. So, for example, the essential development of the brain and the cardiovascular and respiratory systems are thought to be almost entirely complete before birth. The birth cohorts have contributed to the increasing evidence in support of these hypotheses. For example, the 1946 and 1958 cohorts have demonstrated links between growth before, and soon after, birth with aspects of health in adulthood, including blood pressure, body mass, respiratory and cognitive function, schizophrenia, breast cancer and premature death (Wadsworth *et al.* 1985; Mann *et al.* 1992; Jones *et al.* 1994; Hardy *et al.* 2000; Power and Li 2000; Richards *et al.* 2001; De Stavola *et al.* 2000).

Using the cohort study data, models have been developed of the pathways from early life risk to adult health (Power and Hertzman 1997; Kuh and Ben Shlomo 1997). One notion is that risk pathways develop as the individual ages, because the adverse socio-economic circumstances associated with poor early life growth are also risk factors for other outcomes, such as low educational attainment. These are in turn risks for health-damaging behaviour such as smoking and the risks associated with obesity (Mann *et al.* 1992; Power and Hertzman 1997). In mental health, the pathway of risk postulated is a cascade, beginning with evident, but small, differences in behaviour that result from developmental delay, which lead in turn to a degree of social isolation, and to insecurity in social situations (Jones *et al.* 1994).

Accumulation of risk and the interaction of risk factors from childhood and adulthood are the most frequently demonstrated processes in the studies referred to. However, they also make it clear that while the idea of biological programming seems well supported, it is not a deterministic process at the beginning of life from which there is no escape.

All three cohort studies provided evidence to the government inquiry that reviewed the evidence for social inequalities in health, and made recommendations for future policy (Acheson 1998). The cohorts' particular contribution to the debate about social inequalities in health lies in their demonstration that the origins of such inequality lie substantially in childhood and the opportunities for education (Power *et al.* 1991; Kuh and Ben Shlomo 1997).

Other policy-related research that uses data from the national birth cohort studies has investigated the links between unemployment and health. This has shown that the risk of unemployment was higher for those with poor educational attainment, from disadvantaged socio-economic circumstances, and of short stature in childhood (Montgomery *et al.*

1996). Unemployment also presents a risk to mental and physical health. Montgomery *et al.* (1998) showed that prolonged unemployment was associated with a raised risk of smoking, problem drinking, and signs of anxiety and depression. Another study showed that the longer-term unemployed scored significantly lower than others on indicators of future potential in health and economic terms (Wadsworth *et al.* 1999).

Cohort data are now beginning to inform studies of the processes of ageing, by repeated measures of physical and cognitive function and disability during middle life, as well as through the study of morbidity and mortality, and the collection of sources of DNA. The birth cohorts will be able to show the extent to which the processes and rates of ageing are driven by socio-economic and biological factors occurring earlier in life, as well as by the adult context of life, in comparison with genetic factors, and will provide a source of information about the midlife health of future generations of the elderly.

Poverty, social disadvantage and social exclusion
Poverty has continued to be a problem that is all too evident in each of the cohort studies, and throughout the period that they cover. All three show poverty to be seriously damaging to health in childhood and adult life, to be a risk to literacy and educational attainment, and, furthermore, to carry a risk for economic hardship to be repeated in the following generation. It is also clear that these effects, for example on educational attainment, are sustained in the most recent cohort (Bynner and Joshi 2002).

Poor home circumstances in childhood and low educational attainment have been shown in each of the three cohorts to be risks for elements of social exclusion in adult life, and a particular concern for each study was to explain how this came about. Douglas observed in the 1946 cohort what has increasingly come to be known as a self-fulfilling prophecy:

> Children who come from well-kept homes and who are themselves clean and well shod, stand a greater chance of being put in the upper streams than their measured ability would seem to justify. Once there they are likely to stay and to improve in performance in succeeding

years. This is in striking contrast to the deterioration noticed in those children of similar initial measured ability who were placed in the lower streams. In this way the validity of the initial selection appears to be confirmed by the subsequent performance of the children, and an element of rigidity is introduced early into the primary school system.

(Douglas 1964: 118)

All three cohort studies have been used to investigate resilience to poor socio-economic circumstances and escape from disadvantage (Essen and Wedge 1982; Osborn 1990; Kuh and Wadsworth 1993; Schoon 2001; Schoon *et al.* 2002). Two investigations based on the 1958 cohort asked why, among all those who had experienced disadvantage in childhood, a proportion apparently escaped its effects. The first (Essen and Wedge 1978) was in response to a contemporary government policy initiative seeking to break a perceived cycle of disadvantage in families across generations. That study showed educational attainment to be the key to escape from disadvantage, although this was hard to achieve in homes that offered 'a prescription for low achieving, poorly behaved, disenchanted or alienated young people'. Pilling (1990) revisited this question when members of the 1958 cohort were aged 27 years. Comparing samples of those who had or had not escaped from poverty, she found that success was associated with strong family cohesion, high parental aspirations and interest in their child's educational progress, together with teachers' strong commitment to the child's educational attainment.

A recent phenomenon of much concern to government has been the sizeable minority of young people who leave education at the minimum age without qualifications and then spend a substantial period of their late teens not in education, employment or training. Using 1970 cohort study data, Bynner and Parsons (2002) were able to show, in research carried out for the Social Exclusion Unit, that such experience had lasting negative consequences for later labour market engagement for young men, and a high risk of early pregnancy and psychological damage for young women. Poor basic skills often accompany these incomplete transitions from school to work, adding to the pressures towards social exclusion in later life that these young people experience (Bynner and Parsons 2001).

Bynner (2001a), summarising the more recent evidence, concluded that policy to reverse the social exclusion process can begin at any age, but prevention ideally should begin in the pre-school years and be developed through links between the home and the school, in order to encourage a positive set of relationships around developmental processes and remove obstacles to the acquisition of capabilities.

Other social problems and social change
After the Second World War, when the National Health Service was established, the basis for future national prosperity was being developed, and current spending power and home ownership were both increasing, the widespread rise in such social problems as anti-social behaviour and delinquency caused surprise and incomprehension, particularly in the light of contemporary increases in earnings and purchasing power (Marwick 1982; Hood and Roddam 2000).

The 1946 study showed that children with behaviour problems at 13 and 15 years had been poor scholars at the age of 8, and were more likely than others to leave school as soon as possible (Douglas *et al.* 1968). Delinquency in that cohort was associated with parental separation and with low parental interest in the study member's education (Wadsworth 1979). Lambert *et al.* (1977) studied the behaviour of children in the 1958 cohort who had been in care, and studies of truancy and its causes and effects were also carried out using data from that cohort (Fogelman 1983).

Changing patterns of family formation and dissolution were also perceived as a social problem in the latter half of the twentieth century. The 1946 study coincided with a postwar boom in divorce and separation, and there was great public concern about the effects of this experience on children. Studies in that cohort showed that parental separation, much more than parental death, adversely affected children's educational attainment (Wadsworth *et al.* 1990). The effects of growing up in a one-parent family were extensively studied in the 1958 and the 1970 cohorts (Ferri 1976; Ferri and Robinson 1976; Osborn *et al.* 1984; Golding 1989), and all three studies gave evidence to the Finer Committee on One-Parent

Families (Department of Health and Social Security 1974). A comparison of the effects of parental separation on children's education showed a similar effect size in all three cohorts (Ely *et al.* 1999a), which, in view of the greatly increased risk of experience of parental separation, is a matter for concern. At the same time, it has been pointed out that the average difference in attainment between children from intact and lone-parent families was relatively small, and that only a minority of those from homes in which one parent was absent were found to have developmental problems (Ferri 1976).

The experience of parental separation has also been shown to be associated with risks to mental and physical health in the adult life of members of the first two cohorts (Wadsworth *et al.* 1990; Rodgers 1994), and with risk of separation in the cohort members' own generation (Kiernan 1997a). A comparison of teenage motherhood among the members of the 1946 and 1958 cohorts showed an association with behavioural, but not emotional, problems in the school years, and also the adverse effect of such early maternity in later adult partnership breakdown, and poor housing (Maughan and Lindelow 1997).

The individual and society

The profound changes in the economy, the labour market and the provision of educational opportunities during the years following the end of the Second World War brought a new social mobility to British society and, for many families, a potential to divide generations.

Contemporary social scientists were concerned to assess whether this change in the social structure would broaden access to opportunities for educational attainment. Glass wrote that 'if we are an affluent society, what better use could be made of part of our affluence – as well as part of our extended expectation of life – than in supplying the foundations for a more instructed citizenship' (Glass 1964: xxv). There was growing interest in such concepts as 'meritocracy', and whether they are any more than a way of justifying existing inequalities. In all three cohorts, studies of education and occupation show that the influence of socio-economic circumstances of the family of origin and the influence of gender have continued to exert unequal pressures on opportunities in the labour market and on income (Joshi and Hinde 1993; Joshi and Paci 1997; Joshi and Paci 1998; Bynner *et al.* 2000; Bynner and Joshi 2002; Bynner *et al.* 2002; Kuh and Wadsworth 1991; Kuh *et al.* 1997; Makepeace *et al.* 1999). Now that women in the 1946 cohort have completed childbearing, it will be possible to see whether currently improved occupational opportunities and expanded 'lifelong learning' opportunities are differentially taken up. Take-up is of interest not only in relation to educational qualifications but also to cognitive function, since this is the cohort with the highest proportion of unqualified women with high measured IQ.

Social capital has been studied in terms both of the development in the individual of socially and culturally valuable capital, as well as the identification of social circumstances that are rich in social capital. The birth cohorts have mostly studied the development of individual capital, through family circumstances, child-rearing practices and educational attainment, and these notions have been tested in relation to such end points as income (Kuh and Wadsworth 1991; Kuh *et al.* 1997), occupation (Bynner *et al.* 1997), voting and religious affiliations (Wadsworth and Freeman 1983) and social participation (Wadsworth 1991). The potential for the loss of individual capital through the experience of unemployment early in working life was shown in the 1958 cohort. Men who experienced three months or more of unemployment by age 26 years scored significantly lower than others on an indicator of social capital at age 30 years (Wadsworth *et al.* 1999).

Cohort members in each study have lived through times of considerable social change. Social attitudes to health-related behaviour changed greatly during the period of these investigations. Smoking, for example, has gone from acceptance to unacceptance, and exercise has become fashionable. Using Giddens's (1984) ideas of structuration and self-identity, Schooling and Wadsworth (forthcoming) created typologies of engagement in the social context. These were found to be associated with engagement in health-associated behaviour, even as the public image of the behaviour changed. For example, those characterised as conformist tended to conform to the prevailing 'good' image, so that when smoking was acceptable they were inclined to smoke, and when it was not acceptable they were inclined not to smoke.

For social scientists, the usual approaches of health and psychological studies too often omit important aspects of their subjects' experience, by using such portmanteau classifications as social class, and ignoring social and historical context. The effect of not taking analysis much beyond social class variation is to be blind to the question of what aspects of social context might be linked to the observed association.

The birth cohort studies, however, have a wide range of data on social context, and so unpacking such compressed descriptions as social class features in many analyses. For example, in all three studies, the social context of school was described in terms of class size and organisation, examination success rate and similar measures, and also in terms of the cohort child's relationships and behaviour in school. In addition, teachers made assessments of parental interest in their child's education, and of the child's behaviour and temperament as observed at school. These assessments gave some indication both of home–school relations and the teacher's expectation for the child. They have also been good indicators of how the individual reacts to other social contexts in adulthood, for example in terms of mental health in relation to adverse life events (van Os and Jones 1999). They were not, however, so good at identifying potential reading problems and especially mathematics problems (Parsons and Bynner 1998).

In recent years there has been increasing recognition of the power of these unique research resources for policy purposes, through the use of statistical modelling of life-course processes and their outcomes. The power of these large sets of data (approximately 13,000 variables in the 1946 study, and 16,000 in each of the two later studies) on representative populations can be used to explore the origins of adult outcomes. For example, econometricians have used the cohorts' data to study the economic and social returns to educational experience and different kinds of qualifications (e.g., Gregg *et al.* 1999; Blundell *et al.* 1997).

Conclusion

This introduction to the work of the first three of Britain's national birth cohort studies gives some idea of the extensive range of topics that they have addressed. The long-term plan is to continue collecting information from the members of all three cohorts, in order to produce comprehensive life histories of these large representative samples. Their continuing value is in the opportunities for studying the impact of early life and the developing years on the mental, social and physical processes of adulthood in its middle and later phases, taking account of factors from all stages of life.

The following chapters continue the themes outlined above. The focus of the new analyses presented in this book is a comparison of findings from the three studies, using information collected in early to middle adult life. The differences between the cohorts are seen as outcomes of differences in earlier life circumstances and influences, and indicators of the success or otherwise of policy applications, in relation to education and the labour market (Chapter 2), the world of paid work (Chapter 3), partnerships and parenthood (Chapter 4), family life (Chapter 5), income (Chapter 6), housing (Chapter 7), health (Chapter 8), lifestyle and health-related behaviour (Chapter 9), and social participation, values and crime (Chapter 10).

The differences between the cohorts reported in the following chapters show how much variation there will be in the future between generations of the elderly, and how much we need now to plan for the effects of those differences.

2 From school to the labour market

Gerry Makepeace, Peter Dolton, Laura Woods, Heather Joshi and Fernando Galinda-Rueda

Introduction

We start the story of the three birth cohorts as they embark on adult life with their educational attainments and their entry into the labour market. We begin by describing the changing opportunities and hurdles that each cohort faced, placing educational attainments in the context of home and social backgrounds.

A major policy objective in education during the postwar period was to improve access to formal schooling and improve the training of young people. The first theme of the chapter investigates the impact of these changes on the activities and achievements of the cohort members. We illustrate the extent to which participation in full-time education has increased over time and describe how performance has improved. We find, for example, that the proportion obtaining the highest grades of qualification (whether through academic or vocational routes) more than doubled from 16 per cent of the 1946 cohort to 36 per cent of the 1970 cohort. The intervening figure was 26 per cent for the 1958 cohort. Home background is correlated with qualification level and it appears that the gap in achievement between those from the most and least privileged backgrounds may not have narrowed, despite the overall improvement in performance. Learning is a continuous process and large numbers of the 1958 cohort achieved new qualifications between 23 and 33 and between 33 and 42, although this typically did not raise the highest level of qualification.

Although the long-term objective has been to improve the competitiveness of the British economy by increasing the depth and breadth of training, there have been tensions in defining the best approach. Two recurrent issues related to increasing the skills of young people who would have traditionally left full-time education at the earliest opportunity, and improving the quality of vocational learning. The original grammar school system distinguished academic from vocational schooling, but valued academic education more highly. Although comprehensive schools may have reduced stigmatism and wasted talent among late developers, they did not raise the profile of vocational training. Within the time span covered by our cohorts, the government had become actively involved in vocational training. Major policy changes such as the development of a national classification for qualifications demonstrate the significance of this issue, while more recent proposals, such as work-orientated schooling beginning prior to 16, and the introduction of educational allowances for 16–18-year-olds, illustrate the continued importance of this topic.

A second major theme of the chapter is the school-to-work transition and the early years spent in the labour market. We summarise data showing the economic status of members of the 1958 and 1970 cohorts for each month between the ages of 16 and 30. The pathway into work from education is broadly similar for the men in the two cohorts over this period, though more men are in full-time education and fewer in work at each point in time in the 1970 cohort. A major difference is that large numbers of young men in the 1970 cohort were on government training schemes between the ages of 16 and 18. Overall, men decreased in the proportion of time spent in full-time employment from 85 per cent to 78 per cent, much of which was accounted for by increases in the time spent in full-time education and on government training schemes. Although the magnitude of the change was similar for women, the way time was re-allocated was different. The time spent out of the labour force (because of family responsibilities) fell from 21 per cent to 14 per cent. In net terms, almost all of this decrease was accounted for by increases in full-time education and part-time employment and, indeed, the proportions in these two states was higher at each age for the 1970 cohort, but the pattern of full-time work has changed. Women in the 1970 cohort were less likely than the 1958 cohort to be in full-time work *before* the age of 23, but more likely to be thereafter. We also classify the employment and unemployment histories of the 1958 and 1970 cohorts, showing *inter alia* that the incidence of the most severe type of unemployment spells may have increased over time.

Each cohort has experienced markedly different economic, social and political conditions that have affected their labour market outcomes. One clear factor is the emerging participation of women. They have typically improved their levels of qualifications more than men. For example, the proportion of women achieving the highest qualification levels was under half that of men in the 1946 cohort, either in their early 30s or 40s. The women in the 1970 cohort bettered the performance of men at age 30, while the women in the 1958 cohort matched that of men at age 42.

Perhaps the most dramatic example of changing economic conditions is the large-scale unemployment of the early 1980s that impacted heavily on the 1970 cohort and, indeed, acted as stimulus for changes in the structure of vocational training. The 1958 cohort initially experienced a favourable labour market, but faced worse conditions as they got older, whereas the opposite was true of those born in 1970. The 1958 cohort encountered a buoyant labour market when they left school, but were hit by the 1981 recession when they were 23. The peak experience of unemployment for men in August of 1981 accounted for 9 per cent of the cohort, and unemployment for men in their late 20s was almost as high as it had been in their late teens. Women's unemployment was about the same as men's in the early years, but from the mid-20s onwards fewer reported themselves to have been seeking work, as more of them left the labour force.

Male unemployment rates for the 1970 cohort were of the same order of magnitude as earlier cohorts but this ignores the large numbers on government training schemes. During the winter of 1986–7, the unemployment rate among men was about 2.6 per cent and the proportion on training schemes was over four times greater at about 12 per cent. The proportion on training schemes fell continuously until it fell below the unemployment rate of 3.5 per cent in October 1988. It continued to fall thereafter, but was still as much as 1 per cent in October 1990. A similar pattern emerges for women. The proportions unemployed and on training

schemes were about 2.2 per cent and 9.2 per cent during the winter of
1986–7. Equality in the proportions unemployed and in training occurred
in October 1988 (2.1 per cent in each) and 1 per cent of women were still
on training schemes in April 1990.

For the 1970 cohort, counting experience in a government training
scheme as on a par with unemployment, it appears that the most acute
period of being involuntarily out of work was in their teenage years.
Many of the potentially unemployed in 1986 who were not diverted onto
training schemes may have stayed on longer at school. The 1970 cohort
missed the peak unemployment of 1981, as they were still at school, and
from age 23 the men experienced falling unemployment along with the
rest of the labour force in the mid-1990s. Recorded unemployment for
women in the 1970 cohort (apart from government training) was low
throughout.

The changing structure of schooling
The parents of children born in 1946 had left school before the 1944
Education Act. Most of them (70 per cent of the mothers and 66 per cent
of fathers) had only attended elementary school, leaving at or before 14
and few (under 3 per cent of fathers and half as many mothers) attained
tertiary qualifications. By contrast, most of the parents of the cohort born
in 1958 had benefited from the expansion of secondary state schooling.
This system was selective in nature, allocating children to grammar and
other secondary schools, and was compulsory to age 15. One in five of the
cohort's fathers and one in four of their mothers stayed on in education
beyond 15. The parents of the 1970 cohort were educated under the same
regime, but the expansion of educational opportunity meant that 38 per
cent of them stayed on at school beyond 15. The trend towards later
school leaving continued and, as we illustrate below, the cohort members
themselves also experienced increasing access to formal schooling in the
postwar era.

Most members of the 1946 cohort passed through a tripartite system
comprising grammar schools, secondary modern schools and a smaller
number of technical schools. Pupils attended schools that reflected their

capabilities as measured by their performance in a public examination at 11. In principle, grammar schools would have provided an academic education, while the remaining schools would have had a more vocational emphasis. The most controversial development in the educational system was the move from this system of secondary schooling, based on selection, to the more inclusive comprehensive system which began during the 1960s and took root the early 1970s. The aim was to create schools attended by pupils of all abilities, facilitating changes in the type and scope of education offered to individuals after the age of 11. This affected the three cohorts in different ways. Most members of the 1946 cohort passed through the tripartite system, while those born in 1970 predominantly experienced the new comprehensive schools. The system was in a state of change for the 1958 cohort, with members attending all types of school depending on where they lived. (This brief review is not exhaustive, since cohort members attended other types of school such as independent schools and special schools, and a slightly different system existed in Scotland. Many qualifications were also obtained after school at colleges.)

The 1958 cohort was the first group of pupils affected by the increase in the school leaving age to 16 in 1974 (although transitional arrangements meant that some could leave at 15). The large expansion of the university system that took place in the late 1960s, following the Robbins Report, arrived slightly too late to have a major impact on the 1946 cohort, although members of 1958 and 1970 cohorts benefited considerably. Similarly, our cohorts will only have been affected by the more recent changes indirectly, if they took qualifications as mature students. More recently, there have been attempts to control the content and quality of education, but innovations such as the introduction of the National Curriculum and active monitoring of school performance, will not have been significant for the education of our cohorts.

Changes in the home background

The title of a renowned early book from the 1946 study (Douglas 1964) indicated that the home, as well as the school, is a vital influence on life chances. This is a complex matter and for this chapter we look very simply at the influence of family of origin on attainment by examining just one measure, the social class of occupation of the cohort members' fathers. During the last half century, the number of men classified as manual workers has decreased dramatically. In 1950, three-quarters of the children born in 1946 had fathers in manual occupations, compared to under a half of those in the two later cohorts. There was also a striking increase in the number of mothers in paid work, but precisely because only a few in the earlier cohorts had mothers reporting occupations (as well as the problems with interpreting those occupations that are recorded) no attempt has been made to incorporate such information at this stage. In general, fathers were the major earners and their occupations dominated the family lifestyles. Thus, this chapter provides only a preliminary investigation of how far class of origin and education compensate, or compound, advantage and disadvantage.

Changes in vocational training

Changes in vocational training made the school-to-work transition experienced by the three birth cohorts very different. Vocational training had been, traditionally, in the hands of employers. Apprenticeships were the flagship of the system for craft workers, although other school leavers received structured training leading to well-paid white-collar jobs: for instance, in banks and local and central government. Apprenticeships were typically five to seven years long and served by the individual with a single employer. This system operated largely unhindered until the early 1960s and would have attracted large numbers of school leavers in the 1946 cohort. In 1964, the Industrial Training Act set up a national system of Industrial Training Boards (ITBs) that had the responsibility of improving the quantity and quality of training within their industry. These had the power to give grants and levy charges on firms according to whether they were training their young employees appropriately or not. The idea was to reward the companies who were training properly and penalise those who either trained badly, or relied only on 'poaching' trained workers from other employers. This system of apprenticeships operated during the time that the 1958 cohort were leaving school. At the end of the

1970s, a substantial minority of youngsters worked as apprentices. The traditional apprenticeship was already in decline during this period.

The main feature of this system of vocational training was the lack of direct government involvement. This changed remarkably during the early 1980s, as youth unemployment rose to dramatically high levels and the government responded with a series of initiatives that represented a direct commitment to training (Gallie 1988; Banks *et al.* 1992).

Over the 1973–9 period there was a variety of special employment measures that attempted to introduce training for young people and foster retraining amongst the long-term unemployed, for example, the Training Opportunities Programme (TOPS). The most radical departure came in 1978, with the setting up of the Youth Opportunity Programme (YOP). This established the principle that all those between the ages of 16 and 18 who had left school, were not in full-time education and were unable to get a job, should have the opportunity of training or participating in a government-funded programme. This scheme was extended with the setting up of the Youth Training Scheme (YTS) in 1983. It started as a one-year, low-level training scheme, but gradually changed its nature and became a two-year scheme. By the time school leavers from the 1970 cohort entered the labour market in 1986, most of them would have been eligible for the two-year extended version of the YTS scheme. However, it is by no means certain that each young person from this cohort would have stayed on the scheme for the full two years. In practice, the scheme was perceived as being a low-status alternative to unemployment and hence many young people exited the programme as soon as a more attractive alternative presented itself.

These changes in the training opportunities of young people in the three cohorts were mirrored in their risk of unemployment. The transition from school to work for young people in the 1980s became more difficult than at any time in postwar Britain. This period saw youth unemployment (not including training schemes) rise from 10 per cent in 1978 to 27 per cent by 1984, back down to 10 per cent in 1989 and rising to 21 per cent by 1992. Manufacturing industry was a mainstay of the apprenticeship system, so its decline in the 1980s saw the numbers entering manufacturing apprenticeships fall from 290,000 in 1975 to 45,000 by 1996. In contrast, numbers on the new YTS averaged 400,000 over the 1983 to 1989 period. However, it would be wrong to imagine that the vocational training experienced by the young people in the 1946 cohort was adequately replaced by the state-funded training alternative experienced by the 1970 cohort. The latter provided much less systematic training and for quite a different client group than the former – namely those with few qualifications and poor prospects on the labour market. It was widely felt that the early versions of these schemes, especially YOPs, but including YTS, were merely alternatives to unemployment rather than real vocational preparation on continental lines (Bynner and Roberts 1991; Dolton 1993).

Entry into the labour market
The 1946 cohort members would have experienced the high levels of employment and low inflation rates typical of the early postwar era. There was a belief in the active management of the economy (in particular to keep the rate of unemployment low), pride in the achievements of the welfare state, and support for the operation of many large industries by the public sector. Economic conditions were much changed by the time the 1958 cohort entered the labour market in the mid-1970s. Although most school leavers found jobs, inflation rates were extraordinarily high and unemployment rose remorselessly from the late 1970s onwards, repeatedly reaching new postwar highs. Equal pay legislation and incomes policies demonstrated the continued commitment to intervention in the labour market, but the consensus was breaking up, with widespread concerns over, *inter alia*, the role of unions and levels of public expenditure.

The 1970 cohort came on to the employment market in the mid-1980s, when unemployment had risen dramatically, with devastating consequences for youth labour markets (Banks *et al.* 1992). The reforming government of Margaret Thatcher had been in power since 1979 and had started to alter the economic landscape, by avoiding active demand management and removing barriers to competition. However, it did, paradoxically, significantly expand the government's role in the youth labour market.

The minimum-age school leavers in the three cohorts thus encountered markedly different economic conditions during their school-to-work transitions. In broad terms, the 1946 cohort faced buoyant labour markets supported by government intervention. The 1958 cohort experienced deteriorating economic conditions, with government policies under pressure, but still relatively full employment, for school leavers in 1974. (The risk of unemployment came later when the cohort had reached their early 20s.) The 1970 cohort entered an economy that was managed by a government committed to free-market principles. There was high unemployment, a rapidly 'vanishing youth labour market' (Ashton and Maguire 1983), a clear business cycle, and a new regime of government youth training schemes with limited credibility as preparation for good quality jobs.

Educational attainment

Highest qualification obtained

Table 2.1 illustrates the change in qualification levels across the three cohorts. Since we wished to compare the structure of qualifications over time at similar ages, we used a broad classification of academic and vocational qualifications based on a scale related to National Vocational Qualification (NVQ) levels. We adopted a definition that related to the 2000 surveys and mapped other survey information onto this scale. The top level, NVQ 4 and 5, covers all tertiary qualifications: diplomas, degrees and post-graduate qualifications, since several subjects like teaching and nursing acquired degree status during the period, and postgraduate degrees remain a minority. NVQ 3 covers two or more A levels, or their academic or vocational equivalent (similar internationally to the baccalaureat or to US High School). NVQ 2 includes academic or vocational qualifications equivalent to GCSE or O levels grades A–C. NVQ 1 includes other qualifications, such as lower grades of GCSE, O level or CSE and the lowest level of vocational certificates. In addition to the educational changes noted earlier, there have been extensive changes in the structure of post-school qualifications awarded as part of vocational training or by higher education institutions. The Appendix to this chapter gives details of some of these changes and describes the clarification.

Changing Britain, Changing Lives

Table 2.1a *Highest qualification attained in each cohort in their 30s*

	1970 cohort Age 30 in 2000		1958 cohort Age 33 in 1991		1946 cohort Age 32 in 1978	
	Men %	Women %	Men %	Women %	Men %	Women %
No qualifications	13	14	11	14	45	45
NVQ 1	9	10	16	15	7	11
NVQ 2	24	30	20	32	14	25
NVQ 3	23	14	27	14	13	9
NVQ 4–5	31	32	26	25	21	10
N (100%)	5,439	5,763	5,563	5,765	3,701	3,683

Table 2.1b *Highest qualification attained in each cohort in their 40s*

	1958 cohort Age 42 in 2000		1946 cohort Age 43 in 1989	
	Men %	Women %	Men %	Women %
No qualifications	11	13	41	43
NVQ 1	13	13	7	11
NVQ 2	20	30	15	25
NVQ 3	26	14	14	10
NVQ 4–5	30	30	23	11
N (100%)	5,620	5,778	3,133	3,271

For the three cohorts shown in their early 30s in Table 2.1a, we can see a clear increase over time in the proportion of each gender in the top bracket of qualifications. There was a substantial increase for men, with the proportion rising from 21 per cent for the 1946 cohort in 1978, to 31 per cent for the 1970 cohort in 2000. The growth was even more spectacular for women, with the proportion with tertiary qualifications rising from 10 per cent among the 1946 cohort in 1978, to 25 per cent for the 1958-born women in 1991, and finishing at 32 per cent for the 1970 cohort in 2000. Indeed, women moved from a position in 1978 where the proportion of those in the highest qualification band was less than half that of men, to one in 2000 where they had *overtaken* men. This broad account of the 'catching up' of women's educational attainment with men's does not reveal the extent of the large differences in the subject studied by gender.

There are clear increases in the proportions of men and women with NVQ level 3 when we compare either of the two later cohorts with the earliest cohort. However, the increase appears to be concentrated in the 1980s, since the proportions remain the same for women and actually fall for men when we compare the statistics for the later cohorts.[1] The relative performance of women fell between 1978 and 2000 at this level of qualification.

Table 2.1b makes the same comparison when the 1946 and 1958 cohort members were in their early 40s. Not surprisingly, the figures reflect the larger percentage for the highest-level qualifications in the 1958 cohort that we observed earlier, but there is some evidence that the upgrading of qualifications became more common over the 1990s. Members of the 1958 cohort increased the average percentages with NVQ 4–5, from 28 per cent to 32 per cent for men and from 25 per cent to 30 per cent for women between the ages of 33 and 42.

There was a dramatic fall in the percentage of the cohort with no qualifications between the 1946 and the later cohorts. Even at age 43, 41 per cent of men in the 1946 cohort had no qualifications, compared with only 11 per cent in the 1958 cohort. This is a remarkable change, given that the 1946 and 1958 cohorts are only 12 years apart. However, when it comes to comparing the 1970 and the 1958 cohort, the proportions with no qualifications seem to have stalled at around 11–14 per cent. As detailed in the Appendix to this chapter, some inconsistencies between the reports of qualifications in the 1970 cohort in the 26- and 30-year surveys suggest the figure for the 1970 cohort should be viewed cautiously.[2] If allowance should, in fact, be made for under-reporting of qualifications at age 30, the argument concerning the increased acquisition of qualifications over time is strengthened.

Age of leaving full-time education

Table 2.2 demonstrates in greater detail the net effect of changing educational structure on the age at which members of the 1958 and 1970 cohorts left continuous full-time education.[3] The 1970 cohort tended to stay longer in full-time education than the 1958 cohort, especially the young women. The proportion of women leaving school at the first available opportunity fell from 60 per cent to 45 per cent. For men, the fall between the 1958 and 1970 cohorts is smaller, but also showed a consistent change over time. More than half the men in the 1970 cohort (54 per cent) left school at or before 16, compared with 66 per cent of those born in 1958. The 1946 cohort, for whom exactly comparable data were not available, were even more likely to have left school at the minimum age, for them 15 years.

All qualifications

Table 2.2 also illustrates the range of qualifications that the surveys cover and reports the incidence of several types of qualification, not just the highest. The list is not comprehensive, but includes the most common ones. The heading for O levels covers: O levels (Ordinary) grades A–E, CSE grade 1, GCSE grades A–C and their Scottish equivalents.[4]

The increasing importance of higher education is apparent from these data. Eighteen per cent of men in the 1970 cohort had a degree, compared with 13 per cent of those born in 1958, while the increase for women – from 11 per cent to 17 per cent – was even larger. The change from the O levels plus CSE regime to GCSEs is reflected in the increased proportions with GCSE. It is clear that women in the 1970 cohort were doing better than men at all sub-degree level qualifications, but this was already largely the case among those born in 1958.

The distribution of vocational qualifications reflects the occupational segregation in the labour market. Women were far more likely to have the mainly clerical RSA qualifications (and, in the 2000 surveys, Pitmans qualifications), while men were more concentrated in City and Guilds at various levels and ONC/OND (Ordinary National Certificate/Diploma) and HNC/HND (Higher National Certificate/Diploma). The take-up of the BTEC (Business Technical Education Council) qualifications is interesting

Table 2.2 *Age of leaving continuous education and all qualifications obtained by early 30s*

	1970 cohort Age 30 in 2000		1958 cohort Age 33 in 1991	
	Men %	Women %	Men %	Women %
Age left school				
16 or under	54	45	66	60
17–18	21	30	17	24
19–22	17	18	14	14
23 or over	8	7	3	2
Total (100%) no. of cases	4,770	5,139	5,598	5,799
Academic	%	%	%	%
CSE at grade 1	16	19	26	28
O level at grades A–C	41	44	45	50
GCSE at grades A–C	11	15	1	2
O levels or O-level equivalent	55	61	62	68
A levels or AS levels	22	24	24	23
Diploma of HE or other teaching certificate	9	11	3	4
Degree	18	17	13	11
Higher degree	3	2	2	1
No. of cases	5,450	5,773	5,563	5,765
Vocational				
RSA Stage 1 or RSA Certificate or Other	4	19	1	19
RSA Stage 2 or RSA First Diploma	0.4	4	0.4	13
RSA Stage 3 or Advanced or Higher	0.1	2	0.3	6
C & G Operative, Part 1, Other, Can't Say	15	9	14	5
C & G Part II or III, Advanced, Final, Full Technological	18	6	21	2
ONC or OND or SNC/SND	5	1	7	2
HNC or HND or SNC/SHND	6	3	5	1
BTEC National Certificate or Diploma, First General Certificate or Diploma	14	11	3	2
BTEC Higher Certificate or Diploma	2	0.1	2	0.6
No. of cases	5,439	5,763	5,563	5,765

All definitions include the equivalent Scottish qualification. For example, A level includes Highers and 6th form certificate and BTEC includes SCOTVEC.

from the perspective of both gender and time. The proportions of men and women who had a BTEC qualification were much higher for the 1970 cohort than for the 1958 cohort. Further, the imbalance between men and women (14 per cent compared with 11 per cent), at least at the lower levels of this qualification, was not so pronounced as that for ONC/OND and HNC/HND, which were taken predominantly by men.

Antecedents of attainment

Social origin to attainment

Obtaining qualifications does not only depend on schooling but, among other things, on home background and the individual's ability and health. In this section we look, in a simple way, at just some of the antecedents and consequences of obtaining qualifications.

We take father's occupation when the cohort member was a young child as a measure of social class, and thus as a crude indicator of social

Table 2.3 *Social class of father in childhood and highest qualifications obtained by early 30s*

	1970 cohort Age 30 in 2000									
	Men					Women				
	No qualifi-cations	NVQ 1–3	NVQ 4+	Total %	N	No qualifi-cations	NVQ 1–3	NVQ 4+	Total %	N
I	2	28	70	100	321	2	28	70	100	304
II	5	49	46	100	865	3	44	53	100	913
III nm	6	52	42	100	403	4	58	38	100	401
III m	11	64	25	100	1,937	10	64	26	100	2,039
IV	12	68	20	100	509	13	63	24	100	565
V	22	68	10	100	180	18	70	12	100	191
No father	14	60	26	100	179	13	62	25	100	232
All	9	58	33	100	4,394	8	57	35	100	4,645

1958 cohort
Age 33 in 1991

	Men					Women				
	No qualifi- cations	NVQ 1–3	NVQ 4+	Total %	N	No qualifi- cations	NVQ 1–3	NVQ 4+	Total %	N
I	1	34	65	100	280	1	36	63	100	266
II	4	54	42	100	743	4	54	42	100	743
III nm	5	60	35	100	475	4	61	35	100	517
III m	11	69	20	100	2,109	13	68	19	100	2,220
IV	17	70	13	100	855	21	64	15	100	865
V	26	62	12	100	248	35	53	12	100	298
No father	19	60	21	100	117	27	55	18	100	131
All	11	63	26	100	4,827	13	62	25	100	5,040

1946 cohort
Age 32 in 1978

	Men					Women				
	No qualifi- cations	NVQ 1–3	NVQ 4+	Total %	N	No qualifi- cations	NVQ 1–3	NVQ 4+	Total %	N
I	12	38	50	100	103	13	48	39	100	89
II	25	39	36	100	402	24	53	23	100	395
III nm	20	42	38	100	251	22	58	20	100	263
III m	49	30	21	100	1,146	46	47	7	100	1,229
IV	54	36	10	100	495	52	42	6	100	524
V	54	39	5	100	262	70	30	0	100	216
No father	48	32	20	100	360	39	49	12	100	407
All	43	34	22	100	3,019	42	47	11	100	3,193

nm = non-manual
m = manual

advantage. The successive classes of the Registrar General's scheme are ranked with professional at the top and unskilled manual at the bottom. Within class III junior non-manual is placed above skilled manual. In particular, we relate father's social class to the highest qualification attained by the cohort member. We make no attempt to allow for mother's occupation or other features of home background. In Table 2.3 we simplify educational achievement into three categories: 'No qualifications', 'NVQ levels 1–3' and 'NVQ levels 4–5', as recorded when cohort members were in their early 30s.

In all cases, the chance of the cohort member gaining the highest level of qualifications increases, and the chance of having no qualifications decreases, with the social class of the family. For example, the chances of a child with a father in social class I getting NVQ level 4–5 are always highest. Indeed, the proportions are 50 per cent or more in all cases except for women born in 1946. Of those born in 1970 from social class I, 70 per cent of both the men and women had these tertiary qualifications. The chances of achieving this level fall steadily with occupation so that individuals from social class V only have a 10 per cent chance of NVQ 4/5 if they are men and 12 per cent if women.

The pattern is qualitatively similar in the 1946 cohort, but the incidence of qualifications is lower throughout the table, and there is a wider gender gap in favour of males. Thus, while the proportions in each social class with the highest qualifications are smaller for men, they are more noticeably so for women. The proportions attaining the highest levels of qualifications have steadily increased over time for all social groups, particularly between the 1946 and 1958 cohorts, and women have made larger gains. Similarly, the proportions with no qualifications have fallen over time; again, particularly between the first two cohorts. Among the 1946 cohort, 54 per cent of the men and 70 per cent of the women from social group V had no qualifications at the age of 32 in 1978, but this had fallen to 22 per cent for men and to 18 per cent for 1970-born women aged 30 in 2000. The corresponding gains for social class IV were larger for men, but still significant for women. Although the chances of individuals from the lowest two classes having obtained tertiary qualifications were at most 24 per cent in 2000, they were much better than in 1978, and a large fraction had benefited by moving out of the 'no qualifications' group.

More individuals from the highest social groups gained high qualifications than did those from the lowest groups. Indeed, despite the expansion of educational opportunities across the board, the gap in the chances of gaining tertiary qualifications for the offspring of fathers in the highest and lowest social classes has widened steadily over time. For sons, the gap grew from 45 per cent in the 1946 cohort to 60 per cent in the 1970 cohort, and for daughters it increased from 39 per cent to 58 per cent.

Early attainment and highest qualification achieved

Another glimpse of how educational outcomes are related to earlier experience in childhood is presented in Figure 2.1, relating formal educational qualifications to assessments made earlier on in the school career. We take, as a measure of early promise, test scores for attainment in reading and maths tests administered at age 10 (1970 cohort), or 11 (1958 and 1946 cohorts). These scores are often loosely treated as indicating 'ability', though we put this in quotes because, although they reflect some useful intellectual capacity, this may result from the input of earlier schooling and home background as well as the cohort members' own aptitudes. We only have an index of two dimensions of academic capacity and are aware that this may not be indicative of other capacities or natural intelligence broadly defined.

The cohort members' scores on each test are ranked in five equally sized groups (quintiles). Each variable takes the value 1 if the child was in the lowest 20 per cent of the scores, up to 5 for those in the top 20 per cent. We then summarise this information by adding the two quintile scores. Thus, a summed ability value of 2 means that the individual was in the *bottom* group for both tests, and a value of 10 that he or she was in the *top* bracket for both tests.

Figure 2.1a shows the distribution of tertiary level qualifications (NVQ 4 and 5) across the 'ability' range in the three cohorts. There is a strong association in all three cohorts between attainment at the end of primary schooling and these post-school qualifications, particularly so

Figure 2.1a *Distribution of individuals attaining tertiary qualifications across the test score range in the three cohorts by their early 30s*

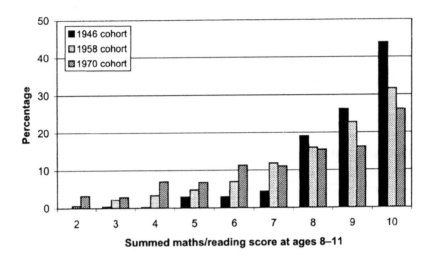

Figure 2.1b *Distribution of individuals attaining no qualifications across the test score range in the three cohorts by their early 30s*

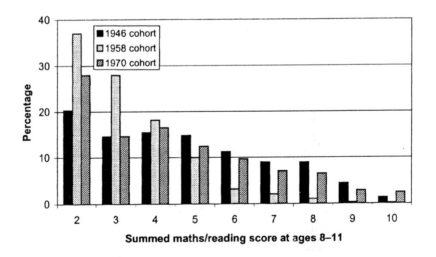

for those born in 1946. Here, 46 per cent of those with a tertiary level qualification in their early 30s come from the top 'ability' group (10). The distribution then falls away quickly with individuals in 'ability' group 7 contributing less than 5 per cent to the highly qualified. This pattern of only the very 'top' individuals in the maths/reading range attaining 'top' qualifications changes through the cohorts, with high qualifications becoming increasingly accessed by those lower down the test score scale, until in the 1970 cohort, 'ability' group 6 contributes over 10 per cent of the highly qualified. The changing relationship between test scores and qualifications between the 1946 and 1970 cohort reflects widening access to higher education, but may also be affected by qualifications not being as comparable across cohorts as we would wish to assume.

The reverse pattern can be seen in relation to those with no qualifications (Figure 2.1b). For the 1946 cohort, having no qualifications was experienced right across the ability range, with even a few high ability individuals remaining unqualified, suggesting talent wasted. In the latter two cohorts, however, the distribution of people with no qualifications becomes increasingly skewed to the left-hand side, representing the fact that, as qualifications become more universal, absence of qualifications becomes confined to individuals with lower and lower scores, and fewer promising candidates fail to achieve some qualification.

Pathways from school to the labour market

Routes to employment
This section summarises the transitions of cohort members from education into paid work. By careful reconstruction of the month-on-month state for each person since age 16, we were able, for the latter two cohorts, to trace movements between full-time work, part-time work, unemployment and being out of the labour force. The production of these profiles was an ambitious undertaking, which faced several practical problems relevant to the interpretation and comparison of the results (see Appendix to this chapter). Unfortunately, these longitudinal pathways are not available for the 1946 cohort.

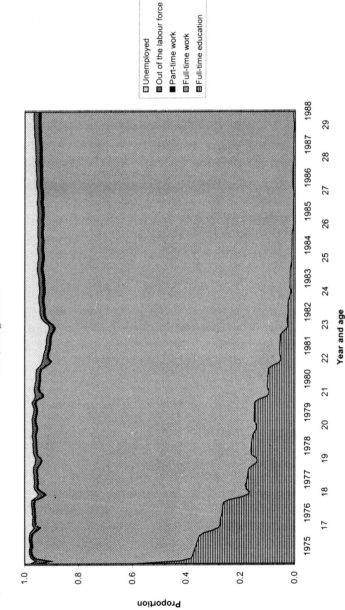

Figure 2.2a *1958 cohort: men's labour market state, at age 16–30*

Legend:
- ☐ Unemployed
- ▨ Out of the labour force
- ■ Part-time work
- ▨ Full-time work
- ▥ Full-time education

Figure 2.2b *1958 cohort: women's labour market state, at age 16–30*

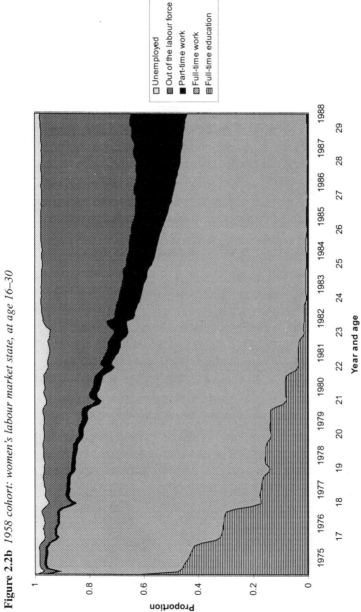

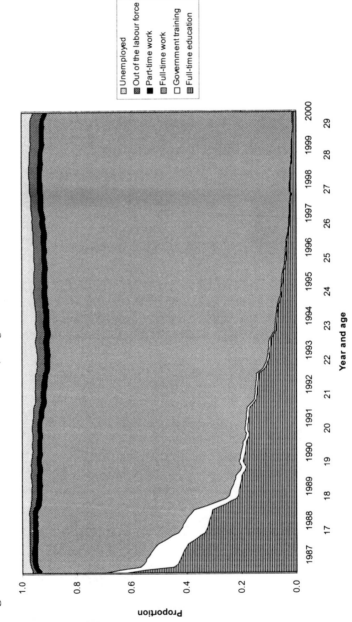

Figure 2.2c *1970 cohort: men's labour market state, at age 16–30*

Figure 2.2d *1970 cohort: women's labour market state, at age 16–30*

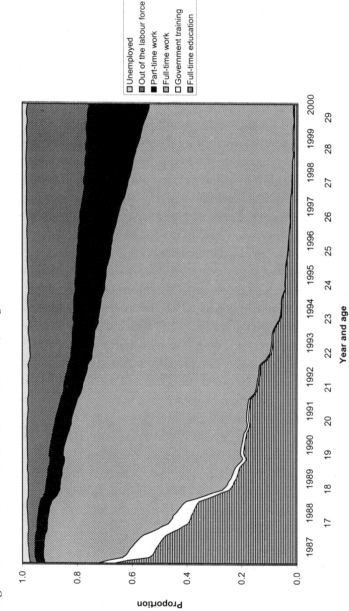

Figure 2.2 summarises the monthly labour market status of young men and women from the summer when they left compulsory education to the beginning of the year in which they were 30. Each month in the history is allocated to one of the following states: full-time education, full-time work, part-time work, government training schemes, unemployment and out of the labour market. The last category includes all reasons for being out of the labour force, such as looking after a family, or, for a few, long-term ill health. Figure 2.2a plots the cumulative proportion across these states at each point in time for men from the 1958 cohort. The greater the vertical distance between any two adjacent horizontal lines the larger is the percentage of the sample in the corresponding state at that point in time. For example, the members of the 1970 cohort were 23 years old in April 1993. The percentage of women (see Figure 2.2d) in each state at that time were 9 per cent (full-time education), less than 1 per cent (training schemes), 65 per cent (full-time work), 8 per cent (part-time work), 16 per cent (out of the labour market) and 2 per cent unemployed. While Figure 2.2 reveals in detail the different timing of the different episodes between age 16 and 30, it may also be convenient to consider the summary of experience provided in Figure 2.3, which takes these years as a whole and reports the average experience by cohort and gender.

Figures 2.2(a)–(d) give another perspective on the expansion of education that took place between the 1958 and 1970 cohorts. There was an increase in the proportion of young people staying in full-time education at each point in time, both in the teenage years and until a much later age, particularly after the age of 24. The increase is similar for both sexes. Not all of this increase in education consists of continuous spells, but involves, for some, returns to education after some time in the labour market. The proportion of all time between 16 and 30 spent in full-time education rose from around 9 per cent to around 13 per cent for both sexes (Figure 2.3). We also see that the young, poorly qualified people in the 1970 cohort who could not find jobs were heavily involved in government training schemes, such at YTS, over the ages 16–19.

Differences emerge in the employment patterns of men and women once they leave full-time education. In both cohorts, the men's employment

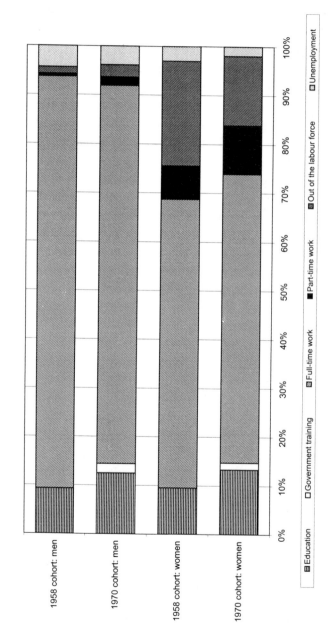

Figure 2.3 *The cumulative proportion of time spent in education and each type of employment activity, between leaving school and 30 years of age, by men and women in the 1970 and 1958 cohorts*

history is dominated by full-time work, with little time being spent in part-time work or out of the labour force. By contrast, the effects of family responsibilities begin to show for women as they get older. 'Out of the labour force' and working part-time account for large proportions of women once they enter their late 20s.

The trajectory from education into work over this part of the life cycle is broadly similar for the two sets of men. The proportions in full-time work increase with age and the proportions in full-time education decline. The proportion of men in full-time work is higher, and the proportion in full-time education is lower, in the 1958 cohort at each age, although the differences decline over time and are small when the men approach 30. Overall, as shown in Figure 2.3, there were increases of 3 per cent in the time spent in education, 2 per cent in government training and 1 per cent in 'out of the labour force'. These were almost matched by a fall in the proportion of time men spent in full-time employment, so that the over-all proportion of time men spent being *unemployed* remained remarkably similar in the two cohorts, despite the 12-year gap separating their experiences.

There is, however, a different story for women. A comparison of Figures 2.2b and 2.2d shows that women were spending less time out of the labour force and more time in paid work. Figure 2.3 shows that the average time spent out of the labour force decreased from 21 per cent to 14 per cent between the two cohorts. The time unemployed decreased by 1 percentage point, and the time on training schemes increased by slightly more, but there was virtually no change in the average time spent in full-time work. In net terms, almost all of the decrease in time spent out of the labour force was accounted for by increases in part-time employment and full-time education.[5]

Figure 2.4 plots the percentages in each state over time, in order to illuminate the rather complex picture of what is happening to women. The trends in part-time work and education are broadly similar for the two cohorts, with the proportions in part-time work increasing over time and the proportions in full-time education decreasing. The proportion of women in part-time work and education is higher in the 1970 cohort for

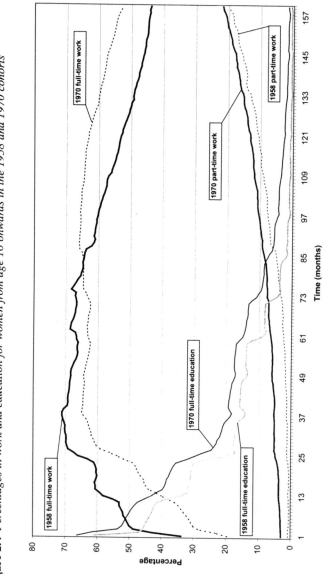

Figure 2.4 *Percentages in work and education for women from age 16 onwards in the 1958 and 1970 cohorts*

the whole period. There is, however, a more interesting change in the pattern of full-time work over time. The proportion of the 1958 cohort in full-time work increases from age 16 to a maximum of about 71 per cent at 19. It then starts to decline, slowly at first to a value of 65 per cent at 23 but then much faster to reach 50 per cent at 27 and 44 per cent at the end of the period. The proportion of the 1970 cohort in full-time work also increases sharply from age 16 to reach 65 per cent at 19. It then fluctuates, but is still around 65 per cent at 23 and remains at that level until the age of 25, when it begins to decline. The net result of this is that young women, approximately under the age of 23, are more likely to work full-time in the 1958 cohort, but the older women are *less* likely to do so. Employment has been prolonged by postponing or avoiding the break from the labour force more commonly made by women in the earlier cohorts. This change is associated with less childbearing before age 30 and, to some extent, more women maintaining continuous employment after maternity leave.

Experience of unemployment
Finally, we consider those individuals who failed to find a secure position in the labour market and spent at least some of their time after leaving school unemployed. One virtue of longitudinal information is that it can, in principle, reveal how many people have ever been unemployed, and for how long these experiences have lasted.

Table 2.4 categorises labour market histories of the 1958 and 1970 cohorts from age 16 to age 30, in terms of the extent to which there had been any unemployment recorded (not counting government training schemes as unemployment). Those with long spells of unemployment are distinguished from those whose unemployment was only short-term. Among those *not* experiencing unemployment are those who were *continuously* employed and those who also had periods in education, in government training and/or out of the labour market. It seems that the experience of *any* unemployment between age 16 and 30 (as with the total number of unemployed months) was greater for the 1958 than the 1970 cohort (among men, 43 per cent as against 24 per cent; among women 41

Table 2.4 *Summary of employment and unemployment record between 16 and 30 years of age*

	1958 cohort Age 16–30 in 1974–1988		1970 cohort Age 16–30 in 1986–2000	
	Men %	Women %	Men %	Women %
Continuously employed	34	10	30	14
Continuously employed except for government training schemes or full-time education	15	10	38	34
Continuously employed except for out of the labour force, government training schemes or full-time education	8	38	7	35
Intermittent employment with some unemployment but no spell over 3 months	16	15	4	4
Unemployment with longest spell 4–11 months	17	17	9	5
Unemployment with longest spell 12–23 months	6	6	5	3
Unemployment with longest spell of two years or over	5	2	6	3
Ever unemployed	43	41	24	15
Never been in work	0	1	1	2
No. of cases	4,462	4,541	5,300	5,620

per cent and 15 per cent). However, *long-term* unemployment, with at least one spell lasting over two years, affected a slightly bigger minority in the 1970 cohort (6 per cent compared with 5 per cent in the 1958 cohort). In both cohorts, the experience of unemployment was also more common for men than women, whose histories are more likely to involve moves out of the labour force.

Unemployment and education

Who becomes unemployed? The histories of unemployment between the ages of 16 and 30 are shown separately for members of the last two cohorts by qualification obtained by age 30 or 33 (Figure 2.5). As we might expect, the higher the level of qualification, the lower the incidence of unemployment spells, and the higher the probability of continuous employment combined with education. In the 1958 cohort, 52 per cent of those with no qualifications had reported some experience of unemployment before they were 30, compared with 40 per cent of those with tertiary qualifications (NVQ 4–5). In the 1970 cohort, 29 per cent of the unqualified reported at least one spell of unemployment compared with 20 per cent of the most qualified (NVQ 4–5). When it comes to long-term unemployment, this experience, too, is concentrated on the unqualified. In both cohorts, they are nearly twice as likely as those with NVQ level 1 to record spells longer than two years. Ten per cent of the unqualified had an unemployment spell lasting two or more years in the 1970 cohort and 9 per cent in the 1958 cohort. By contrast, among the most qualified, the corresponding rates were 1 per cent (1970) and 2 per cent (1958). Thus, a good education protects against labour market difficulties, particularly in the 1970 cohort.

The other side of the coin is an increasingly strong relationship between qualifications and continuous employment. In the 1970 cohort in particular, highly qualified women are more likely to remain in continuous employment than both their less qualified contemporaries and their predecessors in the 1958 cohort. Differential trends in women's labour force participation by education are also evident in national statistics (Twomey 2002).

Lifelong learning

Globalisation and the emergence of new computer technologies have placed great strains on economies in recent years. The belief that the pace of change will continue has led many commentators to stress the need for a highly skilled and flexible workforce that recognises the importance of lifelong learning. In this section, we begin to explore the acquisition of

Figure 2.5a *Unemployment history between 16 and 30 by highest qualification: 1958 cohort*

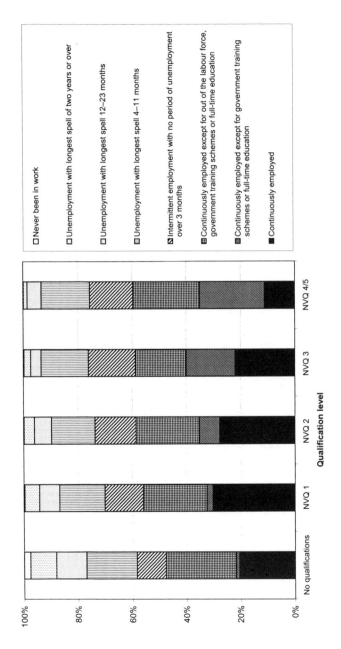

Figure 2.5b *Unemployment history between 16 and 30 by highest qualification: 1970 cohort*

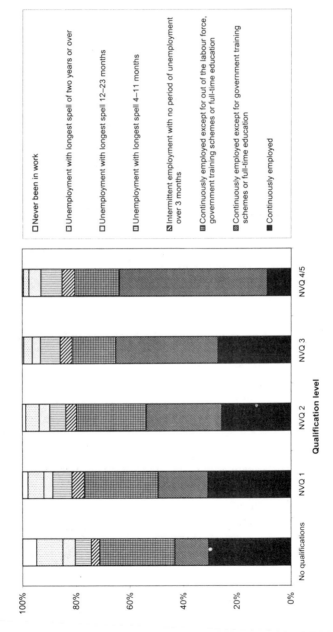

qualifications as an adult. This approach has certain limitations. Adult learning may or may not involve further formal qualifications, and we do not investigate the potential value of unaccredited learning for the individuals involved. At this stage also, we confine our analysis to the 1958 cohort, in order to examine adult learning up to age 42. (Full details have been collected of the adult learning experiences of the 1970 cohort up to age 30 (Feinstein *et al.* forthcoming).)

Table 2.5 examines different aspects of adult learning for the 1958 cohort. Part a shows the percentage gaining *any* formal qualification between the ages of 23 and 33 and between 33 and 42, whether or not the highest level of qualification is thereby increased. It shows a high incidence of adult learning for men and women in both periods. Depending on the sample, 38 per cent or 39 per cent of men obtained a qualification between 23 and 33, falling to 35 per cent between 33 and 42.[6] The position for women was reversed, with the percentage increasing from 28 per cent to 39 per cent. It is not clear whether the qualifications obtained were work or leisure related (although it is often difficult to make this distinction). Nor can we be sure whether the increase reflects the fact that older women are more committed to the labour market, or whether adult learning is low during the earlier childbearing years.

Table 2.5b demonstrates that individuals who are already more highly qualified are also more likely to obtain further qualifications. The effect is particularly noticeable for ages 23–33, when many people are establishing themselves in the labour market. The percentage of men who obtain a qualification in their 30s and early 40s increases steadily with NVQ level, from 23 per cent for those with no qualifications to 39 per cent for those with NVQ 4/5. A similar pattern is observed for women, except that there is no increase at the highest NVQ levels. Unqualified women are less likely to obtain a qualification than unqualified men, while, at NVQ level 1, the pattern for men and women is the same. At the other end of the scale, women with higher levels of qualification are far *more* likely than highly qualified men to obtain a further qualification.

Table 2.5c illustrates that most of this learning does not in fact raise NVQ levels. Overall, only 10 per cent of the men and 12 per cent of the

Table 2.5a *Percentage of 1958 cohort obtaining any qualification in the specified period*

	Men 23–33	Women 23–33	Men 33–42	Women 33–42
Present in 1991	38	28		
Present in 1991 and 2000	39	28	35	39
No. of cases	5,563	5,765	4,702	5,062

These samples are restricted to those with no missing values for qualifications over the relevant time periods

Table 2.5b *Percentage of 1958 cohort obtaining any qualification in the specified period by highest qualification at 33*

	Men 23–33	Women 23–33	Men 33–42	Women 33–42
Highest qualification at 33				
No qualifications	0	0	23	17
NVQ 1	28	16	32	32
NVQ 2	29	22	34	40
NVQ 3	35	34	36	49
NVQ 4–5	70	53	39	48
All	38	28	35	39
No. of cases	5,563	5,765	4,702	5,062

Table 2.5c *Percentage of 1958 cohort who increase their qualification level by highest qualification at 33*

	Men 23–33	Women 23–33	Men 33–42	Women 33–42
Highest qualification at 33				
No qualifications	0	0	23	17
NVQ 1	15	9	17	19
NVQ 2	9	9	14	14
NVQ 3	17	17	8	15
NVQ 4–5	42	27	0	0
All	20	14	10	12
No. of cases	5,563	5,765	4,702	5,062

women increase their NVQ level between the ages of 33 and 42. This is half the rate for men between 23 and 33, although it represents only a moderate fall for women.

It is clear that the importance of lifelong skills will continue to influence mid-life labour market trends, and it will be interesting to see if the patterns described above are repeated for the 1970 cohort as they reach their 40s over the next decade.

Conclusion

This chapter has followed our three birth cohorts from their childhood origins over the threshold of their educational experience and into their adult lives. The cohort studies can show how the process of embarking on adult life has changed over time for successive generations and how it has varied across individuals within them. They contain evidence on two major sources of social and economic inequality in the lives of British people, two accidents of birth: class of origin and gender.

Successive cohorts have faced, on average, better opportunities for education than their own parents, particularly their mothers, but it is not obvious whether the relative gains have been any greater for children from less advantaged origins. The evidence assembled here still suggests unequal *outcomes*. More of these qualifications are available, but they are disproportionately achieved by those who come from more favourable backgrounds. They are also being achieved by those with a wider spread of primary school attainments, rather than concentrated among the most promising children. Enhancement of qualifications through adult learning also tends to *widen* differentials rather than compensate for them. These trends are very similar for men and women born in 1958 and 1970. Women born in 1946 from all backgrounds were less qualified than men. Women's 'catching up' with men's educational attainments is one of the major trends recorded by examination of the three cohorts.

We have followed the two more recent cohorts into their early years on the labour market, where the impact of their education can be seen in the increasingly polarised histories of unemployment (and, for women, employment). Further differentials in family building and other domains will be presented in later chapters. Details of each cohort's employment experience, and their occupational attainment as adults, are presented in Chapter 3.

Notes

1   This result is sensitive to the classification of City and Guilds qualifications.
2   Incorporating the age 26 information would lower the percentages of men and women with no qualifications to about 9 per cent in each case and raise the percentages with NVQ 4–5 to about 34 per cent.
3   'Continuous' may include a 'gap' year.
4   Details of the definitions and underlying complexity of this measurement are reported in the Appendix to this chapter.
5   The increases are 3 per cent for part-time employment and just under 4 per cent for full-time education.
6   Our sample for the 33–42 period is restricted to those present in both surveys because the answers for respondents to the 2000 survey, who were not present in the 1991 survey, cover the whole period from March 1974.

Appendix: Technical issues in chapter 2

1 The measurement and classification of qualifications

Glossary

CSE Certificate of Secondary Education
O level Ordinary level
GCSE General Certificate of Secondary Education
A level Advanced level
AS level Advanced Supplementary level
Diploma of HE Higher Education Diploma
RSA Royal Society of Arts
C & G City and Guilds
ONC Ordinary National Certificate
OND Ordinary National Diploma
SNC Scottish National Certificate
SND Scottish National Diploma
HNC Higher National Certificate
HND Higher National Diploma
SHND Scottish Higher National Diploma
BTEC Business and Technical Education Council
SCOTVEC Scottish Technical and Vocational Education Certificate
GNVQ General National Vocational Qualification

In the 1946 study questions about qualifications obtained were asked in all the adult surveys, but this chapter relies on responses given at age 26. The 1958 study has regularly collected information on qualifications. The questions in 2000 asked 'whether the qualification has been obtained since the age of 33' for individuals who were present in 1991. The 1991 survey collected information about all qualifications obtained up to that age so the combined information gives a record of educational achievement at the ages of 33 and 42. These data are used here and elsewhere in the book.

The 1970 cohort was asked in the 2000 survey about all qualifications obtained back to age 16. The 1996 postal survey, had presented this cohort with a list of academic qualifications ranging from CSE grade 1 to postgraduate degree (MA, MSc, PhD, etc.). For each qualification the respondents were asked to tick a box if they had the qualification and, if any, to write the number of qualifications gained in another column. Another question asked if the respondent had gained any other qualifications since leaving school. It prompted the respondent to include HGV, PSV, RSA, Pitmans, City & Guilds, TEC, BEC, SEN, SRN, NNEB, membership of professional institutions, or any similar technical, vocational or professional qualifications. If the answer was yes, the respondent was asked to write in the names of the qualifications.

The 2000 survey was more structured, involving a face-to-face interview with the answers subject to simple checks. The individual was presented with a list of academic qualifications (GCSE, GCE O level, CSE, A/S level, GCE A level, etc.) preceded by a 'routing question': 'Have you obtained any of the qualifications on this card since April 1986?' They were then asked for more detailed information about each qualification identified in turn. These questions included the date when they were awarded and place of study. A similar procedure was followed for vocational qualifications.

The book and this chapter use the answers to the 2000 survey as the primary source of information on qualifications, because the survey had a higher response rate and, like the previous surveys of the 1958 cohort, it involved face-to-face interviews. This decision has some implications that we will return to below. Comparisons of the 1958 and 1970 cohort data on qualifications are not straightforward because the 2000 survey provided the first comprehensive data on qualifications for the 1970 cohort. The survey at age 16 took place before the summer examinations and only deals with expectations about future performance. The postal survey undertaken at age 26 had a relatively low response rate. More importantly, there are differences in the structure of the vocational questions and the form of survey.

In practice, there have been some significant changes in the structure of qualifications over time as the system of qualifications evolved. There were, for example, changes in the form of qualifications offered by RSA and City and Guilds and the introduction of Pitmans qualifications as a separate category. (Indeed, 6 per cent of the women in 1970 said they had a Pitmans level 1 qualification.) BTEC qualifications replaced the previous system based on ONC/OND and HNC/HND. The designation of polytechnics as universities has made the distinction between CNAA and university qualifications less relevant, while the introduction of AS levels has increased the range of options available. Over time, these changes have affected the form of the questions asked. For instance, the question about nursing in the 2000 survey is the last in a series of questions and asks for any nursing or paramedic qualification not covered elsewhere (for example, as a degree).

Possible under-reporting of qualifications in the 1970 cohort

A surprising feature of Table 2.1 is the decline in the proportion with O levels. Although the 1970 cohort finished schooling before the surge in pass rates that followed the advent of GCSEs, national figures suggest a steady improvement in the performance of school-leavers from 1974 to 1986. Indeed the percentage reporting an O-level equivalent qualification in the 1996 survey is much higher than in the 2000 survey and these large differences remain even if we allow for the change in the composition of the samples. Indeed, quite large numbers of individuals reported a qualification in 1996 but did not do so in 2000. There are reasons why this might occur. The significance of a low-level qualification may diminish over time, or it may be due to the differences between a face-to-face interview and a postal survey. Nonetheless, the gap between the surveys is only four years and the possession of an important qualification like an O level is not a difficult concept to recall.

One partial source of under-reporting of O-level and CSE qualifications is the change in the system of basic academic examinations to GCSEs. Substantial numbers of individuals obtain this type of qualification after leaving school. The 1958 cohort would have been able to take O levels until they were 30. GCSEs were introduced when the 1970 cohort were 18, so members of this cohort would have taken GCSEs on day release or in night classes. This is borne out by the large difference in the percentages of each cohort with GCSEs. Any confusion between the GCE and GCSE examination regimes would mostly have impacted on the 1970 cohort.

In Table 2.1 the percentage with no qualifications has apparently stabilised at around 12–14 per cent when we compare the 1970 with the 1958 cohort. This may partly reflect an under-reporting of low-level qualifications in the 2000 survey for 1970 cohort members suggested above. Here we find that 497 men and 870 women report a higher value for their highest qualification in 1996 than in 2000. If we take maximum value for the highest qualification the percentages of men and women with no qualifications fall to 10 per cent (13 per cent) and 9 per cent (14 per cent) respectively. (The figures from Table 2.1 are in parentheses.) The percentages with NVQ level 3 increases to 24 per cent (23 per cent) for men and 16 per cent (14 per cent) for women and the percentage with NVQ levels 4–6 increases to 33 per cent (31 per cent) for men and to 35 per cent (32 per cent) for women. It might be argued that these individuals are unreliable and that we should ignore the information they provide. If they are completely excluded from the analysis, the percentages of men and women with no qualifications are 11 per cent (13 per cent) and 11 per cent (14 per cent) respectively. Rather surprisingly, the percentages for NVQ levels 3 and 4–6 are the same when rounded as those quoted for analysis using the maximum of the 1996 and 2000 figures.

Mapping to NVQ levels

Level 1   City & Guilds Other, RSA Certificate/Other, Pitmans level 1, other vocational qualifications, NVQ level 1, GNVQ Foundation, other grades in GCSE, CSE, Scottish school qualifications, and O levels

Level 2   BTEC First Certificate or Diploma, City & Guilds Part 1, RSA First Diploma, Pitmans level 2, Apprenticeship, Intermediate GNVQ, NVQ level 2, 1 A level, 2 or more AS levels, GCSE or O level grades A–C, CSE grade 1, Scottish Standard 1–3, Scottish lower or ordinary grades

Level 3 BTEC National Diploma, ONC/OND, City & Guilds Parts 2–4 (or equivalent), RSA Advanced Diploma, Pitmans level 3, Advanced GNVQ, NVQ level 3, 2 or more A levels, Scottish Highers or Certificate of 6th Year Studies

Level 4 BTEC Higher Certificate/Diploma, HNC/HND, Professional degree level qualifications, Nursing qualifications, RSA Higher Diploma, NVQ level 4, Degree, HE Diploma, PGCE, other teaching qualification

Level 5 NVQ level 5, Higher degree

The 1946 study employed an eight-point scale. The categories (with the corresponding NVQ level in parentheses) are: None (0); Nominal (1); Sub-O level (1); O levels or training equivalent (2); A level (3), Professional (4); First degree, Dip Tech, etc. (4); Masters (5); Doctorate (5).

2 Employment history data

Unlike most of the other data used in this book, an attempt was made to combine data from earlier sweeps with those collected in 2000 in order to reconstruct the longitudinal work histories of the 1958 and 1970 cohort members. This was a complex and tricky operation involving a number of assumptions where data are missing or inconsistent, which have not yet been fully evaluated. Almost all the information on the 1970 cohort profiles derives from data collected in 2000 that give a single retrospective history covering all the 14 years of interest. This has been supplemented by data from earlier surveys giving partial information on work histories for subsets of the sample, including a fully dated history for 10 per cent of the sample up to age 21. The 1958 cohort histories have been reconstructed from diary information reported at ages 23, 33 and 42. Thus the 1970 cohort avoids the considerable problems of splicing histories which are not always consistent because dates are not reliably reconciled. However it is more likely to suffer from the problems of recall over long periods. It is known that short episodes tend to be forgotten, and therefore omitted from employment histories going back more than about four or five years (see Dolton and Taylor (2000) for a detailed examination of the biases involved in recording the length of different labour market spells in the 1958 data). We suspect therefore that these estimates are somewhat biased against the experience of unemployment in short episodes in the teens and early 20s for the 1970 cohort. There are further limits to the comparability of data from differences in the phrasing of the questions at different dates, in missing information and of incomplete response whose full implications require further detailed research. See Galinda-Rueda (2002) for a description of the calculation of the work history data for the 1970 and 1958 cohorts.

An important difficulty is that the 2000 surveys only record the starting dates of each spell in a new activity. In contrast, sweeps 4 and 5 of the 1958 study asked for start and end dates of spells. It is possible that the 2000 survey may systematically under-report short spells particularly of unemployment. This means direct comparison of these cohorts over the 16–30 age range should be made with caution. No comparison has yet been made between the early school-to-work transitions of the sub-sample reported at age 21 and those reported at age 30. There may well be inconsistencies between the results presented in earlier studies based on the restricted sample at age 21 and those presented here.

3 The world of paid work

Laura Woods, Gerry Makepeace, Heather Joshi and Peter Dolton

Introduction

We now take up the story of the members of our three cohorts in adulthood, concentrating in this chapter on their experience of paid work. We look at the situation of people as they reached their early 30s, in three snapshots of time: the late 1970s, the early 1990s and the turn of the Millennium. At the latter two dates we also show the position for the two older cohorts when they had reached their early 40s.

We describe participation in employment for the cohort members relative to their gender, qualifications and social class; their jobs in terms of occupation, the hours they worked and their fringe benefits; the employment of individuals in relation to their family and household characteristics and finally their own labour market achievement relative to that of their family of origin. We turn first to the economic and policy backdrop to these experiences.

The economic context

The period spanned starts in the 1970s, which presented a series of economic challenges that eventually shattered the relative economic stability of the postwar decades in Britain. Successive governments had accepted that the welfare state should be supported, and large parts of industry were publicly run. Although the rates of unemployment and inflation had fluctuated, they had never been particularly high and there was a growing belief in the benefits of active social and economic policy. In the 1970s, unemployment rose consistently, to rates that would have been perceived as catastrophic ten years earlier and were matched by equally disturbing rates of inflation.

In 1979, one year after the first point of observation in this chapter, the first Thatcher government was elected and wide-ranging changes in economic and political philosophy resulted. Many traditional institutions and practices were altered and many manufacturing businesses disappeared. A partial list of labour market 'reforms' would include: reduction in union power, privatisation of publicly owned industries, abandonment of wage and price controls, cuts in public expenditure and cuts in social security payments relative to earnings. These changes were driven in part by a general ideological shift away from state welfare provision to individual (and family) responsibility. Unemployment still remained high. The effects of this regime were in force for most of the years up to the time we look at the 43-year-olds in the 1946 cohort (1989) and the 33-year-olds in the 1958 cohort (1991). They also applied in many ways over the 1990s, leading up to our final observations in 1999/2000.

Economic policy in the 1990s was based on free-market principles, with particular emphasis on a deregulated labour market and on skills development. The Thatcher era heralded a period of 'personal' career development, in which individuals were expected to strive ambitiously for advancement through qualifications and the pursuit of promotion. The period from 1979–97 saw an unprecedented growth in the inequality of income generated by a wider dispersion of skills and human capital (see Chapter 6). There was also a price to pay for the notorious under-investment in new technology in British industry, which had contributed to continental European and Far Eastern economies' competitive advantage (Hutton 1995) and a work force that was considered under-trained compared with its major European competitors (CBI 1989).

In addition to the general trends identified above, there were a number of specific changes relating to employment and skills that affected the three cohorts discussed in this book. Technological innovation, particularly the advent of communications and information technology, had profound implications for the structure and organisation of work (Gallie 1988). Except for specialists, members of the first two cohorts would have had to acquire any computing skills after leaving school, whilst those born in 1970 were the first to have come into active contact with computers in secondary school and thus would have entered the labour market with this additional skill over their predecessors. Globalisation and technological change also altered the structure of the labour force. Over the period experienced by our cohorts, there was a decline of engineering and manufacturing industry and a significant increase in the proportion of the workforce in service industries. These changes altered the stance of government policy and most governments now use the concept of a 'knowledge economy' to emphasise the importance of high skill levels and job mobility. For example, in the UK, there has been continuous intervention in education and the development of lifelong learning strategies (whose impact on the cohorts is discussed in Chapter 2).

Traditional labour market institutions changed substantially in the last quarter of the twentieth century, reflecting the political and economic trends outlined above. Broadly speaking, there was a move from an interventionist stance to a more free-market view. Such changes included the rejection of incomes policies, substantial changes to the tax-credit system, and the restriction in powers, then decline in membership, of trade unions. Towards the end of our period, we saw the incorporation of European approaches to policy, which brought back a degree of regulation, with the acceptance of the Social Charter and the Minimum Wage.

However, a major shift took place in relation to job security. A 'job for life' is no longer expected or likely. Increasingly, people have more jobs in their working life and even several changes of career. Another notable feature has been the huge increase in the labour-force participation of women, particularly those who are married and have children. There has been an equalising out of job prospects between men and women employees, and a reduction in the pay gap between them that has meant increasing financial independence for women.

Accompanying these changes, there has been a substantial shift in attitudes about women's roles (Scott 1999). Whether its origins lie in cultural or economic change, women are now much more likely to work full time or part time, for pay, at all points in their lifetime, while labour market inactivity amongst men has increased.

Participation in the labour market

In each adult survey, the current labour force status of the cohort members has been assessed. Table 3.1 shows snapshots of labour force membership in their early 30s and 40s. Within the economically active, we distinguish the unemployed from the employed, who are further subdivided into employees and self-employed, and for women into full- and part-time workers. The proportion of men working part-time is not shown separately, as it is never above 2 per cent of the cohort.

At all points, well over nine out of ten men were economically active, with the majority working full time, mostly as employees. The proportion of men working as self-employed rose as men moved from their 30s into their 40s, to around one-fifth. A larger minority of men than women reported unemployment at the time of the interviews (the peak at 6 per cent for 33-year-old men in 1991, when national unemployment rates were very high). The largest identifiable group among economically inactive men includes the permanently sick or disabled, which rose for the 1958 cohort from 2 per cent at 33 to 5 per cent at age 42.

The economic activity rates for women were lower and much more variable across cohort and age. They were closer to men's at ages after 40 than around age 30, where female labour-force participation has traditionally dipped, coinciding with peak child-rearing responsibilities. Taking first the women in their 30s (Table 3.1a), the proportion economically inactive (largely looking after home and family) was 46 per cent for the 1946 cohort (age 32 in 1978), falling through 29 per cent for the 1958 cohort in 1991, to 21 per cent for the 1970 cohort (age 30 in 2000). The corresponding increase was found particularly in full-time work as an employee. Among the cohorts at 30-something, in 1978 part-time work was more common than full-time; by 1991, full-time work was slightly more common, and by 2000, it was more than twice so.

There is a clear upward trend in women's participation rate, over calendar time across cohorts at ages around 30, reflecting the accumulated qualifications and postponed childbearing of the later cohorts. There is also a clear trend within the life course of rising participation in

Table 3.1a *Labour force participation and employment status in each cohort at interview in their early 30s*

	1970 cohort Age 30 in 2000		1958 cohort Age 33 in 1991		1946 cohort Age 32 in 1978	
	Men %	Women %	Men %	Women %	Men %	Women %
Economically active	**94**	**76**	**96**	**70**	**99**	**54**
Employee	79	69	74	61	86	49
Full-time		*48*		*33*		*22*
Part-time		*21*		*29*		*27*
Self-employed	11	5	16	7	13	5
Full-time		*3*		*4*		*3*
Part-time		*2*		*3*		*2*
Unemployed and seeking work	4	2	6	2	0	0
Economically inactive	**4**	**21**	**2**	**29**	**1**	**46**
Other	**2**	**3**	**1**	**1**		
N (100%)	5,447	5,772	5,583	5,786	2,751	2,875

Table 3.1b *Labour force participation and employment status in each cohort at interview in their early 40s*

	1958 cohort Age 42 in 2000		1946 cohort Age 43 in 1989	
	Men %	Women %	Men %	Women %
Economically active	**93**	**80**	**98**	**90**
Employee	73	71	71	75
Full-time		*40*		*40*
Part-time		*31*		*35*
Self-employed	18	7	25	9
Full-time		*4*		*6*
Part-time		*3*		*3*
Unemployed and seeking work	3	2	2	6
Economically inactive	**5**	**18**	**2**	**10**
Other	**1**	**2**		
N (100%)	5,604	5,778	2,993	3,055

mid-life, brought about by returning to the labour market as children grow older, to be seen in the 1946 and 1958 cohorts in their 40s (see Macran *et al.* 1996; and Joshi and Hinde 1993, for a comparison of employment after childbearing by the mothers of the 1946 cohort and their daughters). There may also be hidden cohort differences among women at 42 and 43, which are masked, in these statistics, by differences in the stage of the child-rearing life course of the 1958 and 1946 cohorts. At 42, the more recent cohort are not only one year younger themselves, but have younger children on average. Thus underlying employment propensities between the two cohorts are likely to be more different than displayed by Table 3.1.

Another interesting feature of Table 3.1 is the changing pattern of self-employment. Women were at all stages less than half as likely as men to be self-employed, the highest proportions being for the 1946-born women at age 43 in 1989: 6 per cent were self-employed full time and 3 per cent part time (Table 3.1b). Among men in their early 30s, 13 per cent of the 1946 cohort were self-employed in 1978, rising to 16 per cent in the 1958 cohort in 1991, but falling back to 11 per cent among the 1970 cohort in 2000 (Table 3.1a). The propensity to be involved in self-employment has clearly changed over the years. This is borne out by the data for the men in their early 40s, where the proportions in self-employment were much higher, especially among the 1946 cohort (Table 3.1b). One major explanation of this may be the array of self-employment policies which started under the Conservative government.

A further aspect of working lives which has changed remarkably over the last 20 years is the extent of job mobility. This increased markedly between the two more recent cohorts, with individuals from the 1970 cohort having on average 3.1 jobs between the ages of 16 and 30, whilst those in the 1958 cohort averaged 2.7. Nearly two-thirds of men in the 1970 cohort had had three or more jobs, compared with 56 per cent of men born in 1958. This trend was broadly the same for women and is all the more dramatic when we consider that the 1970 cohort had spent a larger proportion of their time since 16 in full-time education.

Employment and education

Both men and women are less likely to be employed if they have low qualifications. Table 3.2 cross classifies the cohort's current employment with their highest qualification obtained up to the survey date. The gap between the most and least qualified increases over time, and becomes widest for women in all cohorts in 2000. For women born in 1970, full-time employment rates at age 30 ranged from 70 per cent for those women with higher education to 30 per cent for those with no qualifications (Table 3.2a). In the 1946 cohort in 1978, the corresponding rates of full-time employment were 35 per cent and 18 per cent. Part-time employment rates show less of a gradient by qualifications. The gradient is sometimes reversed as the more qualified tend to be less likely to work part time than full time.

It is the most qualified who display the greatest increase in full-time employment across cohorts around age 30. However, if we look *within* cohorts as they pass from their 30s to their 40s it is, by contrast, the unqualified who increase their full-time employment the most. The more qualified women more often remain continuously in the labour market and already have a higher labour market attachment in their early 30s. The larger increases in the other groups reflect a pattern of returning to employment among mothers.

That the more qualified women should display more attachment to paid work can be explained, at least in part, by the enhancement of their earning power through their education (see Chapter 6). For the qualified, their higher earning power means that there is, in turn, more to be gained from the improvement of women's pay and opportunities by participating in employment (Rake 2000). They have less need, economically and, perhaps, psychologically, to rely on being supported by a husband or the state, and more of a chance to afford childcare when children are young. Changes in employment and opportunities have occurred alongside changes in attitudes and expectations, and in the nature of marriage. As the cohort data show, these changes have occurred at a different pace for those in different social or educational groups (Macran *et al.* 1996).

Table 3.2a *Labour force status at interview by highest educational level in each cohort in their early 30s*

Women

NVQ level	1970 cohort Age 30 in 2000					1958 cohort Age 33 in 1991					1946 cohort Age 32 in 1978				
	None %	1 %	2 %	3 %	4 %	None %	1 %	2 %	3 %	4 %	None %	1 %	2 %	3 %	4 %
Economically active															
Full-time	30	38	44	54	70	21	28	34	40	51	18	20	27	27	35
Part-time	25	30	27	22	15	31	37	36	27	26	37	25	31	25	18
Unemployed	4	1	2	2	2	4	2	2	2	1	1	3	1	1	0
Economically inactive	41	31	27	22	13	44	33	29	32	21	44	53	41	47	47
N (100%)	824	562	1,738	809	1,837	827	846	1,865	761	1,420	1,215	309	764	274	314

Men

NVQ level	1970 cohort Age 30 in 2000					1958 cohort Age 33 in 1991					1946 cohort Age 32 in 1978				
	None %	1 %	2 %	3 %	4 %	None %	1 %	2 %	3 %	4 %	None %	1 %	2 %	3 %	4 %
Economically active															
Full-time	78	84	88	91	92	73	88	90	93	94	94	96	96	97	98
Part-time	2	3	2	1	1	1	1	1	1	1	0	0	0	0	0
Unemployed	8	7	5	4	3	16	7	6	4	3	6	4	2	2	1
Economically inactive	12	7	6	4	4	11	3	3	2	2	0	0	2	1	1
N (100%)	724	464	1,305	1,242	1,712	688	823	1,434	1,012	1,553	1,172	188	387	381	616

Table 3.2b *Labour force status at interview by highest educational level in each cohort in their early 40s*

Women

NVQ level	1958 cohort Age 42 in 2000					1946 cohort Age 43 in 1989				
	None %	1 %	2 %	3 %	4 %	None %	1 %	2 %	3 %	4 %
Economically active										
Full-time	31	38	44	45	54	36	47	53	44	59
Part-time	32	40	36	36	30	42	35	33	36	30
Worker status unknown						0	0	1	1	1
Unemployed						5	2	2	3	2
Economically inactive	3	2	2	1	1	14	15	12	15	8
Non-worker status unknown	34	20	18	18	15	2	0	0	2	0
N (100%)	812	731	1,706	795	1,734	1,353	331	784	307	337

Men

NVQ level	1958 cohort Age 42 in 2000					1946 cohort Age 43 in 1989				
	None %	1 %	2 %	3 %	4 %	None %	1 %	2 %	3 %	4 %
Economically active										
Full-time	73	88	87	91	93	90	89	93	97	97
Part-time	3	3	3	1	2	2	0	1	0	0
Worker status unknown						0	2	0	1	1
Unemployed						4	5	1	0	0
Economically inactive	6	3	4	3	1	2	1	2	1	2
Non-worker status unknown	17	7	7	5	4	2	4	2	0	0
N (100%)	665	673	1,325	1,144	1,797	1,217	192	433	422	672

Key: None = No qualifications　　1 = NVQ Level 1, CSE 2–5　　2 = NVQ Level 2, O Level/CSE 1
3 = NVQ Level 3, A Level　　4 = NVQ Level 4, Degree Level +

Employment and social class of origin

If, as we have seen in Chapter 2, social background leaves a trace in the distribution of education qualifications, are there also differentials to be seen in the labour market position of the cohort members as adults? When we examined the cohort members' economic activity status with relation to their fathers' social class of origin, we found some tendency for both men and women from 'humbler backgrounds' to be out of employment in all cohorts, with more variation for women. For daughters of fathers from different class backgrounds, a class gradient emerges between the 1946 and 1970 cohorts in the chances of their being in full-time work in their early 30s. From the flat profile at age 32 in 1978 of around 25 per cent, a steep contrast develops among 30-year-olds in 2000, from 42 per cent for the daughters of fathers in unskilled occupations to 65 per cent of those with fathers in professional occupations. These patterns reflect the influence of class-related differences in education and the timing of childbearing, and suggest an extension of the accumulation of economic advantages across generations. However, as the differences by class of origin in the employment participation of women born in 1958 were reduced as they moved from 33 to 42, it remains to be seen whether the wide disparities among the 1970 cohort at 30 will persist.

Employment and occupation

To enable us to look at the secular change in employment structure, Table 3.3 shows employed individuals in each cohort at each age, and the fathers of each cohort a generation earlier, by occupational social class, as ranked by the Registrar General's classification in the year of survey. Information on women's employment is further separated by whether they work full time or part time, since the occupations of women part-timers tend to have lower grades. There is a striking change in the proportion of men with manual occupations (classes III manual; IV and V: skilled, semi-skilled and unskilled). These accounted for about three-quarters of the fathers of the 1946 cohort in 1950, but two-thirds of the fathers of the 1958 cohort in 1965 and for 62 per cent of fathers of the 1970 cohort in 1975. Information

Table 3.3 *Occupation grade of current employment: men and women employed full-time; and women employed part-time*

Cohort and age	Occupational social class of father						
	I %	II %	III nm %	III m %	IV %	V %	N (100%)
Fathers of the 1946 cohort	3	13	10	45	20	9	6,344
Fathers of the 1958 cohort	6	16	11	45	18	5	8,640
Fathers of the 1970 cohort	7	21	9	46	12	4	9,081
	Occupational social class of cohort members' current job						
1946 cohort at 32 in 1978							
Male workers	10	28	9	42	9	1	2,660
Female full-time workers	2	36	46	5	11	0	667
Female part-time workers	1	17	32	8	35	8	837
1958 cohort at 33 in 1991							
Male workers	8	34	11	33	11	2	4,125
Female full-time workers	4	45	32	7	11	1	1,788
Female part-time workers	1	22	38	7	23	9	1,605
1970 cohort at 30 in 2000							
Male workers	8	34	13	32	11	2	4,834
Female full-time workers	6	43	37	7	7	0	2,944
Female part-time workers	2	19	44	9	21	6	1,297
1946 cohort at 43 in 1989							
Male workers	10	39	9	33	8	2	2,888
Female full-time workers	2	41	34	8	13	2	1,436
Female part-time workers	1	20	43	7	19	11	1,196
1958 cohort at 42 in 2000							
Male workers	7	40	10	32	8	3	5,040
Female full-time workers	4	45	31	7	11	1	2,570
Female part-time workers	2	22	38	7	23	8	1,978

Note

Social class categories are given by the RG social class:
I = Professional   II = Intermediate   III nm = Skilled non-manual
III m = Skilled manual   IV = Semi-skilled   V = Unskilled

comparing the occupations of individual pairs or fathers and sons is shown in Table 3.8.

When the male cohort members were in their 30s, 52 per cent of the 1946 cohort were in manual occupations in 1978, falling to 46 per cent of the 1958 cohort in 1991 and 45 per cent of the 1970 cohort in 2000. The first two cohorts, especially those born in 1946, showed small shifts out of manual work between their 30s and 40s.

For women cohort members working full time, there was no clear trend in the proportion in manual work (around one in six for those in their 30s) between 1978 and 2000. However, unlike men, women in the 1958 cohort show no net movement out of manual jobs within the life course. Manual work accounted for half the part-time jobs of 32-year-old women working in 1978, but for only around one in three female part-time jobs at the other adult surveys.

The above findings indicate that structural change is more pronounced in the longer time scale of intergenerational comparison than in the inter-cohort comparisons from the last two decades of the twentieth century. *Within*-cohort change is not great on the surface of these comparisons of averages, but the analysis does not (yet) reveal the extent to which individuals have experienced changes of occupation or moves in and out of the workforce.

For employed men and women working full-time among the non-manual classes (I, II and II non-manual), the biggest group was in social class II (intermediate). This group includes a wide range of white-collar jobs, including teaching, nursing and management, which are neither professional (social class I: medicine, law, senior civil servant) nor 'junior' (mainly clerical and sales). Only small numbers of cohort members (or their parents) are recorded as having occupations in social class I. About one in ten of the employed men in each adult cohort had a job classed as professional, which is considerably more frequent than among their fathers in the 1950s and 1960s. There has been more of an upward trend in the status of women's occupations compared to men's, but even among women employed full time, the highest proportion in social class I occupations was only 6 per cent among the 30-year-olds born in 1970. Professional jobs held by women part-timers remain extremely rare, and women part-timers are concentrated in the junior and manual jobs.

For those working in manual occupations, the highest proportion of men work in skilled manual jobs, whilst for women, full- and, particularly, part-time, the greatest numbers are in semi-skilled occupations. The lower occupational grade of the women working part time is common to other age groups (Twomey 2002). Note that in the case of these cohorts, most of the women working part time are mothers of dependent children; the low status of their jobs will entail low earnings (see Chapter 6). This will arise partly because of their current domestic circumstances, partly out of their lesser educational attainments, and partly from other features of their past history yet to be as fully explored for the situation in 2000 as it has been for 1991 and 1978 by Joshi and Paci (1998).

Working lives

Working hours

How much paid work were the cohort members doing? Do the patterns in these data fit with the prevailing view that we work longer hours than our parents? The real story is more complicated. Johnes and Taylor (1992) have reported that working hours of manual workers have been steadily declining over the last 40 years. In contrast, Harkness (1999) reports a significant increase in the proportion of men and women working over 50 hours a week, by comparing the Labour Force Survey data from 1988 and 1998. What is lost in comparisons of this kind is the facility to be able to examine comparable individuals. In addition, a somewhat more complex situation is revealed if one looks at the whole distribution of weekly working hours, rather than simply focusing on those who work long hours. Both these analyses are possible with the longitudinal cohort data.

The pattern of men's weekly working hours in their early 30s, for all three cohorts, is captured in Figure 3.1a. Here we see that the 1958 cohort men at 33 reported fewer hours than their counterparts in the 1946 cohort 12 years earlier. Indeed, the whole distribution had shifted to the left: on average, men in the 1946 cohort reported working 47.2 hours per week

Figure 3.1a *Weekly hours worked by men in the three cohorts in their early 30s*

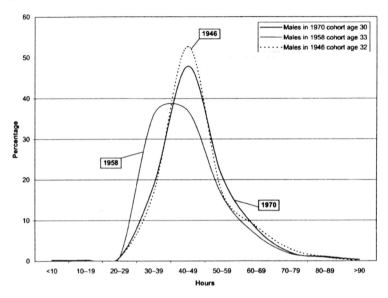

Figure 3.1b *Weekly hours worked by women in the three cohorts in their early 30s*

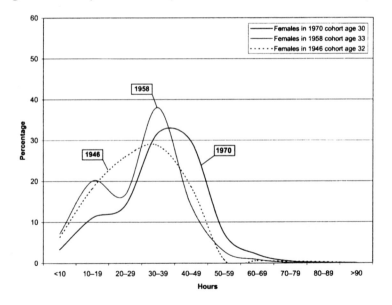

Figure 3.1c *Weekly hours worked by men in the two cohorts in their early 40s*

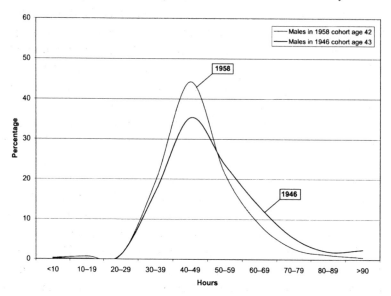

Figure 3.1d *Weekly hours worked by women in the two cohorts in their early 40s*

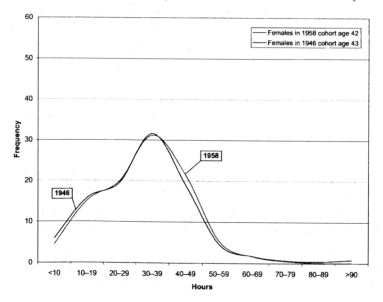

compared to the 1958 cohort, whose reported hours averaged 44.6. However, looking at the 1970 cohort aged 30, we see that the distribution of hours worked has shifted back to the right. The mean went back up to 47.1 hours: approximately the same as in 1978 for the 1946 cohort. One possible explanation for these shifts is that the depressed state of the economy in 1991 may have meant that hours of work at that time were limited, with less overtime and even shorter working weeks.

Figure 3.1b graphs the pattern of women's weekly working hours in their 30s. Initially, in the 1946 cohort, women's hours were fairly evenly spread around a mean of 29 hours per week, at a time when more than half the women working were part-timers. The distribution of hours for the 1958 cohort in 1991 shows the development of two peaks, as more women were working full-time. A cluster of hours of part-timers (around 15 hours per week) appeared distinct from those of full-timers (around 35) in 1991. By 2000, the left-hand peak was less pronounced. The relatively small number of part-timers reported a more even spread of hours up to 30, and the full-timers' hours peaked around 40 hours. This shows the same increase over time as for men in this age group, although 5 hours per week fewer than for the men between the 1970 and 1958 cohort. The increase in full-time jobs in women's employment at this age has helped to raise the hours worked by the average employed woman in the cohort studies from 32.2 in 1978, and 29.1 in 1991, to 35.3 hours per week in 2000.

Looking at weekly working hours of men and women in their 40s, we see from Figure 3.1c that men aged 42 in 2000 (the 1958 cohort) worked considerably fewer hours, on average 3.7 fewer, than their counterparts (the 1946 cohort) in 1989. This comes about because very long hours were less common in the second cohort. In contrast, Figure 3.1d shows that there is very little difference in the distribution of weekly working hours of women aged 42 in the 1958 cohort and women aged 43 in the 1946 cohort. Each peaks around 35 hours, with a secondary peak for part-timers around 15 hours. The similarity of the two distributions reflects the fact that the proportion of women working part-time changed less for the cohorts in their 40s than it did at the earlier age (Figure 3.1a).

Fringe benefits of employment

Information on fringe benefits received by cohort members was available for the 1970 cohort at age 30, for the 1958 cohort at ages 33 and 42, and for the 1946 cohort at 32 and 43. Numbers of individuals reporting at least one benefit were higher for full-timers than part-timers. Among full-timers, more women than men reported at least one benefit, but men were more likely to have large numbers of benefits. In their 30s, coverage of company pensions fell for men from 33 per cent among the 1946 cohort in 1978, to 27 per cent among the 1970 cohort in 2000, while the proportion of women employees with company pensions rose from 10 per cent to 34 per cent, reflecting the relative decline in part-time employment among women at these ages and, possibly, a greater share of public sector employers for women than men. Once they were over 40, membership of employer pension schemes rose for both sexes in the 1946 cohort and for women in the 1958 cohort (to 40 per cent in the latter case). Amongst 43-year-olds in 1989, employed men had 78 per cent coverage by employer pension compared to 48 per cent of women. This suggests that people take more interest in getting pension coverage as they get older, but also that the more recent cohorts will be placing more reliance on forms of pension other than their employers', such as personal pensions. Men were more likely than women to have had a company car, especially in 1989. Help with childcare was only listed in this context of the 1958 cohort women in 1991 when a mere 1 per cent reported having this fringe benefit.

The labour market and the family

This section of the chapter looks at some aspects of the cohort members' employment in conjunction with their own family position in adulthood.

Marital status and labour-force participation

When considered by marital status, men are generally more likely to be out of work, either unemployed or inactive, if they have no current partner. The converse is approximately true: that women living with a partner are less likely to have paid work than women who have never had a partner. Previously partnered women, many of whom are lone mothers, also show relatively low labour-force attachment. Cohabitees are more likely to be employed, and full-time, than legally married women. The trends across, and within, cohorts resemble the overall trends in female participation for the largest sub-group, those married at the time of the survey, but for those who were not married, the patterns vary (compare Table 3.4 with Table 3.1). For example, whereas never-married women in the 1946 cohort were in a small minority, at both 32 and 43, their participation in full-time employment was higher than among the larger never-married groups in the succeeding cohorts, probably reflecting changing patterns in the timing and selectivity of marriage.

Children

Table 3.5 affords another glimpse of the interaction of life cycle patterns in the different cohorts. Women are cross classified by whether they have a child under 5 living with them, any child over 5 but under 18, or no co-resident child under 18. (This also shows women only, as men's employment patterns are not greatly differentiated by their parental status.)

In the early 30s, this threefold classification roughly distinguishes (i) those who have never (yet) had children, (ii) those whose last child so far was born up to their late 20s and (iii) those whose most recent, including their first, child was born within five years of the most recent survey (after 25–28 years of age, depending on the cohort). The third group have children who are least likely to be in school and most likely to be looked after by their mothers staying full-time out of paid work. By the early 40s, it will almost certainly be different women who, at that stage, have a child under 5. (Note that the tables do not follow the same women within sub-groups across waves.)

The contrasts in economic activity rates according to the woman's motherhood status are more marked than they were by marital status. The presence of children is more likely to inhibit paid work than the presence of a partner. The comparison at '30 something' clearly shows the well-known and expected pattern that mothers with young children are less

Table 3.4a *Labour force status at interview by marital status: women in their early 30s*

Marital status	1970 cohort Age 30 in 2000				1958 cohort Age 33 in 1991				1946 cohort Age 36 in 1982			
	Single, never partnered %	Married with partner %	Cohabit-ing %	Previously partnered %	Single, never partnered %	Married with partner %	Cohabit-ing %	Previously partnered %	Single, never partnered %	Married with partner %	Cohabit-ing %	Previously partnered %
Economically active												
Full-time	64	41	61	42	73	29	53	37	79	18	17	50
Part-time	10	31	17	22	8	38	20	25	6	33	66	19
Unemployed	5	1	1	4	4	1	3	3	8	1	0	1
Economically inactive	21	27	21	32	15	32	23	35	7	49	17	30
N (100%)	1,367	2,737	1,335	315	580	4,143	564	489	206	2,653	6	93

Table 3.4b *Labour force status at interview by marital status: women in their early 40s*

Marital status	1958 cohort Age 42 in 2000				1946 cohort Age 43 in 1989			
	Single, never partnered %	Married with partner %	Cohabiting %	Previously partnered %	Single, never partnered %	Married with partner %	Cohabiting %	Previously partnered %
Economically active								
Full-time	65	40	59	48	73	40	60	63
Part-time	11	40	24	23	5	41	28	20
Worker status unknown		1	1		0	1	0	0
Unemployed	6			3	2	3	12	5
Economically inactive	19	19	16	26	15	13	0	11
Non-worker status unknown					5	2	0	1
Total (100%) no. of cases	392	4,028	625	712	107	2,661	87	369

Note

These marital status codings try to reflect as much as possible the current living arrangements of the CM. Thus, those who have previously been married/ widowed/separated/divorced but are living with people at the time of survey are included under 'cohabiting'; those on their first or second marriage who are still living with their spouse will be included under 'married'; those not currently living with anyone but who have previously been married or cohabiting are included under 'previously partnered'. Only 'single, never partnered' will all be the same with regards to their legal married status – all legally single people who have never lived with anyone.

Table 3.5a *Labour force status at interview, by dependent children in household: women in their early 30s*

Age of youngest child	1970 cohort Age 30 in 2000			1958 cohort Age 33 in 1991			1946 cohort Age 32 in 1978		
	Under 5 %	5–17 %	No child %	Under 5 %	5–17 %	No child %	Under 5 %	5–17 %	No child %
Economically active									
Full-time	20	28	86	16	28	83	6	25	73
Part-time	37	37	6	35	45	7	28	41	17
Unemployed	1	5	2	1	2	4	1	1	2
Economically inactive	42	30	7	48	26	6	67	33	8
N (100%)	2,312	801	2,639	2,330	2,058	1,369	1,419	970	369

Table 3.5b *Labour force status at interview, by dependent children in household: women in their early 40s*

Age of youngest child	1958 cohort Age 42 in 2000			1946 cohort Age 43 in 1989		
	Under 5 %	5–17 %	No child %	Under 5 %	5–17 %	No child %
Economically active						
Full-time	25	38	67	18	39	69
Part-time	37	42	15	49	42	18
Worker status unknown				0	1	0
Unemployed	1	1	3	0	4	4
Economically inactive	38	18	16	22	13	8
Non-worker status unknown				11	1	1
N (100%)	566	3,674	1,522	45	2,467	656

likely to be in paid work than mothers with children over school age, or those with no dependent children. It also corroborates other evidence (for example, from the Labour Force Survey, Twomey 2002) that growth in employment is particularly strong amongst the mothers of young children. The economic activity rate for mothers of children under 5 increased by 25 percentage points between the 32-year-olds of 1978 (1946 cohort) and the 30-year-olds of 2000 (1970 cohort), compared with an overall increase of three points among those with older children and one point among those with no dependent children. The increased proportion across cohorts of women with no children – presumably childless – at this stage (13 per cent in 1978 (1946 cohort); 24 per cent in 1991 (1958 cohort); and 46 per cent in 2000 (1970 cohort)) also contributes to the overall rise in activity.

Looking *within* cohorts from 30 to 40 something, we see that the economic activity (and full-time employment) of mothers of each age group of children has gone up in both the 1946 and 1958 cohorts. This is to be expected, as the average age of the children will be higher and because those who postpone childbearing to their late 30s are likely to have greater labour-force attachment. There has also been a general trend towards more employment of mothers of young children, with the growth from the mid-1980s of family-friendly employment practices and of childcare facilities (Forth *et al.* 1997). In 2000, over half the mothers of children under 5 in the cohorts had paid jobs; 20 per cent of the 1970-born 30-year-olds were in full-time jobs and 37 per cent in part-time jobs. In the 1958 cohort, mothers aged 42 with children under 5 had the same proportion (37 per cent) working part time, but 25 per cent in full-time jobs, bringing their employment rate up to 62 per cent, and reflecting the higher levels of qualification held by women who had postponed child-bearing. What was not expected in the results for women in their 40s was the lack of much difference between 1989 (1946 cohort) and 2000 (1958 cohort) for mothers of school-age children. This may reflect the fact that the children concerned were, on average, older in 1989 than 2000.

The overall fall in economic activity between the ages of 30 and 40 for women without dependent children is likely to be due to changes in the composition of this sub-sample, with those whose children have passed 18 joining those who remained childless.

The employment participation of mothers is also affected by whether they are in a two- or one-parent family. In the 1970s, lone mothers were generally more likely to be employed, and employed full time, than married mothers. Our data on 32-year-olds (1946 cohort) in 1978 conforms with this pattern: 70 per cent of lone mothers in the 1946 cohort were employed full time and 10 per cent part-time; compared with 18 per cent and 33 per cent of the partnered (married) mothers. The subsequent cohorts display the reversal of differentials with those which occurred generally in the 1980s: only 18 per cent of lone mothers aged 30 in 2000 (1970 cohort) had full-time jobs and 27 per cent part-time, in contrast to 23 per cent and 29 per cent among partnered mothers. From the observations at age 42 (1958 cohort) and 43 (1946 cohort), lone mothers also show less of a propensity to be in paid work than partnered mothers. The reverse trend in labour force participation for lone mothers has been attributed to the structure of benefits, the shortage of childcare facilities and the difficulty of taking advantage of part-time employment when there is only one parent in the home (Joshi 1990; Kiernan *et al.* 1998; Bradshaw *et al.* 1996). Although policies have been introduced since 1997 to encourage lone parents into the workforce, these data do not show that they had, by 2000, had the result of removing differences between one- and two-parent families. We would therefore expect lower income among lone parents than those who were married or cohabiting.

Employment and childcare

Information was also available for the 1958 and 1970 cohorts on the childcare arrangements which permitted employed mothers to undertake paid work. Apart from school, employed mothers often reported a combination of formal and informal arrangements for childcare. The most frequent mention, by these and other mothers, was informal care, alone or in combination with other arrangements. This included care by fathers, grandparents and neighbours. Formal provision, including child minders, nurseries, and nannies, was most frequently, but not exclusively, mentioned by mothers of children under 5 working full time. The increasing use of formal care derives mainly from the increased full-time employment of mothers, rather than an increased use of this type of care within the group of working mothers. The mix of childcare arrangements reported by mothers in the 2000 surveys is not much different from those reported in 1991, given the age of the child and the mother's hours of work (for a detailed study of the use of childcare by the 1958 cohort at 33, see Ward *et al.* 1996).

The employment, household composition and income of couples

Changes in the distribution of employment among adults, more jobs for women but also more joblessness, manifest themselves in changes in the distribution of employment among couples. The rise in women's employment implies more two-earner couples, and the rise in joblessness tends to lead to a rise in the proportion of couples in which no one earns, especially if one spouse is more likely to be out of employment at the same time as the other than would arise from pure chance. An association of partners' joblessness is a well-known feature the British labour market (Gregg and Wadsworth 1996; Davies *et al.* 1998). It is thought to be partly due to the disincentives to wives' working enshrined in the benefit system, but also possibly reflecting the tendency of people with poor employment prospects to find similar partners and the influence of unfavourable local labour markets.

The cohort members in couples conform to the phenomenon. For example, in 1978, 50 per cent of the 32-year-old women in the 1946 cohort with employed husbands were themselves employed, compared with 28 per cent of those with unemployed husbands. For the 1970 cohort in 2000, employed husbands had employed wives in 77 per cent of cases, but the proportion was less than half, 38 per cent, among unemployed husbands. For a detailed study of spouses relative contributions to joint income among the 1958 cohort at 33, see Joshi *et al.* (1995). The most common arrangement found in this study was for the wife to be a part-time secondary earner, neither totally independent of nor totally dependent on her partner. The growth of full-time employment in 2000 is likely to have increased the minority of wives earning as much as, or more than, their husbands. At this point, we take a less detailed scrutiny, classifying couples simply by the number of them who are earning.

Pooling the information on male and female cohort members' partnerships, there is confirmation of the tendency for the proportion of cohort members in couples with two earners to rise over time within cohort, and at the younger ages, across cohorts. At the older age, the proportion with

Table 3.6 *Couples with two, one and no earners, and % of each with children in the household*

	1970 cohort Age 30 in 2000		1958 cohort Age 33 in 1991		1946 cohort Age 32 in 1978	
	All couples	With children ≤17 years	All couples	With children ≤17 years	All couples	With children ≤17 years
	%	%	%	%	%	%
2 earners	70	48	61	71	50	81
1 earner	26	85	34	92	49	94
No earner	4	88	5	90	1	92
N (100%)	7,530	7,530	9,187	9,187	4,514	3,947

	1958 cohort Age 42 in 2000		1946 cohort Age 43 in 1989	
	All couples	With children ≤17 years	All couples	With children ≤17 years
	%	%	%	%
2 earners	74	78	79	83
1 earner	22	84	19	75
No earner	4	75	2	73
N (100%)	9,178	9,178	5,392	4,379

two earners is highest (79 per cent) in the 1946 cohort at age 43 in 1989, reflecting the relatively high female participation rates in this survey. There are fewest dual-earner couples (50 per cent) in the earliest survey, age 32 in 1978, when one-earner couples were almost as numerous (49 per cent). The couples with no earner range from less than 2 per cent in the 1946 cohort in 1989, to 5 per cent for the 1958 cohort at age 33 in 1991, which reflects the high unemployment at the time of that survey. Hence, there is some sign of the national polarisation of employment opportunities towards dual earner couples, but, in these snapshots across life cycles, the jobs of the dual earners seem to have come as much at the expense of single-earner couples as workless couples.

In their 30s and 40s, most couples have dependent children, but fewer two-earner couples have children than couples with only one or no earner, and where the woman is likely to be at home. For the couples at 30-ish, around nine out of ten of those with one or no earner had children. Almost as large a proportion of the dual earner couples also had children, although this varied from 48 per cent for 30-year-olds in the 1970 cohort through 71 per cent for 33-year-olds in 1991 and 81 per cent for the 43-year-olds in 1989.

Occupational attainment, education and family of origin

In this section we look at the occupational level attained by the time of the adult surveys, including the level of the last occupation of those who were not currently employed, still using the Registrar General's schema as a rough guide to the degree of achievement.

Qualifications and social class attained
How far have qualifications been passports to success in the labour market? Table 3.7 relates the highest qualification attained to a summary of occupational attainment in the form of the proportions attaining jobs in one of the top two classes. Those with tertiary qualifications (NVQ 4–5) have the strongest chances by far of obtaining jobs in the top stratum. Around three-quarters of the tertiary qualified men had such occupations: more

in the 1946 cohort than their successors, and more in their 40s than in their 30s. The figures for women were somewhat lower (apart from the 86 per cent at age 43 for the small number of highly qualified women in the 1946 cohort). Nevertheless, it is not unheard of for those with fewer, or even no, qualifications to reach this part of the labour market. Among the unqualified, about one in seven of the men (and one in ten of the women) in the 1970 and 1958 cohorts held social class I or II occupations in 2000. Among those with A-level-type qualifications (NVQ 3), 37 per cent of men from the 1958 cohort had attained this level of occupation by age 33 and 41 per cent by age 42. Men's lead over women was particularly marked at this level of qualifications. Among women with NVQ 3 in the 1958 cohort, the proportion with 'top' occupations was 26 per cent at age 33 and 28 per cent at age 42. Looked at in terms of the proportions of those with top stratum occupations who had different levels of qualifications, in the two most recent cohorts there is an excess of 50 to 60 percentage points in the proportion with tertiary qualifications over the proportion with none. In the 1946 cohort, however, there is less concentration on the highly qualified, particularly women, among whom there were not enough with tertiary qualifications to fill all the top occupation slots achieved.

Early attainment and occupational status in adult life

The links between education and attainment will be partly due to qualifications that reflect the acquisition of skills which give access to the top jobs, but may also be due to earlier advantages that gave access to the qualifications as well as the higher occupations. We saw in Chapter 2 how test scores of primary school achievement or 'ability' led to different levels of qualification. Now, as an illustration of one part of a more complex set of relationships, we relate these early test scores directly to occupational attainment. Figure 3.2 displays, by 'ability' score, the distribution of cohort members in two extreme occupational groups: the 'top' professional, managerial and intermediate white collar jobs of I and II in Figure 3.2a, and the least skilled (semi- and unskilled) jobs (IV and V) in Figure 3.2b.

Figure 3.2a *Distribution of individuals in social class I and II across the attainment range in the three cohorts in their early 30s*

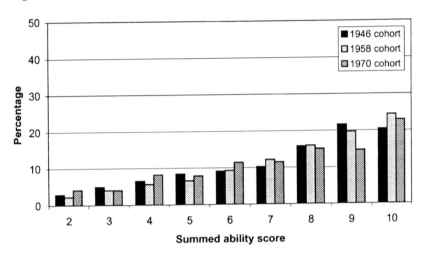

Figure 3.2b *Distribution of individuals in social class IV and V across the attainment range in the three cohorts in their early 30s*

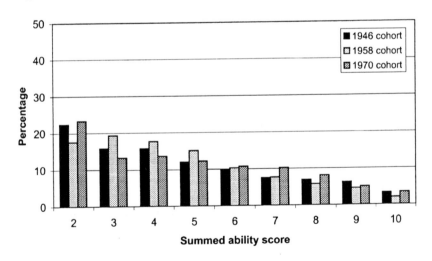

Table 3.7 *Percentages attaining professional or intermediate level occupations (current or most recent jobs) by highest qualification attained*

		No qualifications	NVQ 1	NVQ 2	NVQ 3	NVQ 4–5	All
1970 cohort at 30							
Men	I or II	15	16	26	29	72	39
N (100%)		727	464	1,305	1,242	1,712	5,450
Women	I or II	10	13	21	27	67	34
N (100%)		827	562	1,738	809	1,837	5,773
1958 cohort at 33							
Men	I or II	9	15	26	37	73	38
N (100%)		688	825	1,434	1,012	1,555	5,514
Women	I or II	7	11	17	26	72	30
N (100%)		826	846	1,865	759	1,423	5,719
1946 cohort at 32							
Men	I or II	13	21	47	45	78	37
N (100%)		1,138	179	355	379	615	2,666
Women	I or II	12	6	15	48	60	12
N (100%)		794	225	575	226	268	2,088
1958 cohort at 42							
Men	I or II	14	22	30	41	77	44
N (100%)		665	673	1,325	1,145	1,797	5,605
Women	I or II	11	13	20	28	69	34
N (100%)		813	731	1,705	793	1,734	5,776
1946 cohort at 43							
Men	I or II	22	34	52	63	84	48
N (100%)		1,111	169	403	414	656	2,754
Women	I or II	19	21	24	58	86	32
N (100%)		1,070	272	676	244	301	2,563

The first thing to notice is that here, too, there is a gradient by ability score, rising for the top jobs, and falling for low-grade jobs, but this gradient is not nearly so marked as the gradient for top qualifications by test score shown in Figure 2.1. Differences between cohorts within test scores are also small by comparison to those associated with qualifications (see Table 3.7). If these scores measure 'merit', they do not support the idea of a 'rising meritocracy' with outcomes increasingly well matched to ability. Following the 1958 and 1946 cohorts into their 40s, the results suggest that there has been little change in the 'ability' composition of the highest occupational status group. Thus, the extent to which early attainment predicts where an individual ends up in the occupational spectrum does not appear to have changed greatly over time. If the influence of early ability remains stable, this suggests little change in social mobility, a topic to which we now turn.

Intergenerational social mobility
Finally, we make the long leap from the occupation of the father in the cohort members' childhood to their own occupational attainment as adults.

The changing structure of men's occupations, with the move away from manual jobs, means that some cohort members, at least, must have experienced a different occupation from their fathers, because of the decline in the number of low ranked 'slots'. But beyond this, is there evidence of social fluidity in movement down as well as up the occupational ladder across generations (Erikson and Goldthorpe 1993)?

The transition, if any, from class of origin to own occupation is summarised in Table 3.8. This shows, for each class of origin, by sex, cohort and time of survey, the proportions whose own class of occupation by the time of the adult survey was graded above, below, or the same as their class of origin. We also display the class position of the cohort member's father. Occupation is ranked extremely crudely, using the Registrar General's scale, making the naive assumption that it represents a generally agreed ordering, and ignoring the fact that it is based on several schemes of occupational classification which have changed over time. The following analyses also have to be interpreted cautiously because we do not have completely comparable snapshots across histories of within-career mobility. The rates of occupational change as measured here are also not completely comparable for men and women, due to the large number of women's jobs in social class III non-manual, and the questionability of ranking it above social class III manual, where men's jobs tend to cluster.

Table 3.8 *Percentage experiencing occupational mobility or stability by father's social class*

Men

Class of job relative to origin	I	II	III nm	III m	IV	V	Total
1970 cohort at 30 in 2000							
Increased	21	11	52	42	77	89	39
Constant	79	47	17	41	19	11	34
Decreased		42	31	17	4		26
N (100%)	318	842	397	1,899	491	175	4,122
1978 cohort at 33 in 1991							
Increased	21	12	53	42	77	90	45
Constant	79	53	17	40	18	10	33
Decreased		35	30	18	5		22
N (100%)	266	699	448	1,993	805	240	4,451
1946 cohort at 32 in 1978							
Increased	33	12	56	38	87	97	51
Constant	67	52	14	47	11	3	32
Decreased		36	30	15	1		16
N (100%)	99	428	356	1,524	737	319	3,463
1978 cohort at 42 in 2000							
Increased	19	11	60	48	83	92	48
Constant	81	59	12	40	13	8	32
Decreased		30	28	13	4		19
N (100%)	247	641	412	1,767	696	198	3,961
1946 cohort at 43 in 1989							
Increased	30	12	67	48	86	92	55
Constant	70	60	12	40	12	8	31
Decreased		28	21	12	3		14
N (100%)	98	411	347	1,575	670	255	3,356

Women

Class of job relative to origin	I	II	III nm	III m	IV	V	Total
1970 cohort at 30 in 2000							
Increased	12	6	39	70	78	92	51
Constant	88	45	43	11	18	8	22
Decreased		50	17	19	4		28
N (100%)	302	902	395	1,996	546	177	4,318
1978 cohort at 33 in 1991							
Increased	11	6	37	66	69	88	52
Constant	89	42	41	8	23	12	20
Decreased		52	22	26	8		28
N (100%)	247	698	489	2,036	777	260	4,507
1946 cohort at 32 in 1978							
Increased	17	2	39	66	71	91	56
Constant	83	35	43	6	25	9	17
Decreased		64	18	29	4		27
N (100%)	71	324	270	1,198	483	204	2,550
1978 cohort at 42 in 2000							
Increased	12	7	41	70	73	90	55
Constant	88	42	38	7	20	10	19
Decreased		51	21	23	8		27
N (100%)	220	612	439	1,820	691	221	4,003
1946 cohort at 43 in 1989							
Increased	9	2	42	71	63	82	57
Constant	91	37	42	6	24	18	19
Decreased		60	15	23	12		25
N (100%)	89	403	318	1,398	608	289	3,105

Has the transformation of educational opportunities in the postwar era produced more 'rags to riches' scenarios for those born later? Looking at men in their early 30s, about one in three in each cohort were in the same position as their fathers. The chances of experiencing upward mobility from a given background were remarkably similar. Nearly all the sons of unskilled manual fathers had achieved occupations at a higher level (89–97 per cent), as had three-quarters of the men whose fathers had semi-skilled jobs, and four in ten of those from skilled manual backgrounds. Over half the sons of the relative minority of men in junior non-manual jobs achieved occupations in social class I or II, but only a little over one in ten moved from a social class II background into social class I. Overall, the chances of experiencing upward mobility are diminished for the more recent cohorts, since more of their fathers were already further up the scale. Likewise, downward intergenerational mobility, which increased from 16 per cent in the 1946 cohort to 26 per cent in the 1970 cohort, reflects the greater number of the latter with fathers in the higher classes, rather than an increased risk of downgrading from a given starting point. Most of the occupational change is short-distance between adjoining categories. Extreme moves in the opposite direction, 'riches to rags', are equally uncommon in all three cohorts.

This picture of little change in the chances of social mobility also applies to women. Their occupational opportunities being weighted towards social class III non-manual, and their fathers' to social class III manual, exaggerates the estimates of women's upward mobility presented here. Women were also more likely than men to record a downward move from their father's occupation, but, as with men, the perhaps unanticipated similarity between cohorts in their 30s remains.

The evidence on men, and to a lesser extent women, in their 40s shows some net upward movement during a career, but still the same story of cross-cohort similarity.

Underlying the ebb and flow of social mobility, the influence of class of origin on adult outcomes remains apparent in all three cohorts. At the age of 30 the offspring of social class I in the 1970 cohort were about eight times more likely than those with fathers in social class V to have an occupation at social class I or II. For the 1958 cohort at 33, there was also an eightfold difference. The families with the higher-class backgrounds tended to produce children gaining higher scores in school tests and higher educational qualifications. These factors help to account for the better outcomes of the higher social classes, but not entirely. Allowing for ability tested at school, and final qualification attained, an individual from a social class I background was still twice as likely to obtain a job classified as I or II than an individual from social class V. The few children with high reading and maths scores who failed to convert them into high qualifications might still end up in a top job (I and II), even if their father was in a low class (IV or V), but the small chances of doing so would be greater if their own father was in a favoured position. Amongst children in the 1958 cohort in the combined top fifth for maths and reading scores, 76 per cent born to fathers in social class I obtained a 'top' job at the age of 33 compared to 26 per cent of those born to fathers classified as social class V. The equivalent proportions in the 1970 cohort at age 30 were 69 per cent and 24 per cent respectively – a roughly threefold advantage in each case. The upper layers of the occupational structure, measured in this way, have recruited from all origins, but children from working-class families have not encountered completely equal access. Opportunities for social advancement appear somewhat greater for women than men, but, over time, these outcomes have not changed much between those growing up in the third and the last quarter of the twentieth century.

Conclusion

In this chapter, we have focused on the paid work of cohort members, in mid-adulthood, in the context of their work places and homes, their families of origin and of destination. There have been bigger changes and differentials in the participation of women in paid work over these ages than for men. Trends in hours of work are also complex. Contrary to the impression of an increasing culture of long hours, those reported by men showed a reduction in very long hours after the 1946 cohort. For women, the trend was in the opposite direction, as more women across cohorts

4 Partnerships and parenthood

Elsa Ferri and Kate Smith

Introduction

Few aspects of the lives of our three cohorts are likely to show sharper contrasts than the domain of family and personal relationships. Many changes took place during the second half of the twentieth century which are likely to be reflected in different experiences of partnership and parenthood, family life and gender relations among those born in 1946, 1958 and 1970.

These include the now familiar demographic changes, such as the huge increase in cohabitation as a precursor, or alternative, to marriage; the seemingly relentless rise in divorce rates, which peaked in 1993 (ONS 2002a); and the linked phenomenon of serial monogamy, since there is little evidence that failed relationships are a disincentive to repartnership or remarriage (Utting 1995).

These trends in partnership behaviour are also reflected in another major demographic change, namely, the timing and context of parenthood. For women, the average age at first birth rose from 24 in the early 1970s to 29 in the year 2000 (ONS 2002a), and it is predicted that an increasing proportion of women will eschew motherhood altogether. The growth in cohabitation has been accompanied by a corresponding increase in the proportion of children born outside marriage – currently approximately two-fifths of all new births (ONS 2002a). The increased fragility of adult relationships, and the propensity to acquire new partners after the break-down of a marriage or cohabitation, have meant that more and more children experience change – in many cases, multiple changes – in their parental care situation and immediate family environment. A further result of this has been that the notion of *social*, as opposed to *biological*, parenting has become a prominent feature of family life at the end of the twentieth century, as more and more adults, especially fathers, find themselves raising children to whom they are not genetically related (Ferri and Smith 1996). For the children involved, this increased complexity of family structures and relationships extends beyond the immediate household to encompass grandparents and other relatives, with the potential for either gain or loss of their network of kin relationships, depending upon the aftermath of the rupture in their parents' relationship.

Inter-cohort comparisons can investigate how far these trends can be traced in the relationships and family lives of those born at different times, and how they link to other changes in the lives and circumstances of the three cohorts. The studies contain a further rich analysis potential: from birth through childhood and adolescence, the data collected at each survey of the three cohorts have recorded the changing parental care situations and family settings in which they themselves grew up. Added to the comprehensive information on the cohort members' own adult experiences of partnerships and parenthood, updated at each adult survey, these family histories make the cohort studies a unique source for investigating inter-generational continuities and discontinuities in family formation and family breakdown.

In considering the part played by experiences in the family of upbringing, it is worth noting at this stage just how different these had been for the members of our three cohorts. To take family stability as an example: despite a postwar surge in divorce rates, children born in 1946 were much less likely to experience the breakdown of their parents' marriage than those born 12 or, especially, 24 years later. Just 3 per cent of the 1946 cohort had experienced parental divorce or separation by the age of 6. Changing family circumstances became an increasingly common occurrence in subsequent cohorts: by the time they were 7, 8 per cent of those born in 1958 were not living with both biological parents (Davie *et al.* 1972); while among the 1970 cohort, 9 per cent had experienced family disruption by the age of 5 (Osborn and Milbank 1987). While parental divorce and separation grew increasingly common, the death of a parent became a much rarer experience.

Over the years, the cohort studies have provided unique data for policy-related research investigating the influence of family experience on children's development. Numerous analyses, drawing on information from all three cohort studies, have informed our knowledge and understanding of the part played by different experiences in the families in which the cohort members grew up (e.g. Ely *et al.* 1999). From the 1960s onwards, social policy relating to families was driven by concern about the impact of increasing rates of divorce and extra-marital births. As noted in Chapter 1, studies of the impact of family disruption have shown that children are, on the whole, resilient to bereavement, whereas the breakdown of their parents' relationship is more likely to be linked to poorer development in childhood (Essen 1979; Ferri 1976; Kiernan 1992), and an increased risk of depression in adulthood (Rodgers 1994). Analyses produced for government enquiries such as the Finer Committee on One-Parent Families (DHSS 1974) were particularly important in demonstrating how any adverse outcomes linked to family breakdown due to either cause were relatively small in magnitude by comparison with the influence of social and economic disadvantage (Ferri 1976; Wadsworth and Maclean 1986).

A further great strength of the longitudinal data provided by the cohort studies lies in the potential for disentangling the sequential influences of different circumstances and experiences. This is demonstrated by investigations which have depicted family breakdown as a *process* rather than an *event*. Thus, Elliott and Richards (1991) found that the relatively poor achievement and social behaviour shown by 16-year-olds born in 1958 whose parents had divorced were already in evidence at the age of 7, some time before the formal break in the family. Similar findings were reported by Cherlin *et al.* (1991), who found lower attainment scores among 7-year-old boys in the 1958 cohort whose parents *subsequently* divorced.

More recently, studies of family demographics and relationships have focused on the cohort members' own experiences of adult partnerships and family life. While negligible numbers nowadays lose a partner through death in early adulthood, rates of separation and divorce have continued to rise. One of the most important findings to emerge from recent research based on the cohort studies has been the link between disrupted adult relationships among the cohort members themselves and divorce or separation in their own families of origin (Buchanan and Ten Brinke 1997; Kiernan 1997b).

In this chapter, we examine a number of key aspects of the demographics of family life for all three cohorts in early adulthood (around the age of 30) and for the two earlier cohorts as they reached early middle age (42/3). This includes their experiences of partnership (marriage or cohabitation); the timing of their transition to parenthood and the number of children they had by each age; and the type of family situation in which those who had become parents were bringing up their children. The aim is to present a broad overview of some of the main trends and patterns in these areas, and to identify some of the emerging questions and issues which future longitudinal analysis will be able to address.

Partnerships

The notion of lifelong marriage as the only socially sanctioned framework for sexual partnerships and the transition to parenthood has come to seem somewhat outdated in recent decades. The increasing prevalence of cohabitation as a precursor, or alternative, to marriage (Buck *et al.* 1994; Kiernan and Estaugh 1993) and of serial monogamy, contributes to the diversity of personal living arrangements which characterises Britain at the start of the twenty-first century. Until very recently, there was a steady downward trend in the number of marriages each year, culminating in an all-time low figure in 2000 (ONS 2002b). It is not yet wholly clear how far this represents merely a delay in embarking upon committed relationships (especially among the growing numbers experiencing higher education and prolonged career establishment) or a principled rejection of more formal and traditional ties (Berrington 2001).

Partnerships in early adult life
Marriage and cohabitation
The trends in partnership relationships which have taken place during the past few decades can be clearly seen in the situation reported by the three

cohorts in early adult life. The growing popularity of cohabitation is evident among the two later born cohorts. The great majority of the men (77 per cent) and women (88 per cent) born in 1946 were married at the age of 31 – about twice as many as in the 1970 cohort (Figure 4.1). In contrast, whilst cohabitation was virtually unreported among the 1946 cohort, about a quarter of the 1970 sample, and a third of those born in 1958, were, at age 30, currently living with partners to whom they were not married.[1] The lower figure for the 1970 cohort does not mean that

Figure 4.1 *Partnership situation of cohort members at age 30*

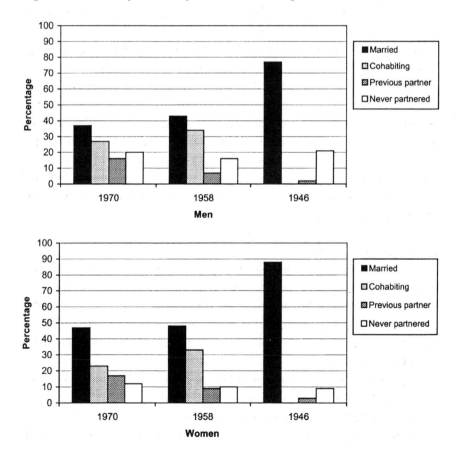

cohabitation was less common in this cohort: a further one in six, although not partnered at 30, had *previously* lived with someone, in most cases in a cohabitation.

Further information from the two later born cohorts revealed that about a third of the men and women born in 1958 who were married by age 30 had lived with their spouse before marrying, while among the 1970 cohort this figure had risen to over 70 per cent. These findings echo comparisons of cohorts born in 1950–62 and 1963–76 in the British Household Panel Study, which found that the proportions marrying directly or cohabiting first were reversed between these two groups, and that, in the latter cohort, cohabitation had become the most common form of first partnership (Ermisch and Francesconi 2000).

It is now well established that cohabitation is a more fragile relationship than marriage and that divorce is more common in marriages preceded by cohabitation (e.g. Haskey 1992). We can thus expect future surveys to show a continuing rise in rates of partnership dissolution among the members of the later born cohorts. The detailed partnership histories collected at the adult surveys, containing start and end dates of all marriages and cohabitations, will be of great importance for analysis of the patterns of partnership formation and dissolution. They will also throw light on the factors associated with positive and negative outcomes in terms of relationship stability.

Age at first partnership
Women born in 1970 were much less likely than those in the earlier cohorts to have entered their first partnership at a very young age. Just over a quarter of the 1970-born women had lived with a partner by the time they were 20. This compared with four out of ten of the women born in 1958, while the same proportion in the 1946 cohort were *married* by age 20 (Figure 4.2).

There was a strong relationship between age at first partnership and educational achievement; for example, among the women born in 1970, nearly a third of those with no formal qualifications had entered their first partnership before they were 20, compared with less than one in 12 of

Figure 4.2 *Age at first partnership: women*

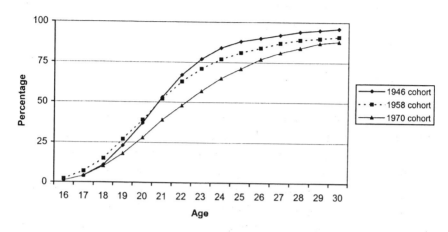

their peers who had obtained a degree. The gradient was even steeper in the 1946 cohort – more than half of those with no qualifications were married by 20, compared with only 6 per cent of the small group of women graduates. The difference in age at first partnership between the 1970 and the earlier born cohorts is thus strongly linked to the huge increase in the proportion of women in the youngest group going on to higher education. Nevertheless, changes in educational experience by no means wholly account for the cohort differences in partnering behaviour. Youthful marriage was very much a feature of British society in the 1960s, when the 1946 cohort reached adulthood. For example, even among the relatively small number of women in this cohort who had obtained a degree, over 80 per cent were married by the age of 25.

Similarly, among the men in the three cohorts, the main overall difference lay in the relatively high proportion of those born in 1946 who had married in their mid to late 20s. As with the women, the great majority of men in the 1946 cohort were married by age 25 – irrespective of their educational experience. This is likely to reflect the opportunities for economic independence available to these young men – in particular the availability of relatively secure and well-paid jobs to those with no, or only minimal, educational qualifications.

As noted above, the family history data collected at various surveys from childhood onwards enable us to investigate *intergenerational* patterns of relationship formation and breakdown – for example, to see whether there are links between cohort members' own partnership experiences and those of their parents. First findings suggest that parental divorce, far from being a deterrent to marriage or cohabitation, was clearly linked with *earlier* partnership. In all three cohorts, those whose parents had divorced or separated contained a much higher proportion who had entered their first partnership aged 20 or under. It may be that moving in with a partner is seen as an attractive alternative to a broken parental home. For the men, this involved about one in five in each cohort – about half as many again as among those whose parents had remained together. Figures for the women were even higher – half of those in the 1958 and 1946 cohorts with divorced parents were partnered by 20, as were 38 per cent of those born in 1970. The lower figures for women in the latest cohort may indicate that rising educational and career opportunities are increasingly seen as an alternative to early partnership. Nonetheless, the figures quoted for all three cohorts are disturbingly high, since the combined influence of early partnership and parental divorce are likely to be seen in high rates of relationship breakdown in the future among the cohort members in these groups (Kiernan 1997b).

Divorce and separation
As Figure 4.1 shows, the 1970 cohort were the least likely to be living with a partner at all at 30, either married or cohabiting. This largely reflects a difference between the cohorts in the experience of relationship *breakdown*: twice as many of those born in 1970, both men and women, had been in at least one partnership which had ended by the time they were 30, as was the case among the 1958 cohort. From the analysis so far, it seems likely that the 1970 cohort had experienced multiple *cohabitations* rather than *marriages*. Almost a fifth (18 per cent) of the women in the 1958 cohort had been divorced by age 33, compared with just 8 per cent of the 1970 cohort women at age 30. The corresponding figures for men were 12 per cent and 5 per cent. However, the total number who had had

previous *partnerships* (i.e. including cohabitations) was much greater in the 1970 cohort. The experience of partnership breakdown, like cohabitation, was extremely uncommon among the 1946 cohort by this stage in their lives: just 2 per cent of men and 3 per cent of women had been divorced or separated by the age of 31.

Number of partners by age 30
From the figures relating to partnership breakdown, it is clear that the person the cohort members were living with at age 30 was not necessarily their first partner. Figures showing the number of partners members of the 1970 and 1958 cohorts had had by this age (this information was not available for the 1946 cohort) reveal a slightly more polarised pattern among the more recent cohort: while rather more had not had a partner at all by age 30, the proportion who had had more than one was also slightly greater.

Members of the 1970 cohort were more likely to have already had two or more partners if their own parents had divorced (26 per cent of women and 23 per cent of men, compared with 17 and 14 per cent respectively of those whose parents had remained together). This pattern was almost identical among the 1958 cohort at the age of 33. However, parental divorce was more common among the 1970 cohort (24 per cent) than among those born 12 years earlier (15 per cent), so we can expect to see even higher rates of partnership change among the latest cohort in future.

Satisfaction with relationship
These first findings concerning partnership experience confirm the considerable fluidity in personal relationships which has come to characterise British society at the end of the twentieth century. There are indications from these preliminary analyses that the partnerships of the most recently born cohort may be especially fragile. Despite the now familiar statistics relating to divorce and separation, however, our knowledge of the underlying causes of relationship breakdown remains fragmentary and inconclusive. Research in this area spans a wide spectrum, from large-scale demographic analysis to investigations based on therapeutic casework.

The detailed data collected in the cohort surveys can contribute greatly
to research seeking to understand the economic, social and personal changes
which lie behind these trends. We have already seen, for example, how
family of origin and educational experience link with differences in the
partnering behaviour of the members of each cohort. More subjective
information is also crucial in this area, however, and the recent surveys
of the 1958 and 1970 cohorts have included questions concerning feelings
of satisfaction or otherwise with various aspects of the cohort members'
lives, including their personal relationships. Table 4.1 compares the
responses of the 1970 cohort at age 30 with those of the 1958 cohort at
age 33 to the question: *'How happy is your relationship with your spouse
or partner?'* This shows a startling difference between the two groups,
with substantial proportions of men and women born in 1970 expressing
dissatisfaction with their relationship, regardless of whether they were in
a first or second marriage or cohabiting, either as a never-married person
or following separation or divorce. Between a fifth and a quarter of the
1970 groups were clearly unhappy with their partner, compared with just
a few per cent of the older cohort. Furthermore, the tendency among the
1958 cohort for the married to be more content than the cohabiting was
not evident among the women born in 1970.

Analysis of the responses of the 1958 cohort to the same question when
they were age 42 showed a marked increase in relationship dissatisfaction,
to levels comparable with the 1970 cohort at age 30. This may indicate a
period effect – that is to say, a more generalised disenchantment with
relationships, as well as other aspects of life, at the time of the 1999–2000
surveys. However, we will need to await future data on the 1970 cohort
to ascertain whether there is also an age effect in operation, reflecting
rising discontent with partnerships in early middle age.

The responses of the 1970 cohort to the question on satisfaction with
their partnership were examined more closely, to see if they were related
to other characteristics, such as the age at which they had first entered a
partnership (not necessarily their current partner), their educational qualifications, the couple's employment situation (one, both or neither in
employment) and lastly, whether they had become parents by age 30.

Table 4.1 *How happy is your relationship with spouse or partner?*

(a) Men

Relationship rating	1970 cohort Age 30 in 2000				1958 cohort Age 33 in 1991				1958 cohort Age 42 in 2000			
	Married		Cohabiting		Married		Cohabiting		Married		Cohabiting	
	1st	2nd	Single	Separated/ divorced	1st	2nd	Single	Separated/ divorced	1st	2nd	Single	Separated/ divorced
	%	%	%	%	%	%	%	%	%	%	%	%
1, 2 (unhappy)	22	18	18	19	3	2	1	4	19	17	13	18
3, 4, 5	14	7	23	12	16	10	25	21	19	14	31	22
6, 7 (happy)	64	75	58	69	81	88	75	76	62	69	55	60
N (100%)	1,926	60	1,273	121	2,827	258	291	231	3,241	549	264	347

(b) Women

Relationship rating	1970 cohort Age 30 in 2000				1958 cohort Age 33 in 1991				1958 cohort Age 42 in 2000			
	Married		Cohabiting		Married		Cohabiting		Married		Cohabiting	
	1st	2nd	Single	Separated/ divorced	1st	2nd	Single	Separated/ divorced	1st	2nd	Single	Separated/ divorced
	%	%	%	%	%	%	%	%	%	%	%	%
1, 2 (unhappy)	24	21	20	27	2	2	6	4	20	21	15	17
3, 4, 5	13	13	18	12	18	13	28	21	18	18	27	21
6, 7 (happy)	63	66	62	61	80	85	66	75	62	61	58	62
N (100%)	2,578	105	1,115	193	3,039	407	205	231	3,299	651	221	380

Overall, the findings showed very little variation; except for slightly less positive relationship assessments among women who had become mothers by 30, among men who had partnered very young, and among both sexes in partnerships in which neither person was employed.

Another question concerning the cohort members' feelings about their relationships asked whether, if they could live their lives over again, they would marry or live as a couple with the same person, with someone else, or not live in a partnership at all. The replies of the 1970 cohort to this question showed a striking difference between the married and cohabiting, with the former much more likely to say they would choose the same partner again. This would seem to accord with the relative fragility of cohabitation already referred to.

Not surprisingly, the great majority of men and women in both cohorts who had expressed high satisfaction with their current relationship said that they would choose the same partner again. More puzzling were the almost identical replies given by those who had clearly indicated that they were *unhappy* with their present partner. It was those in the 'middle' group (claiming to be neither happy nor unhappy) who were least likely to say that they would repeat their choice.

Further analysis will be able to investigate the 'unhappily partnered' groups more closely, to try and discover whether their disillusionment is linked to other aspects of their family situation, their economic circumstances and/or their personal wellbeing. Future surveys will also be able to show the outcome of these relationships, and what factors are associated with their survival or termination.

Partnerships in early middle life

Information from the new surveys carried out in 1999–2000 enabled the partnership experiences of the 1958 cohort by the time they reached early middle age (42) to be compared with those of the 1946 cohort at approximately the same age. The picture here showed much greater similarities than had been the case in their early 30s. The great majority (about eight out of ten) of men and women in both cohorts were living with a partner in their early 40s (Figure 4.3). For those born in 1958, the ratio of marriages to cohabitations (about seven to one) was much greater at 42 than it had been at 30. We will need to wait for longitudinally linked data to discover whether earlier cohabitations had been converted to marriages, or whether these were new relationships. It was not possible to distinguish the married and the cohabiting in the 1946 cohort.

Figure 4.3 *Partnership situation of cohort members at age 42/3*

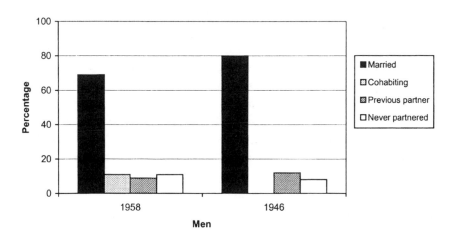

Men

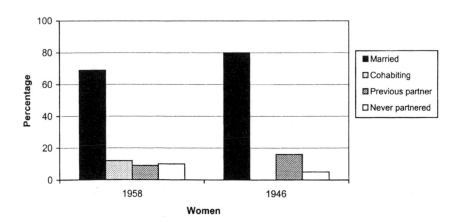

Women

Perhaps the most interesting finding here was the emergence of relationship breakdown as a significant category among the 1946 cohort. Whilst divorce and separation had been virtually non-existent at age 31 (see Figure 4.1), by their early 40s, 12 per cent of the men and 16 per cent of the women were no longer living in a partnership – higher figures than for their 1958 peers (and a likely underestimate of the total, since those with a spouse or partner at the time of the survey may previously have experienced a relationship breakdown).

The 'single lifestyle'

Before leaving the topic of partnership, it is interesting to turn our attention to those who were neither married nor cohabiting at the time of the surveys. As we have seen, although most members of each cohort were living with a spouse or partner at age 30, a substantial minority (up to a fifth) had never done so (Figure 4.1). This reflects another significant demographic trend in recent years: the emergence of the 'single lifestyle'. The number of single person households is currently estimated to be nearly one in three (ONS 2002a). In the younger age groups, this is likely to reflect the delay of marriage or cohabitation in favour of career and personal development, or, alternatively, difficulty in making the transition to independent living. Among those in middle age it is linked to the continuing increase in divorce and relationship breakdown, and among the elderly, to increased longevity, particularly among women. At all ages, solo living may also be associated with other personal characteristics or circumstances associated with never having married or lived with a partner, such as illness.

The 'single lifestyle' was clearly evident among the 1970 cohort at age 30, and most particularly among the men. About one in seven of these men were living alone at that time, and around one in 11 of the women. These figures are much higher than for the 1958 cohort, of whom just 9 per cent of men and 6 per cent of women were living on their own at age 33, while the figures for the 1946 cohort at 36 were just 5 and 2 per cent respectively.

While solo living was quite common among the men born in 1970, living under their parents' roof was even more so. One in six of the men in this cohort were living with their parents at 30 – more than twice as many as among the women. This gender difference was apparent in the earlier born cohorts, too, although the numbers involved were lower. Eleven per cent of the men and 5 per cent of the women born in 1946 were living with their parents at age 36, while this was an even less frequent arrangement among the cohort born in 1958, of whom 8 per cent of men and just 3 per cent of women lived with their parents at 33.

There were striking differences between the groups experiencing solo living at age 30 and those who were living with their parents. For example, in the 1970 cohort, they differed markedly in terms of their educational and occupational achievement: for both sexes, those living alone were more than twice as likely to have a degree as those living with their parents; whilst those still in the family home were twice as likely to be in semi- or unskilled jobs. Thus, solo living at 30 links with high qualifications and high status occupations, while living in the parental home is, by comparison, associated with low achievement, a poor job, and the consequent limited opportunities in terms of human capital to establish an independent lifestyle (Jones 1995).

About half of the men and women living alone at 30 had previously lived with at least one partner, compared with only a third of those living with their parents. This points to an important distinction which the longitudinal data will make possible to analyse within the latter group – those who had never left their parental home by age 30 and those who had lived independently for a period and then returned to live with their parents. Di Salvo (1996) found marked differences between these two groups in a study of the 1958 cohort at age 33. 'Returning' was likely to be a response to adverse circumstances, such as unemployment or relationship breakdown, while those who had never left, especially men, were characterised by a lack of economic and social independence which would support the transition to autonomous living.

Other longitudinal studies, for example the British Household Panel Study, have noted an increased tendency since the 1980s for young adults to return to their parental home (Ermisch and Francesconi 2000), and it seems likely that the relatively high numbers in the 1970 cohort living with their parents at age 30 reflect this trend. Future analysis will be able to explore how this relates to the high proportion of this cohort experiencing higher education, their subsequent employment patterns and delays in other adult transitions such as partnership and family formation.

Parenthood

The trend in Britain in recent years, as in most other western societies, has been towards fewer births, and the postponement, or even rejection, of parenthood. Many analysts and commentators have linked this with the growth of materialism and individualism, with their emphasis on self-fulfilment, as opposed to the supposedly altruistic nature of parenthood. From this perspective, parenthood can be seen, perhaps, as the ultimate consumer choice (Brannen 1992). Others see the trend towards smaller families of just one or two children as rooted in the intensity of modern parent–child relationships and the importance of 'quality' time and interaction (Pelz 1992). In one of the few studies to focus on those who opt to remain child-free, McAllister and Clarke (1998) found that highly qualified women were less likely to become mothers, but that 'career identity did not emerge as central to personal identity or personal fulfillment'. The child-free were, however, 'averse to taking risks' and 'parenthood was identified with disruption, change, poverty and dependency'. The authors note that national statistics rarely differentiate between voluntary and involuntary childlessness. This is an area in which the cohort studies have collected relevant data, and thus provide a key resource for investigating the relationship between a wide range of factors – education, employment, housing, values and aspirations – and cohort members' fertility choices.

Parenthood in early adult life
The delays in forming partnerships which characterise those born in 1970 are matched by a later transition to parenthood among the members of this cohort. By age 30, just a third of the men and a little over half of the women in the 1970 cohort had had their first child (Figure 4.4). This was considerably fewer than among those born 12 years earlier: half of the

Figure 4.4 *Age at first child*

a) Men

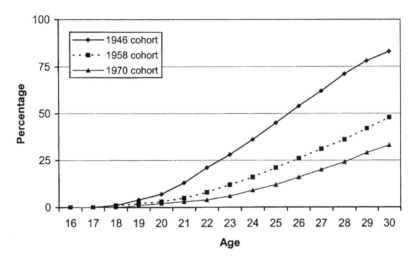

b) Women

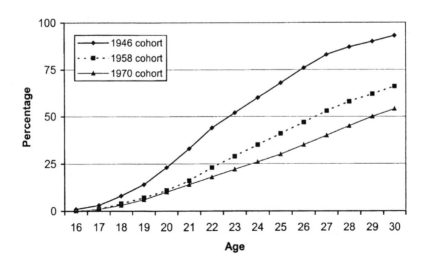

men and two-thirds of the women born in 1958 had had at least one child by the time they reached 30, while for the 1946 cohort, the respective figures were 83 per cent and 92 per cent.

Despite this marked overall trend towards later parenthood, there was much less difference between the 1958 and the 1970 cohorts in the number who had made the transition at a very young age: about one in ten of the women in each case had had their first child at 20 or younger. For those born in 1946, however, the figure was nearly one in four.

Far fewer men had become fathers by 20; just 2 to 3 per cent in the two later born cohorts and 8 per cent in the 1946 group. However, the figures are based at this stage on children *living in the cohort members' household* at 30, and so will exclude men who had fathered children with whom they were not living at that time.

As with their partnership experience, there was a strong link between the timing of the transition to parenthood and the educational qualifications the cohort members had achieved – again, especially for women. In the 1970 cohort, nearly a quarter of the women with no qualifications at all had had their first child at or before the age of 20; for women who were graduates by 30, the figure was just 2 per cent. The pattern was similar in the other two cohorts, though at each level of qualification, there was still a trend for later motherhood among the more recent cohorts. This may suggest that career development and alternatives to family life are increasingly important to the later cohorts.

Among men, the relationship between qualifications and age at becoming a father showed a similar, but much less marked, pattern than for the women. It would seem from this that the changing shape of family life is much more the product of the changing roles and aspirations of women than of men.

Family size
As well as the age at which they became parents, the changing size of the family was evident from figures showing the number of children in the households of the three cohorts when they were aged 30 or thereabouts. As well as the sharp gradient in the number still childless, the trend towards

smaller families was also marked: only 7 per cent of women born in 1970 had three or more children by age 30, compared with 20 per cent of those in the 1946 cohort at age 31 (Figure 4.5). The 1958 cohort were closer to the 1946 than the 1970 cohort in this respect, although their figures refer to age 33.

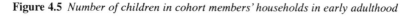

Figure 4.5 *Number of children in cohort members' households in early adulthood*

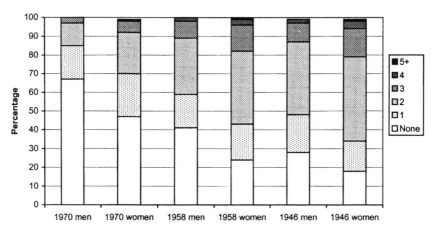

Just as the timing of the transition to parenthood was strongly associated with educational attainment, so the number of children born to members of each cohort showed a clear gradient, with graduates least likely to have three or more children by the time they were 30 and those with no qualifications having the largest families. The pattern was the same in all three cohorts. However, even after allowing for educational qualifications, the 1970 cohort were less likely to have children at all, and had considerably fewer children, than their peers born in 1958. The differences between the 1946 and 1958 cohort were much less marked when qualifications were taken into account, suggesting that there has been a real cohort shift in reproductive behaviour.

At age 30, families are not likely to be complete, and we will have to await further follow-ups to see how many of the 1970 cohort have just delayed childbearing or rejected parenthood altogether. It is also interesting to look at the cohort members' expressed attitudes to having children. The recent surveys of the 1958 and 1970 cohorts included a number of statements concerning views about having children, to which respondents were asked to indicate their agreement or disagreement. One of these was: *'People who never have children are missing an important part of life.'* The responses of the 1970 cohort showed, predictably, a much stronger commitment to parenthood among those who already had children, and especially among those with larger families of three or more. More surprisingly, perhaps, there was also a marked sex difference, with men showing much more enthusiasm for parenthood than women – particularly those with three or more children. It is not inconceivable that these differing attitudes relate to parenting roles and the realities and responsibilities of child-rearing, which are discussed in Chapter 5.

Family type
The preceding accounts of the partnership experiences of our three cohorts have underlined the increasing instability of adult relationships during the latter decades of the twentieth century. By the age of 30, considerable proportions of the later born cohorts had already lived with more than one partner. In this section, we look at how these trends were reflected in the patterns of family life of the members of the cohorts who had become parents. Change and diversity in family arrangements have become familiar themes in social commentary and social policy in recent years, with concern expressed about the impact of these trends upon the well-being and development of children, as well as the economic and social costs of family breakdown.

Just how far have the successive cohorts moved away from the 'traditional' nuclear family represented by a married couple and their offspring living under the same roof? Official figures show that only about one in five households in Britain today fall into this category (although this includes people of all ages) (ONS 2001). Table 4.2 identifies three main types of family arrangement found among the cohorts at or around age 30. These include the 'traditional' nuclear family comprising mother,

Table 4.2 *Family type of cohort member parents at age 30*

	1970 cohort		1958 cohort[a]		1946 cohort[b]	
	Men %	Women %	Men %	Women %	Men %	Women %
'Nuclear'						
Married, own children only	63	59	85	80	97	94
Cohabiting, own children only	18	18	5	7	1	2
'Simple' stepfamily						
Married, stepchildren only	2	1	2	<1		
Cohabiting, stepchildren only	7	<1	2	<1		
'Complex' stepfamily						
Married, own+stepchildren	4	<1	4	1		
Cohabiting, own+stepchildren	4	<1	1	<1		
Lone parent					2	4
Previously partnered	2	15	<1	12		
Never partnered	<1	4				
N (100%)	1,954	3,118	3,446	4,389	1,231	1,323

a   At age 33.
b   At age 36.
Note: The 1946 data do not distinguish own and stepchildren, nor between previously and never partnered among lone parents.

father and the children of their union. (A very small number of cohort members had become adoptive parents by this age – for example, just 14 in the 1970 cohort – and these have been included in the figures for 'own' children.)

The figures in Table 4.2 show that the 'nuclear' family remained by far the most common arrangement in all three cohorts. There were marked differences between them, however: almost 100 per cent of parents in the 1946 cohort were living with a husband or wife and their children; in the 1970 cohort this had dropped to 60 per cent. There has been a steep increase in the proportion of cohabiting unions that produce children (Ermisch and Francesconi 2000), and if cohabiting couples living with their children are included in the 'nuclear' family group, the differences between the cohorts are smaller, but still remain. Child-raising by an unmarried couple was three times more common among the 1970 cohort than the 1958, while, as with cohabitation generally, parenting together outside marriage was almost unreported when the 1946 cohort were in their 30s.

Another major category is families headed by one parent, usually a mother. This was the main source of family policy concerns from the 1970s onwards (DHSS 1974), with the main focus on the aftermath of the surging divorce rates and the increasing numbers of children born to single, unsupported mothers. Although the 'traditional' nuclear family remained the statistical norm as each cohort reached their early 30s, the proportion of lone mothers rose markedly, from just one in 25 among the mothers born in 1946 to nearly one in five among those born 24 years later. It is also worth noting, however, that within the lone mother group in the 1970 cohort, four out of five had previously had a partner. We cannot assume at this stage that a former partner was the father of the child(ren) involved, but these figures do give the lie to the suggestion that lone mothers today are typically young women choosing single, unsupported parenthood.

The number of lone fathers was tiny in all three cohorts (between 1 and 2 per cent). Some of these would be widowers, although there has also been a slight increase in recent years in the number of fathers awarded care of their children following a breakdown in the parents' relationship. However, when the cohort members were aged 30 or so, the great majority of the children involved would be very young, thus increasing the likelihood that they would remain with their mother.

The fastest growing family type in the last few decades has been the stepfamily; the combined result of the continuing rise in partnership breakdown and of re-partnering and the formation of new family units. Recent estimates suggest that one child in eight will experience stepfamily life at some stage in their first 16 years (Haskey 1994). Family policy in the past few years has belatedly begun to recognise the particular characteristics and needs of such families, albeit within a limited framework of the respective rights and obligations of 'biological' and 'social' parents, more specifically fathers (Ferri and Smith 1998).

By the time they were 30, 17 per cent of the men born in 1970 who were bringing up children were stepfathers – nearly twice as many as among men born 12 years earlier. The data for the 1946 cohort do not distinguish between biological and stepchildren – reflecting the comparative rarity of this family type in earlier years and its 'invisibility' as a social issue. Stepfamilies in the 1970 cohort in which a male cohort member was the stepfather were almost equally divided into those which included only the children of the cohort member's new partner (referred to as 'simple' stepfamilies), and those in which the new partnership had also produced children. It is interesting to note that the men in these 'complex' stepfamilies were as likely to be married to, as cohabiting with, their new partners, while in households which involved only the woman's children, cohabitation was much more common. Event history analysis will show whether marriage preceded or followed the birth of the couple's own child(ren).

It is well established that second marriages, as well as cohabitations, are more vulnerable to breakdown than first unions, and previous analysis of stepfamilies in the 1958 cohort have shown more problems and relationship conflict among those in which children have been born to the new couple (Ferri and Smith 1998). Future follow-up surveys will be able to chart the stability of these new partnerships, and the factors associated with their survival or demise.

The numbers of women who were stepmothers by age 30 was tiny in both cohorts – reflecting the fact that most children remain with their mothers after a breakdown in their family of origin. However, cases can be identified from the survey data in which the cohort member (male or female) was step-parent to children living *outside* their own household, and this includes a considerable number of women whose current partner had children living elsewhere (Ferri and Smith 1998). The information available makes the cohort studies a uniquely rich source of data for comprehensive sub-samples of this increasingly important family form, including investigations of male cohort members raising other men's children, while their own offspring are being brought up in other households.

Parenthood in early middle life

By the time they reach their early 40s, cohort members who had become parents before their mid-20s will be moving beyond the stage of having dependent children (under 18) in the household. However, the trend towards delayed family formation which has taken place in recent years will mean that the increasing numbers who put off childbearing until their middle or late 30s will still be caring for relatively young children as they enter middle age.

There was very little difference between the 1946 and 1958 cohorts in the overall numbers with dependent children in the household when they were in their early 40s: about four out of five women and seven out of ten men in each case. Where they did differ was in the tendency for the 1958 cohort to have younger children: for example, at the age of 42, 10 per cent of the women and 15 per cent of the men in the 1958 cohort had children under 5, compared with just 2 per cent and 4 per cent respectively of the 1946 cohort at age 43.

These figures point to a shift in the family life cycles of two cohorts born just 12 years apart. For the group born in 1946, many will, by their early 40s, be starting to emerge from the period when children still living at home make demands upon their financial, material and time resources, although the delayed transitions to independent living noted among the 1970 cohort may prolong this stage in the family life cycle of those born in 1946. Further analysis will reveal how many of this cohort had already become grandparents, and in how many cases this had created a four-generation family, with, as we shall see in the next section, the oldest generation – the cohort members' own parents – themselves moving into a role of dependency.

In the 1958 cohort, however, the above figures confirm that for many of them, the years with dependent children in the household were far from over. This will clearly have economic and social implications for these parents, including their employment roles, their responsibilities and relationships within the home and, as we consider in Chapter 5, their roles in respect of their own, ageing, mothers and fathers.

Family type

The type of family in which the 1958 and 1946 cohort members who were parents were living in their early 40s looked a little different from what we saw in their 30s. For the men born in 1946, the nuclear family was still almost universal, with 95 per cent living with their wife and children (Table 4.3). For the women in this cohort, however, the proportion bringing up children on their own had almost trebled, to 11 per cent, reflecting the impact of divorce or separation which we saw in the partnership data. This was only slightly lower than the figure for the 1958-born women, of whom 14 per cent were lone mothers at age 42. It is worth noting that lone fatherhood, almost non-existent among these two cohorts

Table 4.3 *Family type of cohort member parents at age 42/3*

	1958 cohort		1946 cohort	
	Men %	Women %	Men %	Women %
'Nuclear'				
Married, own children only	81	75	95	86
Cohabiting, own children only	5	9	3	3
'Simple' stepfamily				
Married, stepchildren only	3	1		
Cohabiting, stepchildren only	3	<1		
'Complex' stepfamily				
Married, own+stepchildren	3	1		
Cohabiting, own+stepchildren	1	<1		
Lone parent	4	14	2	11
N (100%)	3,902	4,614	1,185	1,247

Note: The 1946 data do not distinguish own and stepchildren.

in the early 30s, was recorded among 4 per cent of men born in 1958, and 2 per cent of those in the 1946 cohort.

Overall, a rather higher proportion of both men and women in the 1958 cohort were living in 'nuclear' families with a spouse and own children at age 42 than was the case among this cohort at 33. It seems likely that many of the cases of cohabitation recorded at the younger age had been converted to marriages by the time of the 42-year survey. Future analysis of partnership histories will throw further light on this, and subsequent surveys will reveal the stability or fragility of these unions.

One in ten of the men born in 1958 were stepfathers at the age of 42, and just over 2 per cent of women were stepmothers, in each case a slight increase on the number reported when they were 33. Again, longitudinal analysis will be needed to link these findings with the family arrangements recorded at the earlier date.

Conclusions

The snapshot view of partnership and parenthood at the time of the 30- and 40-year surveys presented in this chapter has revealed a number of dramatic changes in the patterns of personal relationships and family life experienced by three cohorts born just 12 years apart. Later transitions to partnership and parenthood, and rising rates of relationship breakdown and serial monogamy, stand out among the demographic trends which have become increasingly prevalent among successive cohorts. Although our findings also show that the 'traditional nuclear family', comprising married parents and their offspring, remains the most common scenario for raising children, the above trends combine to produce a growing diversity of family living arrangements. Lone parenthood (in most cases, lone motherhood) and a complex variety of stepfamily arrangements have become increasingly common experiences in each successive cohort.

In many respects, the demographic changes reported here can be seen as part of the transformation that has occurred in the lives of women in the latter half of the twentieth century. As earlier chapters have shown, women have made spectacular advances in educational and occupational achievement. Changes in the economic context have impacted \ differently on men and women, with the collapse of the labour market framework which sustained men's role as family breadwinner and the simultaneous growth of employment opportunities for women. Together, these changes have presented women with an ever-increasing range of alternative options to economic dependency in the traditional roles of domestic work and child-rearing. The changes in the private domain of partnership and family formation, particularly the delays in partnership and parenthood, are inextricably linked to women's changing public role, especially in the labour market.

However, the picture presented here, particularly that relating to the youngest, 1970-born, cohort, shows that the advance of women has not been universal. Their overall gains in educational and occupational achievement disguise a polarisation in the position of women, which draws a striking contrast between those who have achieved high qualifications and occupational success and those who have not. For the latter minority, the life trajectory revealed in this chapter appears to remain the traditional one of early partnership and (often unsupported) motherhood, a scenario which now carries a high risk of social exclusion based on lack of marketable skills, low income and isolation. Government policy initiatives such as the 'New Deal for Lone Parents' introduced in 1998, and measures concerned with teenage pregnancy, were targeted especially at this vulnerable group, and the 1970 cohort will provide a valuable source of information on how the future life chances of unqualified young mothers will be influenced by such policy initiatives.

One of the most striking findings to emerge from the comparisons described in this chapter relates to the growing fragility of personal relationships. Each successive cohort reveals an increasing instability in marriage and cohabitation. While the later born cohorts show fewer and later marriages, they are no less inclined to embark upon live-in relationships. However, the figures – especially those from the 1970 cohort – suggest that these are likely to be impermanent. A further contrast between the 1970 cohort and their peers born 12 years earlier lies in the high degree of unhappiness and dissatisfaction which appeared to characterise the younger cohort's relationships at age 30 or so. Further analysis will be needed to try and account for the relative disillusionment with personal relationships among the 1970 cohort at 30 – and among the 1958 cohort as they entered middle age. For example, to what extent is it linked to the pressures on relationships created by competing demands of employment and domestic roles, an aspect of family life which we examine in the next chapter? Whatever the explanation, the apparent growth in negative perceptions of personal relationships, together with the increasing impermanence of partnerships, both married and cohabiting, can be seen as indicative of uncertainty and insecurity permeating family life in Britain at the start of the twenty-first century.

Note

1   While most measures of the 1958 cohort come from the survey at age 33, event history data relating to e.g. partnerships and births enable comparisons to be made at age 30.

5 Family life

Elsa Ferri and Kate Smith

Introduction

The demographic changes in the family discussed in the preceding chapter have been matched by other economic, social and personal changes in the lives of men, women and children that transformed British family life in the last decades of the twentieth century. One of the most significant of these concerns the roles, aspirations and expectations of women, most notable in the huge increase in the employment rates of women, particularly mothers with young children (see Chapter 3). A key factor here has been women's continuing advances in educational achievement, which have underpinned their position at all levels of the occupational spectrum (Chapter 2). As described in the introduction to this book, the restructuring of the labour market, with the growth of service industries, IT and part-time work, also operated in favour of women's employment. In contrast, the labour market experience of men has been much less positive, particularly in the 1980s, with high unemployment and skill redundancy based upon the collapse of the manufacturing sector. The demise of so much heavy industry removed great swathes of semi- and unskilled jobs from the labour market. An important result of these changes was that, for many young men at this time, the opportunity to move into the role of family breadwinner via a traditional manual occupation requiring minimal qualifications, became more and more elusive.

One of the most striking features of this changing employment context has been the rise of the 'dual earner' family, reflecting the increase in the labour market participation of women, and of mothers in particular. For a high proportion of British families, two earned incomes have become essential in order to achieve and maintain what would be considered satisfactory living standards in the last decades of the twentieth century. In contrast to these 'work rich' households, there also remains a persistent minority living in homes in which no adult is in employment – the 'work poor' – who thereby suffer the other disadvantages and problems of social exclusion (Gregg and Wadsworth 1995).

The involvement of both parents in work outside the home has implications for more than the material aspects of family life. A study of nuclear families among the 1958 cohort at age 33 found that one in three mothers worked 35 or more hours a week, while a quarter of fathers worked 50 or more hours (Ferri and Smith 1996). This high level of involvement in the labour market has produced the 'work rich/time poor' household, in which the opportunities for families to spend time together and undertake joint activities have become severely constrained.

These developments, and the contrasting changes in the employment position of men and women, have implications for their respective roles in the domestic domain: in particular, the extent to which women's increased involvement in work outside the home is echoed in a more egalitarian sharing of household and child-rearing tasks. The concept of 'parenting time' has emerged as a key factor in relation to the domestic roles of mothers and fathers, particularly those in dual earner households. Recent studies have indicated that, whilst there has been a discernible shift towards greater role-sharing in families with both parents in employment, this has fallen far short of counterbalancing women's involvement in the labour market (Brannen and Moss 1991; Man-Yee Kan 2001; Ferri and Smith 1996). To a very large extent, childcare and domestic work remain primarily a maternal responsibility.

Many questions arise about how these trends are evident in differing patterns of family life among parents born at different times, and in their roles as mothers and fathers. A wide-ranging series of questions on these topics were included in the adult surveys of those born in 1958 and 1970, from which we can compare the parental behaviour of these two cohorts in their early 30s. (Comparable information was not available for the 1946 cohort.)

The 'new dad'

One of the key concepts in the discourse concerning changing gender roles in recent decades has been the emergence – or otherwise – of the 'new man'. Within the context of the family, this somewhat chimeric figure is an integral part of the supposed shift towards equitable sharing of domestic and childcare roles by more 'emotionally literate' men, in response to the increasing demands of paid work on women's time and energies. However, both theoretical and empirical views of the paternal role at the end of the twentieth century were highly contradictory. While some analysts found evidence of the more caring, nurturing father (e.g. O'Brien 1992), others perceived him as an increasingly marginalised figure, rendered almost redundant by the loss of economic power and patriarchal authority (e.g. Bjornberg 1992).

One of the questions which addressed this issue in the 1958 and 1970 surveys asked cohort members whether the father or the mother was mainly responsible for general childcare, or whether this was shared more or less equally. Unsurprisingly, very few respondents said that the father took the lead role, but there were some striking differences in the numbers claiming that it was a maternal, or a joint, responsibility (Table 5.1). A major factor here was the couples' employment situation: in both cohorts, almost twice as many reported shared care when both parents were in employment as in families with only one parent (in almost all cases the father) in paid work. This echoes the findings of other studies showing that men's participation in domestic work rises in line with their partners' earnings (Man-Yee Kan 2001). Earlier analysis of the 1958 cohort also showed that fathers' contribution to childcare was considerably greater when mothers worked full-time than when they were in part-time employment (Ferri and Smith 1996).

The responses of the two cohorts were broadly similar, except that mothers in the 1970 cohort were slightly *less* likely to report shared caring at age 30 than their counterparts born in 1958. Differences among fathers were less marked, but it is interesting to note that in both cohorts, and especially those born in 1970, fathers were more likely than mothers to

Table 5.1 *Person normally responsible for generally being with and looking after children, by couples' employment situation*

(a) Men

	1970 cohort Age 30 in 2000			1958 cohort Age 33 in 1991		
	Both employed %	One employed %	Neither employed %	Both employed %	One employed %	Neither employed %
Mostly father	1	2	2	1	1	3
Mostly mother	39	67	31	37	66	45
Shared equally	59	30	67	61	33	53
Someone else	1	<1	–	1	<1	–
N (100%)	901	695	96	1,390	1,052	78

(b) Women

	1970 cohort Age 30 in 2000			1958 cohort Age 33 in 1991		
	Both employed %	One employed %	Neither employed %	Both employed %	One employed %	Neither employed %
Mostly father	2	2	1	<1	1	1
Mostly mother	51	74	47	46	69	45
Shared equally	46	24	52	53	30	54
Someone else	1	<1	–	<1	<1	–
N (100%)	1,446	857	140	1,793	1,019	83

claim that childcare was a shared responsibility. The variation was greatest among those in dual earner families. The responses to these questions were, of course, subjective perceptions rather than detailed records of the actual time spent by each parent in various aspects of childcare. It may be that fathers whose partners also worked outside the home were most eager to testify to their own domestic contribution, while on the other hand, the pressures on employed mothers led them to have more stringent criteria for acknowledging an equal childcare role in their partners. In an area such as this, perception is at least as important as objective reality, and earlier work on the 1958 cohort found that women who reported little domestic involvement by their partners showed a high degree of unhappiness in their relationships (Ferri and Smith 1996).

Earlier analysis of the 1958 cohort also revealed that, perhaps counter to popular perception, the 'new dad' was less likely to be found among the highly educated middle classes. Indeed, the lowest level of participation in childcare was recorded for graduate fathers in professional and managerial occupations (Ferri and Smith 1996). Looking more closely at father involvement in the 1970 cohort echoed these findings: there was a sharp gradient in the level of shared childcare according to educational achievement, from 59 per cent of fathers with no qualifications to just 37 per cent of graduate fathers. The pattern according to their social class of occupation was almost identical: 60 per cent of fathers in semi- and unskilled jobs reported that they played an equal part in childcare, but the figure dropped to 39 per cent among fathers in the professional and managerial sector. The other key factor associated with father involvement was their own working hours: the longer the hours fathers spent at work, the lower their contribution to childcare and family life – irrespective of their partners' employment situation and working hours (Ferri and Smith 1996). Further analysis of the new data will be able to show whether the relatively long hours worked by the men in the 1970 cohort compared with their counterparts born in 1958 are also associated with less involvement by young fathers with their children and families. Future investigation will also be able to explore whether there is any link between the slightly lower level of participation reported here for fathers in the 1970 cohort and the remarkably high proportion of unhappy relationships among this cohort reported in Chapter 4.

Intergenerational patterns in family life

In the preceding chapter, we drew attention to the opportunities provided by the cohort studies' data for intergenerational analysis of trends in family demographics. It is also possible to compare information collected at the childhood and adult surveys of the cohorts to explore the relationship between the home setting in which the cohort members grew up and the patterns of parenting and family life which they themselves have adopted. There are contrasting theoretical perspectives to be tested here: on the one hand the view that individuals tend to internalise and repeat the patterns of parenting which they themselves experienced; on the other, that many reject their parents' style of child-rearing and deliberately adopt a different approach.

Little investigation has been carried out to date in this area. Ferri and Smith (1996) found a link between the employment patterns at age 33 of mothers in the 1958 cohort and those of their own mothers. Those in full-time employment, and those who were the household's sole earner, were the most likely to have mothers who went out to work before they started school. By contrast, there was no relationship between the level of involvement with children of 33-year-old fathers and what they experienced from their own fathers at ages 7 or 11. It is worth noting that in 1965, when the 1958 cohort were aged 7, as many as six out of ten of their fathers were reported to play an equal part in managing children – a figure which further challenges the claim that fatherhood has changed dramatically over the past generation.

Family cohesiveness

The demands of paid employment on the time and energies of parents has become a familiar topic in relation to the 'work/life balance' and many questions arise concerning the impact of work outside the home upon the family lives of the members of our cohorts. Information about a number of aspects of home life and family functioning was gathered at recent adult surveys of both the 1970 and 1958 cohorts. This included a series of questions on activities which all members of the family undertook together, ranging from eating to shopping, and from outings to visiting relatives. One of the frequent social comments on recent trends in family life bemoans the demise of the family meal, with the advent of 'grazing' and individual family members helping themselves to the contents of fridge or freezer – usually to be eaten in front of the TV. However, the survey findings suggest that the family meal is far from defunct. Over 70 per cent of the 1970 cohort who were parents at age 30 said that their whole family ate together at least once a day – rather more than among the comparable group in the 1958 cohort when they were 33. In both cohorts, those in households in which both parents were employed ate together slightly less frequently than those where only one (mostly the father) worked outside the home. Not surprisingly, families in which neither parent was in employment recorded the highest level of communal eating.

Contact with the extended family also appeared to be flourishing among the 1970 cohort, with nearly seven out of ten cohort members indicating that they, their partner and children together visited relatives at least once a week, compared with just over half of their counterparts in the 1958 cohort. There was very little difference in either cohort between the dual earner and single earner families – if anything, the former showed a slightly *higher* level of family visiting. The main point of difference according to employment situation among the 1970 cohort was the small, but relatively high, proportion in 'no earner' families who said that they seldom or never visited relatives. It was this group among the 1958 cohort at age 33 which showed the lowest level of participation in activities entailing expenditure, such as shopping, or going to the cinema; presumably reflecting the social exclusion suffered by families as well as individuals whose lives are restricted by economic hardship (Ferri and Smith 1996).

As the above figures show, the overall level of joint family activities reported here among the 1970 cohort was rather higher than that found in the 1958 cohort at age 33. The most likely explanation for this lies in the fact that the later born cohort at age 30 had fewer and younger children. A smaller family unit would make it more practicable for all members to be involved jointly, while the younger the children, the more likely that they and their parents would participate in activities together. Whatever the reasons underlying the differences, it would seem that, although fathers in the later born cohort did not seem to be as heavily involved in child-care as their older peers, as far as joint activities were concerned, their family lives were no less cohesive.

The extended family

Changes in family structure and functioning over the past decades have implications for the role and relationships of wider kin – especially, perhaps, grandparents. Marital breakdown may result in the loss of other relation-ships if ties are severed with one half of the parental family. By contrast, repartnering and the formation of stepfamilies is likely to create an enlarged network of extended family relationships, involving step-grandparents and other step-kin.

The birth cohorts present a unique opportunity to study family life over three generations. The cohort members' relationship with their own parents will be an important part of this changing mosaic of family life – and is likely to have a different significance in their lives at different stages. In the early 30s, for instance, the role of their parents is likely to be one of support – material, practical and emotional – towards sons and daughters as they embark upon independent living, and themselves make the transi-tion to parenthood.

The supportive role of parents was confirmed by the 30-year survey of the 1970 cohort (this information was not available for the other two cohorts at age 30). This showed that, since leaving full-time education, exactly half of the men and 55 per cent of the women in the cohort had received financial help from their parents. Among the men, those who were married or cohabiting at age 30 were more likely to have been helped financially than those who had never partnered or who had had a broken relationship. Among the women, however, only those who had never partnered reported a lower level of parental assistance, no doubt reflect-ing the more precarious financial position of women experiencing divorce or separation. A similar picture emerged with regard to accommodation. Just over half of all respondents said that their parents had helped them in this way. This was more frequently reported by men and women who were married or cohabiting at 30, and by women who had experienced partnership breakdown. Again, this would suggest that women are more likely than men to have accommodation problems in the aftermath of divorce or separation.

Among those in the 1970 cohort who had children at age 30, four out of ten men and six out of ten women said they had been helped with childcare by their parents. This sizeable sex difference no doubt reflects the fact that it is *maternal* grandparents who are most likely to provide this kind of support. The major support role of grandparents revealed by these figures is consistent with the findings reported for the 1958 cohort at age 33, which showed that cohort members' parents were the principal source of extra-familial childcare (Ferri and Smith 1996).

Contact with own parents in middle age

As the cohort members move into their 40s, their parents may be reaching a stage in their own lives at which their relationship with their children becomes characterised more by dependency. How has this relationship changed across the cohorts as they have moved through early adulthood and the establishment of their own careers and families, and into middle age? This can be investigated in terms of cohort members' contact with their parents, their perceived emotional closeness, and concerns about their parents' own wellbeing.

By the age of 43, 85 per cent of those born in 1946 still had a mother living, but only 68 per cent had a living father. These figures were higher, however, than among the 1958 cohort, for whom the figures were 79 per cent and 60 per cent respectively. (This could reflect an older age profile among the parents of the 1958 cohort.)

From the information on how often the cohort members saw each of their parents, it seemed that contact was fairly frequent and very similar in the two cohorts. About four out of ten men and women in each case saw their parents at least once a week (Table 5.2). The most frequent

Table 5.2 *Contact with own parents at age 42/3*

	1958 cohort		1946 cohort	
	Men %	Women %	Men %	Women %
Mother:				
Once a week or more	38	52	41	41
Once a month or more	28	20	22	20
Less than once a month	28	23	27	23
Rarely/never	2	3	4	2
Lives with	4	2	6	4
N (100%)	4,405	4,525	1,163	1,197
Father:				
Once a week or more	35	43	39	43
Once a month or more	25	22	22	22
Less than once a month	31	28	28	25
Rarely/never	5	6	6	7
Lives with	3	1	5	3
N (100%)	3,324	3,397	760	757

contact was between the 1958-born women and their mothers – presumably reflecting the fact that more of the women in this cohort had young children, and, as earlier research has indicated, were heavily dependent on their mothers for support in childcare. The numbers who had no contact with their fathers was low in each case, but higher than that for non-contact with mothers – no doubt the aftermath of divorce or separation in their families of origin.

For both cohorts and both sexes, however, there was a difference in contact with parents according to the cohort members' educational level. The higher the qualifications, the less frequent the contact, and this was especially marked among the graduate men in both cohorts and the graduate women in the 1946 group. Among the 1958-born women, although the same trend was evident, even the graduate women were likely to see their mothers more than once a week. It may be that the high achievers in the older cohort were more likely to have moved away from the localities in which they grew up and thus to be living at a distance from parents. The wealth of data collected on the cohort members' current and past residential locations could not be explored for this study but further investigation will be able to link their geographical mobility with their parental contact later in life.

Apart from geographical distance, there may well also have been a comparatively wide 'cultural gulf' between the 1946 cohort and their parents. This cohort were more likely to be the first generation in their family to experience university education and consequently to have achieved upward social mobility. Three-quarters of their fathers had had manual jobs and very few of their mothers would have been in paid employment, and these factors may have acted to lessen the ties to their families of origin.

Emotional closeness to each parent

It is important to note that frequency of face-to-face contact is only one indicator of the relationship between cohort members and their parents.

In the 2000 survey, the 42-year-old members of the 1958 cohort were also asked how close they felt to each of their parents. Comparing their responses with those of the 1946 cohort to the same questions at age 43, revealed further differences between the sexes and the cohorts (Table 5.3).

While both men and women felt closer to their mothers than to their fathers, a higher proportion of women than men claimed a very close relationship with their parents. More unexpectedly, perhaps, both men and women in the 1958 cohort were more likely to feel close to their parents than their counterparts born 12 years earlier. Those in the 1946 cohort were almost twice as likely to say that they did not feel close to their parents at all. This may also be part of the 'cultural gulf' separating the generations, which, as suggested above, may have explained their less frequent contact with parents. Another possible explanation may lie in an

Table 5.3 *Emotional closeness to own parents at age 42/3*

	1958 cohort		1946 cohort	
	Men %	Women %	Men %	Women %
Mother:				
Very close	38	53	29	45
Close	48	35	46	36
Not very close	13	10	25	19
No contact	2	3		
N (100%)	4,402	4,525	1,157	1,179
Father:				
Very close	31	44	26	40
Close	49	38	43	37
Not very close	16	13	31	23
No contact	4	5		
N (100%)	3,325	3,396	770	768

increase in 'emotionality' – at least in terms of its public expression – during the last two decades of the twentieth century, since, as we have seen, there was little evidence of different relationships between the cohort members and their parents in terms of the more objective indicator of frequency of contact. However, earlier investigation of the 1946 cohort has shown complex patterns of association, differing for men and women, between adult relationships with parents and aspects of childhood experience in the family of origin (Wadsworth 1996), and this will be an important area for further analysis of the family lives and relationship networks of the three cohorts.

Concerns about parents

Finally, the interviews with the 1958 and 1946 cohorts when they were in their early 40s asked whether there were any aspects of their parents' lives which worried them.

Among the 1958 cohort (excluding the very small percentage actually living with their parents at age 42), their parents' health was the main source of anxiety, mentioned by about seven out of ten respondents. Concerns about self-care (no doubt related to health worries) were expressed by four out of ten; while money problems featured much less, with only about one in ten saying that they worried about this. It may be that a considerable proportion of the parental generation enjoyed the security of home ownership and occupational pensions. There was very little difference in the responses of men and women cohort members, except that women were particularly likely to worry about their parents' health; and on all measures, slightly more concern was expressed about mothers than about fathers. This may link with their greater emotional closeness to mothers as much as with objectively grounded anxieties.

A very similar pattern of concerns was expressed by the men and women in the 1946 cohort at the age of 43, although on each measure (health, self-care and finance) the overall numbers who worried about these aspects of their parents' lives were slightly lower than in the 1958 cohort. It may be that the parents of those born in 1946 tended to be younger than those of their 1958 counterparts at this stage in the cohort members' lives, and thus to be giving less rise to anxiety, or the difference may be linked to the more distant emotional relationships between the 1946 cohort and their parents referred to above.

From the responses of both cohorts, however, it is clear that a majority of these 40+ year-olds felt some concern about the wellbeing of parents who had entered, or were approaching, old age and dependency. For the 1958 cohort in particular, with the great majority still having young dependent children, it seems clear that the shift towards later family formation has produced a change in the life cycle which creates simultaneous pressure for support from both the younger and the older generations. From what we have seen of the partnering and parenting experiences of those born in 1970, this trend is likely to be exacerbated in the latest of our three cohorts, and this topic will an important focus of questioning and analysis in future surveys.

Conclusions

This chapter has provided glimpses of a number of aspects of the family roles and domestic lives of the three birth cohorts in early and middle adulthood. We have seen that, despite less gendered roles in dual earner households, the huge increase in women's involvement in work outside the home does not appear to have been matched by the contribution of men in the domestic arena. This raises the question of how far changes outside the family – in employment practices, and attitudes and expectations in the wider society – support or inhibit change in the balance of domestic roles. Further analysis of the cohort data will be able to explore how different patterns of parenting, family life and the quality of relationships link to the experience, or otherwise, of 'family-friendly' employment conditions and to fiscal and other policies aimed at supporting families (for example Working Families Tax Credit, or the expansion of childcare provision). How do social policy measures such as these impinge upon family life in terms of partnership satisfaction, personal wellbeing and family stability?

Within the personal domain, to what extent are the negative assessments of relationships, seen among the 1970 cohort in Chapter 4, rooted in conflict or dissonance concerning the respective domestic roles of men and women? Are such dissatisfactions associated with the growth of values such as individualism and cynicism, and different constructs of identity, which are explored in Chapter 10?

Much social concern has been expressed in recent years, at all points on the political spectrum, about a perceived 'crisis in the family', most especially in terms of a 'parenting deficit' with regard to the raising of tomorrow's citizens (Etzioni 1993).

The cohort study data are able to encompass the complexity of this area, including the importance of the personal dimensions which have been examined in this and the preceding chapter. Future research using the cohort studies to investigate family life and parenting should enable policy thinking to develop beyond the hitherto somewhat simplistic notion of strengthening and supporting the institution of marriage.

Finally, this preliminary analysis has shed some interesting light on the extended family in contemporary Britain. The important role played by parents in supporting transitions to independent living and family formation is highlighted by the 1970 cohort. As the two earlier born cohorts reached middle age, a majority had regular contact with their own parents and felt emotionally close to them. But perhaps the most significant aspect of the findings in this area was the implication of the delay in transition to parenthood shown by the younger cohorts for their own roles and responsibilities as they reach middle age – in terms of dependency of both their children and their parents. By the age of 42, the great majority of the 1958-born cohort, unlike their 1946-born predecessors, still had young dependent children living at home; while a majority also were expressing anxieties about the wellbeing of their own parents. With age at first birth and life expectancy both continuing to rise, it could be predicted that this situation will be even more common among the cohort born in 1970. One of the key family-related issues for future studies based on the cohort data will concern the economic, social and health costs in middle life for men and women who find themselves 'sandwiched' in between two dependent generations.

6 Income and living standards

Lorraine Dearden, Alissa Goodman and Phillippa Saunders

Introduction

Alongside the important changes in education, the labour market, and people's family lives, the pattern of living standards in Britain has also changed over recent decades. After a period of relative stability over the 1960s and 1970s, income inequality rose rapidly in the 1980s, as rising living standards for many went hand in hand with growing differences between incomes of different families. For example, Goodman *et al.* (1997) have shown that the increase in income inequality which took place over the 1980s was unprecedented in recent times, affecting all groups in the population. Over the 1990s, it continued to rise, though at a much less rapid rate than in the preceding decade (Clark and Goodman 2001). Alongside the rapid changes in income inequality were large rises in relative poverty over the 1980s: as the living standards of the poorest fell further behind the rest of the population, the number recorded in relative poverty (measured, for example, by the proportion of people in households living below 60 per cent median income) doubled over the period from the late 1970s to the early 1990s, while families with children saw even more marked increases in the incidence of relative poverty (Clark and Goodman 2001).

What explanations are there for these trends? The most important drivers of rising living standards and income inequality in Britain have been changes in the labour market. New technologies favouring more highly skilled workers, together with increased world trade have both led to rising demand for skilled workers compared to their unskilled counterparts (Machin 1995; Chennels and Van Reenen 1998). This has led, in turn, to growing differences in wages across workers in different education groups, particularly amongst males (Gosling *et al.* 2000). Over the 1990s, evidence on these education-related wage differentials was more mixed, though some studies pointed to a declining premium in wages for highly educated workers as an increasing number of graduates entered the labour market. In addition, there have been other important labour market trends which are thought to have increased the differences in living standards between different workers. The decline in trade union membership and union power, which previously had an equalising force on workers wages (Gosling and Machin 1995), the dismantling of the power of wages councils over the 1980s (Machin and Manning 1994), and the decline in the public sector workforce as the result of large-scale privatisations and 'contracting out' of public sector activities (Disney *et al.* 1998) have all been identified as reasons why inequality in wages grew so rapidly over the 1980s. The introduction of the National Minimum Wage in the late 1990s may, by contrast, have been an equalising force (Dickens 2001).

Important changes in labour-market participation have also lain behind some of the dramatic changes in living standards and inequality that we have seen in recent decades. In particular, a decline in the participation rate of (particularly older) men in the labour force over both the early 1980s and the early 1990s, alongside rising employment amongst women, is also thought to have led to increasing polarisation in family incomes, with an emerging gap between 'work rich' and 'work poor' families (Gregg and Wadsworth 2000).

Changes in family life have also had an impact. An increase in the number of people living alone – as more people enter into relationships later in life, as more marriages and relationships break down, and also as people live longer – has led to growing dispersion in living standards amongst a larger number of separate household units. Of particular note has been the increase in the number of lone parents, many of whom are on very low incomes (Banks *et al.* 2001).

The tax and benefit system, too, has an important part to play in explaining the differences in living standards which people enjoy. Large cuts in direct taxes benefiting the highest earners, together with only modest increases in benefit levels for those on low incomes in the 1980s, contributed to rising inequality over this time (Johnson and Webb 1993).

By contrast, over the late 1990s, tax and benefit reforms have been progressive, benefiting low income households the most (Clark *et al.* 2001).

Although differences in wages and incomes have risen enormously over the time period in which the cohorts have entered and progressed through their adult lives, one important gap has been narrowing over time, namely the gap in the wages of men and women. Recent research has shown that since the 1970s, women working full time have experienced significant gains in their relative earnings, although those working part time have not done quite so well (Harkness 1996).

The cohort studies are able to paint a rich picture of all of these changes, since the experiences of the three generations who are the subject of this book reflect the very important trends in the structure of wages and living standards which took place over the 1980s and 1990s. As noted above, rising wages since the late 1970s went hand in hand with rising inequality over the 1980s on a scale unprecedented in recent times. This growth in inequality also continued over the 1990s, although to a lesser degree. These changes have had an important bearing on each of the three cohorts.

Men's and women's wages: rising wage levels and growing inequality

One of the most important comparisons between our three cohorts is that of wages from employment. Although wages do not capture a full picture of people's living standards, they give important information about the resources that people from different generations have been able to command in the labour market, and are a very important factor in determining living standards for those who are employed.[1] (Details of the wage and other measures used in this chapter are given in the Appendix to this chapter.)

Men's wages
For men in their early 30s, the most important changes were those that took place between the 1946 and 1958 cohorts. Bearing in mind the differences in age of cohort members when the wage information was collected, some of the important trends in men's wages can be seen clearly from

Figure 6.1, which compares the distribution of hourly and weekly wages for men and women in each cohort in their early 30s (wages have been adjusted to January 2001 prices). For men, the biggest rise in wages across the generations can be seen between those born in 1946, who were in their early 30s at the end of the 1970s, and those born in 1958, who were in their early 30s at the start of the 1990s. This can be seen from the shift of the wage distributions (both hourly and weekly wages) to the right – showing that a considerably larger proportion of men born in 1958 had higher wages in their early 30s compared to those born in 1946, and fewer were on very low wages.

Inequality in men's wages also rose considerably between these two birth cohorts. This can be seen from the difference in the shape of the wage distributions between the groups born in 1946 and 1958. In particular, the peak of the distribution of wages of the 1958 cohort is much lower, meaning that men in employment were much more widely spread across the entire distribution of wages, rather than clustered within a smaller wage range. In contrast, the structure of wages has been much more stable between those born in 1958 and those born in 1970. This reflects the fact that the changes in the labour market and in inequality were much less dramatic for men over the 1990s than they had been over the 1980s.

Table 6.1 confirms these trends, showing the mean hourly wage for men rising from £7.40 amongst the 1946 cohort at age 31, to just under £10 for the 1958 cohort at age 33 – a real increase of just over a third. Average wages for men in the 1970 cohort at age 30 were not much different from this, at just over £10 per hour. Table 6.1 also shows that, compared to these changes in the average wage, the gains across successive generations at the lower end of the wage distribution have been considerably smaller: 10 per cent of male workers were on wages below around £4.50 per hour in the 1946 cohort (the 10th percentile wage), compared to a comparable wage level of around £5.10 and £5.30 per hour in the 1958 and 1970 cohorts at a similar age. By contrast, at the top end of the wage distribution the growth in wages has been much stronger.

Changes in inequality are summarised by the two measures of inequality provided in Table 6.1. Reflecting the differences in the experiences of

Changing Britain, Changing Lives

Figure 6.1 *Hourly and weekly wages for men and women in their early 30s*

a) Hourly pay, men

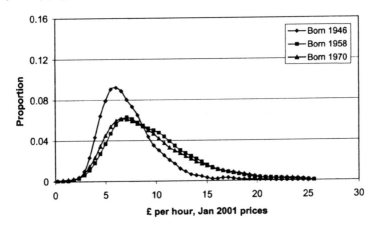

Proportions in employment:
1946 cohort: 82%
1958 cohort: 74%
1970 cohort: 78%

b) Hourly pay, women

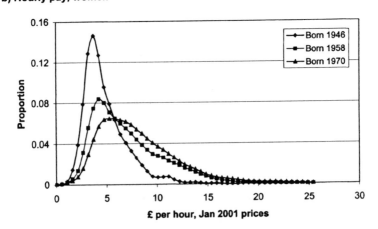

Proportions in employment:
1946 cohort: 46%
1958 cohort: 61%
1970 cohort: 69%

c) Weekly pay, men

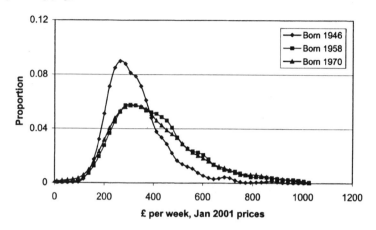

Proportion of whom working part-time:
1946 cohort: 0.3%
1958 cohort: 1%
1970 cohort: 2%

d) Weekly pay, women

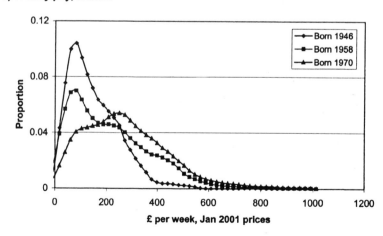

Proportion of whom working part-time:
1946 cohort: 45%
1958 cohort: 47%
1970 cohort: 29%

Table 6.1 *Gross hourly and weekly wages (January 2001 prices) for men in employment*

	Hourly			Weekly		
	1970 cohort Age 30	1958 cohort Age 33	1946 cohort Age 31	1970 cohort Age 30	1958 cohort Age 33	1946 cohort Age 31
Wage levels (£):						
Mean	10.30	9.98	7.40	437.37	433.55	335.22
10th percentile	5.08	5.28	4.48	221.01	229.68	213.75
90th percentile	16.41	15.28	10.95	684.57	662.54	480.11
Inequality:						
'90/10' ratio	3.23	2.89	2.44	3.1	2.88	2.25
Gini coefficient	0.289	0.248	0.203	0.275	0.253	0.197
Sample size	3,973	3,708	1,164	3,974	3,708	1,225

low- and high-paid workers, inequality in men's wages rose across each of the cohorts, although the jump between the 1946 cohort and the 1958 cohort was much bigger (reflecting changes taking place over the 1980s) than that between the 1958 and 1970 cohort (reflecting changes in the 1990s). Table 6.1 also provides some similar summary statistics for the distribution of weekly wages. The average weekly pay for male employees was £335 for those in their early 30s born in 1946, compared to £434 per week for those born in 1958, and £437 for those born in 1970. Again, inequality was much higher for the 1958 cohort compared to the 1946, but did not change much between the 1958 cohort and the 1970 cohort.

Women's wages

The changes in the distribution of wages for women in their early 30s have been even more marked than the changes for men. Against a backdrop of rising female participation in the labour market, women's wages have risen considerably – faster than the rise in men's wages – and have also become more unequal. Looking at hourly wages first (rates have been adjusted to January 2001 prices) Figure 6.1 shows that for the 1946 cohort, those women who were in employment in their early 30s (46 per cent of women) were heavily clustered around wages of around £3.60 per hour. Very few had wages of more than £10 per hour. By the time the 1958 cohort were in their early 30s, the picture had changed considerably. With 61 per cent of women working, the largest cluster of employed women were now earning around £5–6 per hour, with a much larger proportion also spread across higher wage rates.

These higher wages for women in their early 30s were also matched by a large jump in inequality between the 1946 and 1958 cohorts – this can be seen by the much lower peak, and longer tail, of the wage distribution of women born in 1958 compared to that of women in the 1946 cohort. By the time the 1970 cohort women reached their early 30s, their wages were considerably higher again than those of the 1958 cohort at a similar age, and, indeed, the distribution of women's wages amongst this cohort appear to be much more similar to the distribution of *men's* wages than was the case for earlier generations.

The changes in the distribution of women's weekly pay, also shown in Figure 6.1, reflects the large increase over time in the proportion of women in their early 30s working full time rather than part time (see Chapter 3). Almost one half of women from the 1958 and 1946 cohorts who were in work in their early 30s were working part time, so that typical weekly pay in these two cohorts (as represented by the peaks of the weekly wage distributions) was considerably below £100. The weekly pay of those working full time in these cohorts can be seen in the much smaller humps in the distribution at higher weekly wages. By contrast, the number of part-time working women in their early 30s amongst the 1970 cohort was less than a third, which meant that there was a much smaller concentration of women at relatively low weekly pay of less than £100 per week, and a much larger hump of full-time workers earning in the region of £250–300 per week.

All of these trends are also reflected in the information provided in Table 6.2. This shows the average (mean) women's hourly wage rising from around £5 per hour for the 1946 cohort to £7.30 per hour for the 1958 cohort (a real terms rise of nearly 50 per cent), and rising again to around £8.60 per hour for women born in 1970 (a further rise of 18 per cent). The growth in wages was not as strong as this at the lower end of the wage distribution, although the 10th percentile of women's wages was almost 25 per cent higher in real terms for the 1958 cohort in their early 30s compared to the 1946 cohort, whilst for those born in 1970, the 10th percentile was around 15 per cent higher again in real terms. At the top of the women's wage distribution, the growth in wages was even stronger: the 90th percentile of women's wages for those born in 1946 was just £7.60 per hour, compared to £12.30 for those born in 1958 (a rise of more than 60 per cent in real terms), and £13.50 for those born in 1970.

The pattern of inequality for women was slightly different to that of men. On both inequality measures shown in Table 6.2, wage inequality was much higher amongst those born in 1958 compared to the 1946 cohort several years before. However, women born in 1970 experienced higher wages, but also slightly *lower* measured wage inequality amongst their peers at age 30 compared with women at age 33 almost a decade before

Table 6.2 *Gross hourly and weekly wages (January 2001 prices) for women in employment*

	Hourly			Weekly		
	1970 cohort Age 30	1958 cohort Age 33	1946 cohort Age 31	1970 cohort Age 30	1958 cohort Age 33	1946 cohort Age 31
Wage levels (£):						
Mean	8.57	7.26	4.95	287.37	220.13	151.74
10th percentile	4.06	3.54	2.87	79.01	46.66	46.58
90th percentile	13.49	12.27	7.60	495.06	441.69	286.64
Inequality:						
'90/10' ratio	3.32	3.46	2.65	6.27	9.47	6.15
Gini coefficient	0.284	0.285	0.238	0.34	0.403	0.354
Sample size	3,657	3,090	612	3,658	3,090	641

– although the difference in the age at which the wage information was collected for the two cohorts is likely to be an important factor in this. The trends in weekly wages shown in Table 6.2 again reflect the important shift towards full-time work for women in their early 30s. Thus, the average weekly wage for women born in 1970 was almost double that of women born in 1946, whilst some of the large drop in inequality in weekly wages amongst the 1970 cohort compared to the 1958 cohort is a result of the much larger cluster of women on full-time weekly pay in this most recent generation.

Is there a declining gender wage gap?

One observation which can be drawn from the wage distributions shown in Figure 6.1, is that, as new generations of workers enter the workforce, the wage experiences of men and women in their early 30s, once quite distinct, have been converging over time. Many of the reasons for this convergence are discussed in other chapters, for example:

- women in more recent generations have achieved more comparable educational qualifications to men (Chapter 2);
- the occupations women now enter into are less distinctly 'female' occupations, characterised by low pay (Chapter 3);
- women are also having children later (Chapter 4), remaining in the workforce longer before they have their children, and staying out of the workforce for less time once their children are born (Chapter 3).

The above trends mean that women's work experience has become more comparable to men's at a similar age than was the case for previous generations, and this is reflected in their pay.

The trend towards convergence in the male and female wage distributions can be seen quite clearly from Figure 6.2, which compares the distribution of men's and women's hourly wages in their early 30s in each cohort. For those born in 1946, women who were in work in their early 30s had much lower, and also more heavily clustered (less unequally distributed), wages than men. The average wage amongst men in this

Figure 6.2 *Gender wage gaps in the early 30s: men and women's hourly wages across the generations*

a) Born 1946

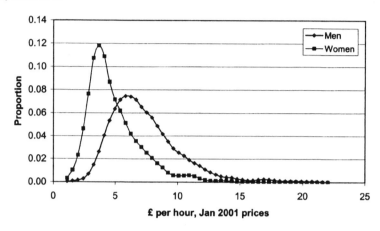

Gap between men and women's wages:
Mean: 49%
10th percentile: 56%
90th percentile: 44%

b) Born 1958

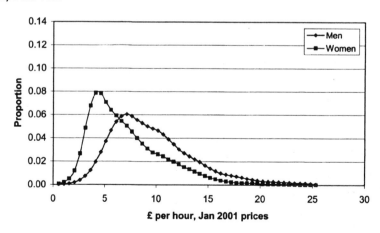

Gap between men and women's wages:
Mean: 37%
10th percentile: 49%
90th percentile: 25%

Figure 6.2 *Gender wage gaps in the early 30s: men and women's hourly wages across the generations (cont'd)*

c) Born 1970

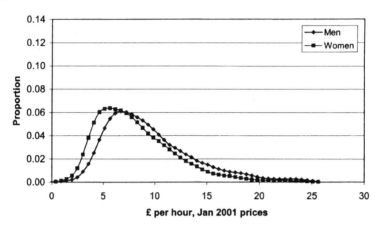

Gap between men and women's wages:
Mean: 20%
10th percentile: 25%
90th percentile: 22%

cohort was 50 per cent higher than the average wage amongst working women, with a larger gap between low-paid women and low-paid men. Indeed, the area of overlap between the men's and women's wage distributions was small, with those at the upper end of the women's wage scale receiving similar hourly wages to men at the lower and middle end of the men's pay range.

For those born in 1958, women's and men's wages in their early 30s were considerably more similar, although the men's wage distribution was still shifted further to the right (higher wages) than that of women, and the average gap between men's and women's wages was 37 per cent. By the time those born in 1970 were in their early 30s, the distributions of men's and women's wages were very much closer than this, although it is clear that significant differences did remain: in particular, there was a much larger concentration of women at relatively low wage rates (below

£5 an hour) compared to men, and a longer, thicker tail of men on relatively high wage rates. The average wage amongst men in this cohort was still 20 per cent higher in real terms than the average women's wage.

Wages and education

One of the most important factors affecting people's wages is their education. There has been much research pinpointing a growing gap between the wages of highly educated and less well educated male workers as one of the major factors behind the dramatic rises in income and wage inequality in the 1980s in the UK. Over the 1990s, this education wage gap appears to have fallen back again, as the number of relatively well qualified workers joining the workforce has continued to grow. The experiences of the three cohorts in their early 30s reflect these important changes.

Across all three cohorts, employees with higher education levels tend to receive higher pay in employment than those with lower qualifications. This is both because education confers skills on workers which make them more productive and valued in the workplace, and also because people who achieve educational qualifications tend to have other characteristics which confer higher wages – for example, higher motivation. The differences in wages of people with different levels of education can be seen from Figure 6.3. For our purposes, we have grouped all cohort members who have no qualifications together with those who have sub-O-level or equivalent qualifications (though there are some differences in the wages of these two groups, particularly amongst the 1946 cohort where a relatively large group of people obtained sub-O-level or equivalent qualifications). It is important to remember that the relative sizes of each of the education groups among employees has changed across the generations: in particular, the proportion of men and women with no, or sub-O-level, qualifications by the time they reach their early 30s has dropped quite dramatically, whilst the number on all higher qualification levels has increased. It is also the case that, amongst those now in their early 30s, men's and women's education levels are quite similar (though there are more men in the 1970s cohort who are educated to A level, whereas more women have ceased their education at O level or equivalent). By contrast, in the earlier cohorts, men in their early 30s on the whole were more highly qualified than women (see Chapter 2 for figures for the whole cohorts).

Figure 6.3 clearly shows a much bigger gap between the wages of highly and less educated workers who were born in 1958 compared to those born in 1946. Whilst the hourly wages of those in the lowest education groups did not change much across these two generations, men with higher education levels, particularly those with degree-level qualifications or above in the 1958 cohort, received much higher wages compared to their more educated counterparts in their early 30s who were born in 1946. An increased demand for skilled workers in the economy has underpinned this change. In particular, changes in technology – for example leading to the increased computerisation of workplaces – and increased globalisation of trade are some of the reasons why skilled workers fared better than unskilled workers over this period. It is also clear from the changing shape of the different wage distributions shown in Figure 6.3 that, compared to the 1946 cohort, inequality was also higher *within* all education groups for the 1958 cohort.

For the 1970 cohort, the picture of wage differences between men in different education groups looks different again. The gap between those with no, or very low, qualifications and the rest appears to have closed somewhat compared to the 1958 cohort at a similar age. It is likely that, amongst younger generations, increasing numbers achieving qualifications (of all levels) has meant that those with qualifications are now able to command less of a wage premium over those without qualifications than in previous generations.

The pattern of wage changes by education group is different for women than for men – with those with no qualifications, as well as those on higher education levels, appearing to see considerable wage growth across the generations.

In order to understand more clearly how the returns to education have been changing over time, Table 6.3 sets out, by cohort, the average wage mark-up for male workers with different qualification levels compared to those with no, or sub-O-level qualifications (the 'raw' returns). In order

Figure 6.3 *Hourly wages for men and women in their early 30s by education group*

a) Born 1946, men

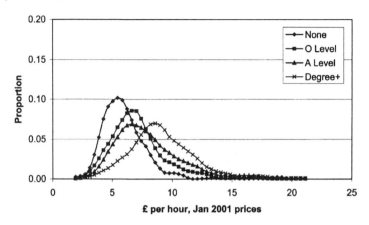

Proportion who have:
No qualifications/sub-O Level: 46%
O Level/equivalent: 15%
A Level/equivalent: 15%
Degree+: 24%

b) Born 1946, women

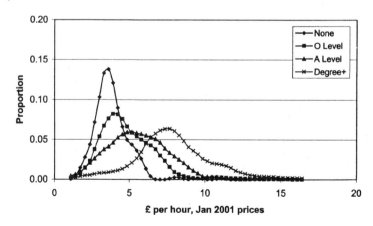

Proportion who have:
No qualifications/sub-O Level: 49%
O Level/equivalent: 24%
A Level/equivalent: 13%
Degree+: 13%

Figure 6.3 *Hourly wages for men and women in their early 30s by education group (cont'd)*

c) Born 1958, men

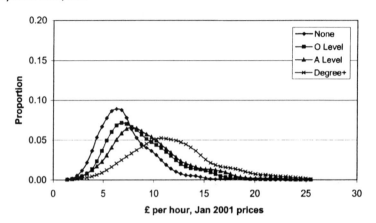

Proportion who have:
No qualifications/sub-O Level: 27%
O Level/equivalent: 26%
A Level/equivalent: 18%
Degree+: 28%

d) Born 1958, women

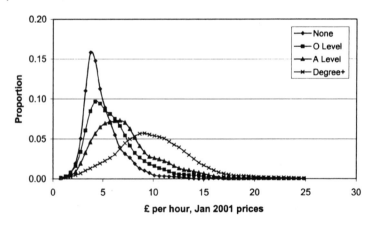

Proportion who have:
No qualifications/sub-O Level: 29%
O Level/equivalent: 33%
A Level/equivalent: 13%
Degree+: 25%

e) Born 1970, men

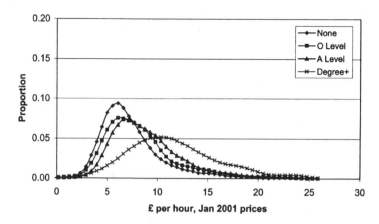

Proportion who have:
No qualifications/sub-O Level: 22%
O Level equivalent: 24%
A Level/equivalent: 23%
Degree+: 31%

f) Born 1970, women

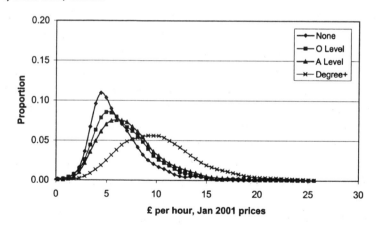

Proportion who have:
No qualifications/sub-O Level: 24%
O Level/equivalent: 30%
A Level/equivalent: 14%
Degree+: 32%

to take into account the fact that some of the differences in wages between workers of different education groups are driven by differences in the characteristics of the workers in each of the groups – for example the region that they live in, their ability, and their parental background – Table 6.3 also shows average wage mark-ups are after controlling for a small number of characteristics of the cohort members, using simple OLS regression techniques. It should be noted that these mark-ups will not be accurate estimates of the true causal impact of education on wages, not least because more educated workers are likely to be different from uneducated workers in more ways than we have controlled for in these simple regressions, and such differences are also likely to be partly responsible for the wage differences we observe.

Looking at both the 'raw' returns to education for men, and those returns estimated using a few simple controls, it is interesting to see that the mark-up for men at each qualification level first rose, and then fell back again across the generations (Table 6.3). For those with O-level and equivalent qualifications, the average wage mark-up for men, after controlling for a few characteristics of the employees, was around 12 per cent amongst those born in the 1946 cohort, rising to around 16 per cent for the 1958 cohort, and falling back to 8 per cent for the 1970 cohort. Similarly, the mark-up for those with A levels, compared to those with no qualifications, was 21 per cent for the 1946 cohort, rising to 24 per cent for the 1958 cohort and falling back to 18 per cent for the 1970 cohort. A similar pattern is seen for those with degrees, although it is only for this group that the return is higher for the 1970 cohort than it was for the 1946 cohort when they were in their early 30s a quarter of a century before.

For women, the picture is quite different, with the returns to education (as measured here) falling between each successive cohort (Table 6.4). Thus, after controlling for a small number of characteristics of the employees, the average wage difference for those with O levels or equivalent, compared to those with no (or low) qualifications, was around 22 per cent amongst those born in the 1946 cohort, falling to around 16 per cent for the 1958 cohort, then falling further to 7 per cent for the 1970 cohort. The mark-up for those in the 1946 cohort with A levels, compared

Table 6.3 *'Returns' to education for men*

	'Raw' returns			Controls for region, ability and father's social class		
	1970 cohort Age 30 %	1958 cohort Age 33 %	1946 cohort Age 31 %	1970 cohort Age 30 %	1958 cohort Age 33 %	1946 cohort Age 31 %
O level	12.6	20.6	18.4	7.9	15.6	12.0
A level	24.5	32.2	31.3	18.0	23.7	20.9
Degree +	66.7	68.8	55.1	46.7	51.4	40.4
Sample size	3,973	3,665	1,120	3,973	3,665	1,120

Note: Controls for ability are test score results quintiles from age 7 (NCDS), 11 (BCS70), and 8 (NSHD). Standard errors are available from the author.

Table 6.4 *'Returns' to education for women*

	'Raw' returns			Controls for region, ability and father's social class		
	1970 cohort Age 30 %	1958 cohort Age 33 %	1946 cohort Age 31 %	1970 cohort Age 30 %	1958 cohort Age 33 %	1946 cohort Age 31 %
O level	12.9	20.7	24.8	7.1	15.6	21.7
A level	22.6	46.7	47.4	14.9	37.8	39.3
Degree +	74.4	110.1	111.9	51.6	88.1	98.0
Sample size	3,657	3,052	583	3,657	3,052	583

Note: Controls for ability are test score results quintiles from age 7 (NCDS), 11 (BCS70), and 8 (NSHD). Standard errors are available from the author.

to those with none, was 39 per cent, about the same for the 1958 cohort
at 38 per cent, and falling back to 15 per cent for the 1970 cohort. Again,
a similar pattern is seen for those with degrees, with the biggest drop in
the average return occurring for the 1970 cohort.

One interesting feature of the education–wage differentials presented
above is that the returns to education for the older two cohorts in their
early 30s were higher for women than for men, whereas amongst the 1970
cohort this was no longer the case. This suggests that education played an
important role in reducing gender–wage differences amongst previous
generations, but no longer plays that role today. Table 6.5 provides further
evidence for this, showing the difference in average hourly pay of men
and women within education groups: the results show clearly that for the
1946 and 1958 cohorts, the gender–wage gap declined significantly with
education. For the 1970 cohort, the gap is similar within all education
levels. Although not shown here, these results remain similar after controlling for other characteristics of men and women within education groups.

Table 6.5 *Percentage male–female wage differences in early 30s, according to level of education*

	1970 cohort %	1958 cohort %	1946 cohort %
None, or sub-O level	19.9	48.9	59.4
O level	22.7	43.6	45.4
A level	17.2	37.7	41.3
Degree +	20.1	22.3	11.0
All qualifications	20.3	37.5	49.5

Family income and poverty

The discussion so far has focused on wages in the early 30s for those who
are in employment. A fuller picture of living standards can be drawn by
looking instead at family income – this includes the income from employment of both the cohort member and their partner (if they have one), as

well as income from other sources, including social security benefits. Trends in family incomes across the generations are affected by a number of important factors, many of which are the subject of other chapters. These include:

- trends in cohort members' *earnings*, as discussed above;

- *demographic patterns*: the age and rate at which cohort members cohabit or marry, have children, separate or divorce will have an important bearing on their family incomes (Chapter 4);

- patterns of *labour market participation*, both of cohort members and their partners (Chapter 3);

- *taxes and benefits*: since incomes are measured net of direct tax, and including state benefits, changes to the tax and benefit system at different times will also have an important impact on the living standards which cohort members enjoy.

Detailed comparisons were made of the living standards in their early 30s of those in the 1958 cohort and the 1970 cohort based on a constructed measure of weekly net family income, adjusted to take family size into account. Although little family income information was collected in their early 30s for those born in 1946, we did have an income measure taken at age 26. It should be noted that all the income and wages information has been expressed in January 2001 prices, so the comparisons between cohorts were not affected by inflation.

Figure 6.4 shows how the distribution of family incomes has changed across the generations. For the purposes of measuring living standards, income is measured net of tax, and adjusted to take account of family size (bigger families have their incomes scaled down, smaller families' incomes are scaled up, or *equivalised* – see the Appendix to this chapter). As we use information about the 1946 cohort's family living standards at age 26, the age gap of seven years between the 1946 cohort and the 1958 cohort is significant, and so the comparisons should be read with some care.

The pattern of rising living standards and growing inequality across the generations is clear from Figure 6.4. The living standards of each generation

Figure 6.4 *Net family income at ages 26, 33 and 30*

All families

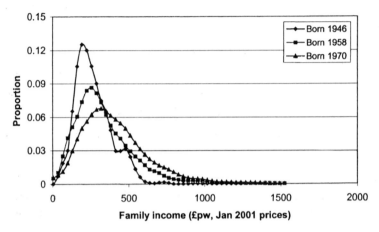

Note   One initial point to notice about Figure 6.4 is that the approximation of family
income derived from the banded income variable for 26-year-olds born in 1946
does not adequately deal with those on the highest incomes – the hump of people
at the top end of the distribution at around £500 per week (in January 2001 prices)
is most likely to be a reflection of the imperfection of our imputation procedure
in dealing with the incomes of people who have placed themselves in the highest
band (£50+ in 1972 prices), rather than a genuine reflection of the top of the
income distribution.

are higher than those of the generation preceding it – this can be seen from
the fact that the distribution of family income of each successive generation
has shifted further to the right. Greater inequality amongst later generations compared to those born in 1946 can also be seen by the lower peak
in the income distributions and an increased spread of incomes over a
wider range. These trends are very similar to those we saw in the distribution of individual's wages, though those born in 1970 received higher
family incomes at age 30 than their 1958-born counterparts at age 33 nine
years earlier – unlike the pattern for men's wages, where the distributions
for the 1958 and 1970 cohorts were about the same. Much of this jump
in living standards in the most recent generation is due to the delaying of

childbirth: by age 30, families were now smaller than they were even a decade before. This means that more women were still participating full-time in the labour market at this age, while any given income had to be shared around fewer people in the family. The three-year difference in the age at which cohort members were interviewed is clearly also a significant factor here, since many women have children (either first or subsequent children) between the ages of 30 and 33.

Our findings also show how income levels and inequality have changed over time. Average family income, as measured by the median, rose from around £250 per week (expressed at January 2001 levels as the equivalent for a childless couple) for 26-year-olds born in 1946, to almost £300 per week at age 33 for those who were born in 1958, and further to around £375 per week for those at age 30 who were born in 1970. The gap between the richest and the poorest cohort members was considerably higher for the 1958 cohort than for the 1946 cohort, but narrowed again for the 1970 cohort. Again, the difference in age at which cohort members were interviewed is likely to be important here, since inequality tends to rise *within* each cohort as they progress through life.

Living standards of different groups
In all three cohorts, incomes vary across education groups, family types, the economic status of the household, and according to the family background of the cohort member. Figure 6.5 illustrates this, by showing the average (as measured by the median and adjusted for family composition) income for different groups within each cohort.

Highest educational qualification
We have already seen that people with higher educational attainment received higher wages from employment across all three cohorts (see Figure 6.3). Not surprisingly, family incomes of cohort members also rose by level of qualification. In fact, since people tend to settle with partners who have similar educational qualifications, differences in family incomes between people of different education levels tend to be even wider than differences in individuals' wages.

Figure 6.5 *Average family income for cohort members in their late 20s and 30s*

a) By highest qualification

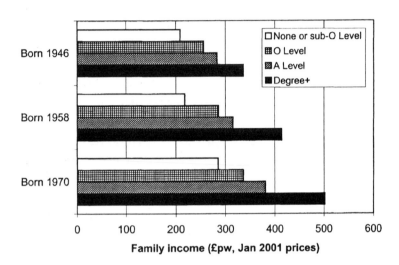

b) By family type

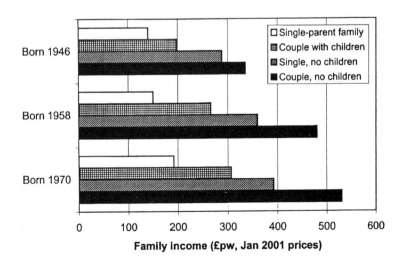

c) By family economic status

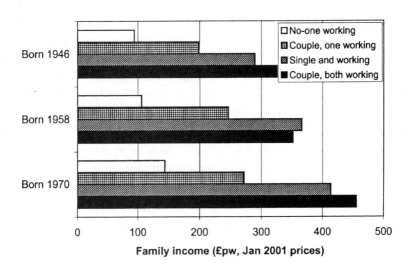

Born 1946

Born 1958

Born 1970

Legend:
- ☐ No-one working
- ⊞ Couple, one working
- ▨ Single and working
- ■ Couple, both working

Family income (£pw, Jan 2001 prices)

d) By father's social class

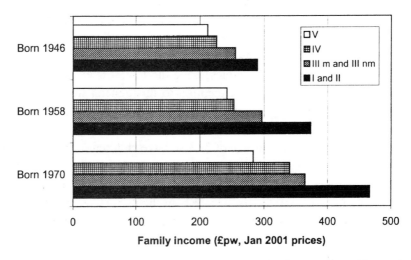

Born 1946

Born 1958

Born 1970

Legend:
- ☐ V
- ⊞ IV
- ▨ III m and III nm
- ■ I and II

Family income (£pw, Jan 2001 prices)

Notes: Average incomes here are measured by the median for each group. Those with no father figure, or whose father was unemployed or social class unknown are not included in this Figure.

Family type

Across all three cohorts, couples without children have the highest family incomes. This is because there are two potential earners within the household, and no extra mouths to feed. Single people without children are next in the family income ranking: their living standards are high on average because they do not have to share their resources amongst other family members (remember, incomes are adjusted to take into account family size). Couples with children are third in the ranking – their lower average living standards reflect the additional costs of children, and also the fact that there are less likely to be two earners in the household amongst these couples. Single-parent families experience the lowest average income of all groups in each generation – reflecting both the additional costs of children, and the relatively small number of single parents in employment. The general rise in living standards across all groups can also be seen here.

Family economic status

In general, couples with two earners are the highest income families across all three generations, followed by single workers. Couples with one earner (many of whom have children) are ranked third according to their average income, while not surprisingly, families in which there are no workers at all (both single people and couples) have the lowest average income of all these groups. There is one exception to this general trend: amongst those born in 1958, single workers at age 33 had higher average income than those in two-earner couples. This reflects the fact that many of those in two-earner couples by the age of 33 also have children – since incomes here are adjusted by the number of mouths to feed, this has the effect of reducing average living standards amongst this group. It is also the case that many of the second earners in these households are likely to have been working part time, providing relatively small additions to family income.

Father's social class

Across all three generations, family incomes also show a significant gradient according to the social class of their origin, as measured by the social class of the cohort member's father when the cohort member was a child. Incomes in all three cohorts are highest on average amongst those whose father was professional or managerial, next highest amongst those whose father's occupation was skilled manual or skilled non-manual, followed by those with fathers in partly skilled occupations and lowest amongst those whose father's occupation was unskilled. Previous research has shown that educational achievement plays a crucial role in the transmission of income and social class status between parents and their children, though this does not explain all of the differences we observe. It is very interesting to note, and consistent with the lack of trend in social mobility noted in Chapter 3, that these income differences appear more pronounced in younger generations.

Two important things to remember when interpreting these trends is that (1) the number of people falling into each of the different categories discussed above has changed across the cohorts, and (2) there is considerable variation in living standards *within* all these groups, as well as *between* them.

The composition of different income groups
As well as understanding how the average incomes of different groups have changed across the generations, we can also examine how the composition of the richest and poorest groups in each generation has changed. Figures 6.6 to 6.8 show where families of different types are to be found across the income distribution. Each cohort's population has been broken down into five different income groups (or quintiles) ranked from poorest to richest, and each figure shows the proportion of each of these income groups made up by different families. For reference, the composition of the entire cohort is also shown.

Figure 6.6 shows the population broken down by family type. Families with children, and particularly single-parent families, were clearly over-represented amongst the lowest income groups and under-represented at the top of the income distribution in all three cohorts (though there were very few one-parent families amongst those born in 1946 when they were aged 26). For example, though single parents made up just 6 per cent of

Figure 6.6 *Family types across the income distribution*

a) Born 1946 (at age 26)

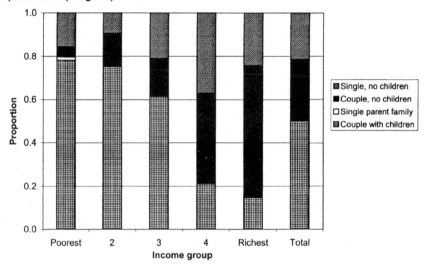

b) Born 1958 (at age 33)

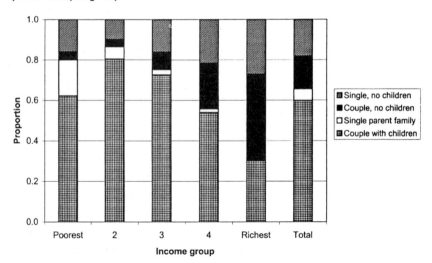

c) Born 1970 (at age 30)

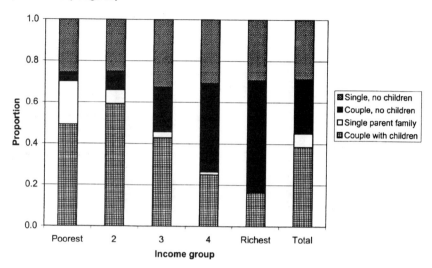

all those born in 1970 by the time they were 30, they made up more than one in five of the bottom income quintile. In this same generation, couples with children made up around 40 per cent of the total cohort, but 50 per cent of the poorest income group. In all three generations shown here, couples without children are over-represented in the richest income groups.

Turning next to the composition of the different income groups by economic status (Figure 6.7), it is clear that workless families were heavily over-represented in the lowest income groups in all generations (though there were very few of them at all amongst the 1946 cohort at 26), while families where all adults were working (either couples or singles) predominate at the top of the income distribution. It is also clear from Figure 6.7 that there were many more single-earner couples amongst the 1946 generation at this age than amongst subsequent cohorts.

Finally, the composition of different income groups is uneven according to family of origin, with those whose fathers were in lower social classes more likely to fall into lower income groups: again this appears to be more pronounced in more recent generations. Though not shown in

Figure 6.7 *Family economic status across the income distribution*

a) Born 1946 (at age 26)

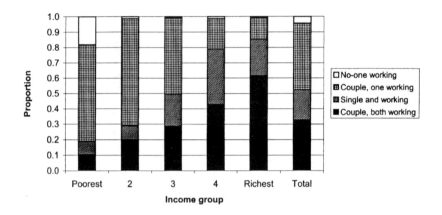

b) Born 1958 (at age 33)

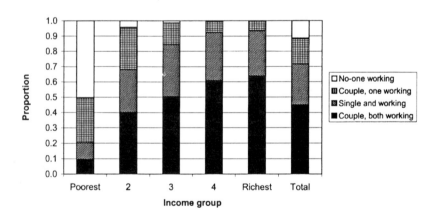

c) Born 1970 (at age 30)

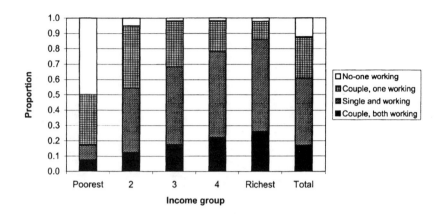

Figure 6.8, around 30 per cent of those whose fathers were in unskilled professions were to be found in the poorest income group amongst those born in 1946, whilst this proportion was around 35 per cent amongst those born in 1970.

Poverty across the generations

Using information about cohort members' living standards, we can also discover how experiences of poverty have changed across the genera-tions. Although there is no single agreed definition of poverty, we can attempt to identify the approximate number and type of people living in poverty in each generation: in order to do this we use one commonly used measure of poverty – the number of people living below 60 per cent of the median family income. Ideally, we would like to identify whether cohort members are in poverty by measuring their incomes relative to the average living standards of the population as a whole at the relevant time (i.e. including people of all ages), rather than just relative to the living standards of other cohort members. However, this is difficult to do in practice, since the cohort studies themselves do not contain information about the living standards of people of other ages, and income information

Figure 6.8 *Father's social class across the income distribution*

a) Born 1946 (at age 26)

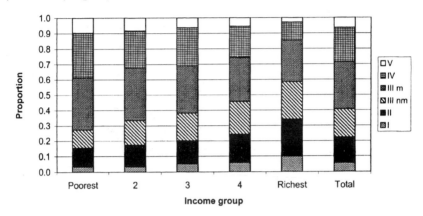

b) Born 1958 (at age 33)

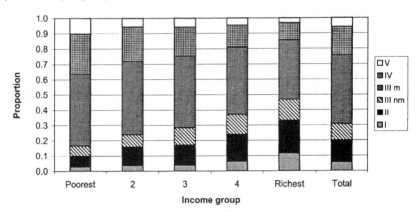

c) Born 1970 (at age 30)

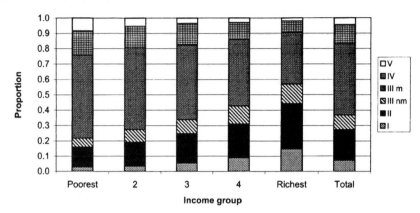

available from other data sources does not tally closely enough with the income measures available in these studies to combine them successfully.

For this reason, we use a rather narrower concept of poverty amongst cohort members for this chapter: namely, the proportion of cohort members falling below 60 per cent of the median 'equivalised' income within each cohort. This is still a relative measure of poverty, since the income below which a cohort member is judged to be in poverty will rise as the average incomes of cohort members go up. In order to compare how experiences of poverty across the generations has changed with respect to a more absolute measure of poverty, we can also examine how the number of people living below fixed income lines has changed across the generations. In this case we have chosen a fixed income poverty line of £151 per week (this was 60 per cent of the median family income at age 26 amongst those born in 1946, expressed as the equivalent for a childless couple in January 2001 prices).

The number of people in their late 20s or early 30s falling into poverty, measured relative to their peers, has risen over time as inequality has grown. Around 12 per cent, or one in eight of all cohort members born in 1946 were in poverty relative to their peers in their mid-20s, compared to around 19 per cent, or almost one in five of those in the later two cohorts.

Surprisingly perhaps, the number falling below this fixed income line was also higher for those born in 1958 when they were 33, compared to those born in 1946 at age 26. This partly reflects the different times in the economic cycle at which the different birth cohorts were interviewed, since 1991 was during a period of recession in which a greater number of 1958 cohort members were out of work and on low incomes compared to the 1946 cohort interviewed in 1972 when they were 26. Amongst those in the 1970 cohort in their early 30s, only around 7 per cent, or around one in 13, were on incomes below £151 per week.

Just as income levels varied systematically across different groups of the population, poverty rates were also quite different across different groups. This is shown in Figure 6.9, which shows how relative poverty rates varied across education, family type, economic status, and family background.

Across all the generations, cohort members with no qualifications were much more likely to be in poverty relative to their peers than those with higher qualifications, and the likelihood of being in poverty was progressively reduced at each higher qualification level. Increasing divergence in the fortunes of different education groups between the 1946 and 1958 cohorts is also clear from Figure 6.9: more than 40 per cent of those with no qualifications were in relative poverty amongst the 1958 cohort in their early 30s, compared to around 20 per cent of those born in 1946. The gap between the rate of poverty amongst those with no qualifications and those with O level or equivalent was also considerably higher amongst the 1958 cohort compared to the 1946 cohort, though the age at interview may play an important role here.

Although single-parent families make up a small proportion of the overall population, they have by far the highest likelihood of falling into relative poverty compared to other groups. In all three cohorts, around 60 per cent of lone parents were in relative poverty using this definition. Couples with children were the group with the next highest likelihood of falling into poverty.

Families with no adult in employment (both singles and couples) were the most likely to be in relative poverty in each generation, though the

Figure 6.9 *Poverty across the generations: relative 'poverty' rates amongst different groups*

a) **By highest qualification**

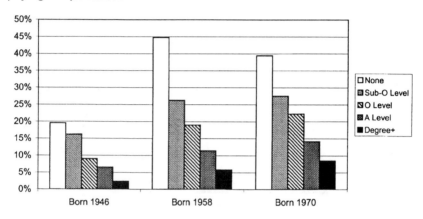

b) **By family type**

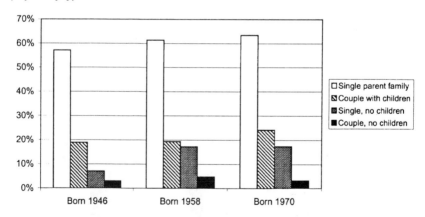

Figure 6.9 *Poverty across the generations: relative 'poverty' rates amongst different groups (cont'd)*

c) By family economic status

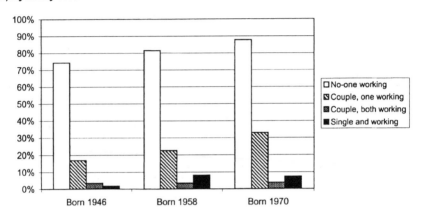

d) By father's social class

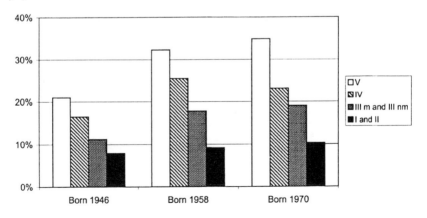

Note:
Those with no father figure, or whose father was unemployed or social class
unknown are not included in this Figure.

incidence of worklessness was the highest at these ages amongst the 1958 cohort compared to those born in 1946 and 1970.

Just as we saw a steep gradient in average family incomes across people from different family backgrounds (Figure 6.5), there was also a much greater incidence of poverty amongst those whose father's social class was lower. Again, much of the explanation for this lies in the poorer educational achievements of those from less skilled backgrounds (see Chapter 2).

Living standards and inequality across the lifetime

Until now, our discussion has focused on the different experiences of men and women around age 30. It is also important to ask how the living standards of each of the cohorts changed as they progressed through life. Figure 6.10 investigates this by showing the average wage (measured here by the median) and wage inequality (measured by the gini coefficient) at different ages across the lifespan of the cohort members up until their early 40s. For this, we have used additional information about 1958 cohort members at age 23 and 1946 cohort members at 26, as well as information from both these cohorts in their early 40s. (Although the 1970 cohort members were also interviewed at age 26, we do not use their wage information here, since the measure of wages collected was not directly comparable.)

Figure 6.10 shows that average wages within each cohort generally rise over time. This is shown by the upward slope of the median wage lines. This wage growth by age arises largely because cohort members' earnings tend to rise over time with their increasing labour market experience. It may also be due to compositional effects, as different people move in and out of the labour market. For women, the increase in the average wage over time is less steep than for men: this is both because the composition of the women's workforce is changing over time, with more low-paid women entering employment by age 43 compared to those working at 31 (for the 1946 cohort); it is also due to slower wage growth for women who remain in work. Figure 6.10 also shows that each generation maintains

Figure 6.10 *Average wages and inequality by age and cohort*

a) Men

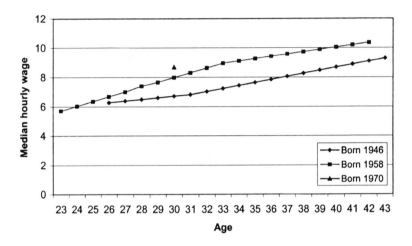

b) Women

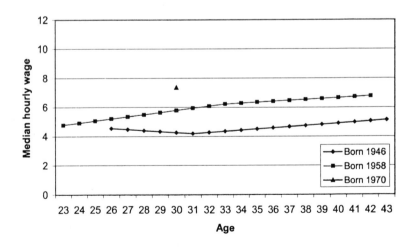

c) Men

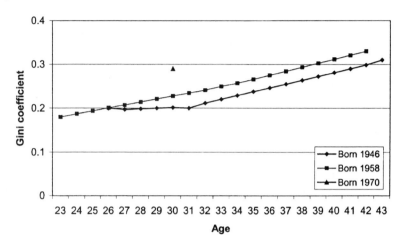

d) Women

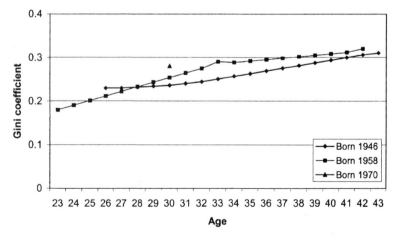

Note The points at which cohort members have been observed are shown by a solid mark. It should be noted that we do not attempt to approximate the profile of cohort members' wages between marks, but instead simply join them together by a straight line as an illustrative guide to the path they have taken over time.

higher wages than the preceding one as they progress to their early 40s. This can be seen from the fact that the wage lines for each more recent generation always lie above that of the generation preceding.

Inequality in wages also rises across the lifetime: as people progress through their working lives, their wage outcomes become more dispersed. This process happens for a number of reasons: as well as changes going on in the general economy which may affect levels of inequality amongst groups of workers (for example changing patterns of unionisation), this widening of fortunes across the life cycle also occurs because of differing accumulation of skills and experience amongst workers on different wages, and because of the accumulated effects of random chance. This increasing inequality over the life cycle can be seen clearly for those born in 1958, though it is less clear for the 1946 cohort (Figure 6.10c and d).

Conclusions

Perhaps the first point to make in summarising our analysis of income and living standards in the three birth cohorts is that successive generations of men and women have experienced rises in their wages and living standards.

At the same time, amongst those in employment, wage inequality has risen. Each birth cohort entered young adult life with wages more unequal than those of the generation preceding them, and this pattern of inequality has been maintained as they progress through their lives.

By far the biggest step change in wage inequality for those in their early 30s can be seen in the differences between the 1946 and 1958 cohorts, reflecting the important changes taking place in the labour market over the 1980s. By contrast, the differences that were found between the 1958 and 1970 cohorts were much less pronounced.

Changes in the returns to educational qualifications have been responsible for many of the trends in inequality we have seen. For men in their early 30s, wage differences between high- and low-skilled workers rose quite sharply between the 1946 and 1958 cohorts, and then fell back again across the three generations. By contrast, for women in their early 30s, education-related wage differentials have fallen successively over time. At the same time, inequality *within* education groups has risen across the generations.

Alongside the rise in inequality, the number of people from each cohort who have been identified as experiencing relative poverty as compared to their peers has also gone up. Poverty rates also vary considerably by education, family type and family background.

Men's and women's wages have been converging over time, though the gender wage gap has remained significant. Women born in 1970 who were in work in their early 30s as the new century dawned, had hourly wages on average approximately 20 per cent lower than working men of the same age. This compares to a gap of 37 per cent amongst those born in 1958 when they were in their early 30s, and of 50 per cent amongst those born in 1946 at a similar age.

Amongst all three generations in their late 20s and early 30s, living standards were highest on average for couples without children, and lowest for single-parent families. This in part reflects the costs of children, and also the number of potential earners in the household. Families in which all adults are working (both singles and couples) were, in general, considerably better off than families in which fewer adults were working.

In conclusion, this chapter has demonstrated quite strikingly that, whilst living standards have, in general, risen steadily with each successive cohort, inequalities in income and wages have also increased. These findings alone represent a significant indicator of the changes in British society in the last decades of the twentieth century. However, it is also important to recall our finding that there was also a significant gradient in the incomes of cohort members according to their own parental background, as measured by their fathers' social class, and that this gradient appeared to have become *steeper* amongst more recent cohorts. Thus, not only has Britain become an increasingly unequal society, but the income achieved by the more recently born is more strongly linked to the social class position of their own parental generation.

Appendix to chapter 6

Data and measurement issues

Before it is possible to set out how living standards have changed across the cohorts, some measurement issues need to be discussed. This section sets out briefly the comparisons which have been possible, and how wages and living standards have been measured for the purposes of this chapter.

Wages from employment

The main comparisons given are of **gross hourly and weekly pay** from employment. It should be noted that the exact measure of pay and hours differ slightly between the generations (see Box 1). In their early 30s, the 1958 respondents were asked the amount they were *usually* paid, 1946 respondents the amount they were paid *on average*, whilst the 1970 respondents were asked about the amount of their *last* pay. Although for many respondents usual, average, and last pay are likely to be the same, there may be some differences in the distributions driven entirely by these definitional differences. In addition to this, in their early 40s, 1946 cohort members were asked to place their average gross pay into one of 26 bands ranging between the lowest band (£0–40 per week) and the highest band (£481 per week and over). We have imputed a continuous wage variable from this banded earnings variable using regression techniques.[2] Box 1 also sets out some differences in the way that weekly hours are measured.

Weekly equivalised net family income

Comparisons of the 1958 and 1970 cohorts are based on a constructed measure of family income – *weekly equivalised net family income*. The

---

Box 1 *Pay variables used from the three cohort studies*

Cohort members in their early 30s:
BCS at 30 (1999–2000)
Last time you were paid, what was your gross pay before deductions?
How many hours per week do you *usually* work in your (main) job/business not including meal breaks? What is your usual overtime? (Variable constructed to include paid overtime only for comparative purposes.)

NCDS at 33 (1991)
What is your *usual* gross pay before deductions? (If no usual pay given, then last gross pay asked for instead.)
How many hours per week do you *usually* work for that pay, excluding meal breaks but including paid overtime?

NSHD at 31 (1977)
On average, how much do you earn a week (including overtime and other payment)?
How many hours do you *usually* work per week including overtime? (Hours at work plus hours at home.)

Cohort members in their early 40s:
NCDS at 42 (1999–2000)
Last time you were paid, what was your gross pay before deductions?
How many hours per week do you *usually* work in your (main) job/business not including meal breaks? What is your usual overtime? (Includes both paid and unpaid.)

NSHD at 43 (1989)
Would you mind telling me which of the letters on this card represents your own *average* gross earnings, before deduction of income tax and national insurance? (Card presents 26 earnings bands.)
How many hours a week on average do you have to work to earn this amount?

---

measure has been *equivalised*, or adjusted to take into account family size.[3] All income levels are expressed as the equivalent income for a childless couple. Comparisons with the 1946 cohort use data collected at age 26. Cohort members were asked to place their income in one of ten different bands, ranging from the lowest band (under £10 per week in 1972 prices) to the highest band (over £50 per week). Again we have imputed this into a continuous variable using regression techniques. We have also equivalised this income measure to take into account family size, though in this case the equivalence scales are only approximations, since the exact family composition of 1946 cohort members at age 26 is not known. For this reason the comparisons must be treated with care; indeed there appear to be particular problems with our approximation of family income for the 1946 cohort at age 26 amongst those in the highest income range (see below).

In constructing the family income measures from the 1958 and 1970 cohorts, it was not possible to include income from self-employment, since this was not collected on a consistent enough basis to make reliable comparisons of family incomes containing self-employment income.

Besides self-employment income, it has been possible to look in more detail at the *sources* of income in the household for the 1958 and 1970 cohorts – including the relative contribution of income from male and female partners within a couple, as well as income from state benefits and other sources. Although the 1946 cohort members were asked questions about their net family income in 1972 and again in 1989, these responses are not sufficiently detailed to form comparisons of the sources of income with the other two birth cohorts.

The timing of wage/income information
A number of important considerations must also be borne in mind regarding the *timing* of the wage and income information presented in this chapter. Firstly, the information about income and wages for each cohort in their early 30s has been collected at somewhat different ages – at 33 for the 1958 cohort, compared to an average age of 30 for the 1970 cohort and 31 for the 1946 cohort (wages only). This means that the 1958 cohort members will have had two or three more years of potential labour market participation and wage growth by the time of interview; for women in particular the comparisons at different ages will also be affected by the timing of childbirth and childcare responsibilities at these different ages. Of course, when comparing family income at 26 for the 1946 cohort

members to family income at 33 for the 1958 cohort and 30 for the 1970, these potential problems become even more pronounced.

Another important point to bear in mind when considering the comparisons between cohorts is that each of the cohorts were entering these stages of their lives at different points in the economic cycle. The year of interview for the 1946 cohort in their early 30s (1977) and for the 1970 cohort (1999–2000) were both years of economic growth. By contrast when the 1958 cohort were interviewed in their early 30s (1991) was at the start of an economic recession. Since wages and employment are strongly related to the economic cycle, this will make an important difference to the comparisons, both in terms of the composition of the workforce, and the pay which workers are able to command.

Notes

1   Although partner's income and income from other sources will also be important determining factors.
2   We imputed a continuous variable by obtaining within-band predictions from an interval regression on the log of the lower and upper weekly wage bounds, with the cohort members' education and wages reported at previous waves as explanatory variables. Imputations were conducted separately for men and women. We also experimented with different specifications including one with only the constant on the right-hand side of the regression equation.
3   The equivalence scale used is the McClements scale, which is also used for the government's official low-income statistics. For the purposes of this book, all children of the head or spouse who are 17 or under and living in the household are counted as dependants.

7 Housing

Kate Smith and Elsa Ferri

The preceding chapter highlighted the rise in living standards experienced by our three successive cohorts, which was nonetheless accompanied by an increasing polarisation in terms of wage inequality. In this chapter, we turn our attention to housing, as another major indicator of economic and social wellbeing. This is a further area in which vast changes have taken place in Britain since the immediate postwar period that saw the birth of the 1946 cohort.

The early years of the three cohorts, especially those born in 1946 and 1958, were very different in terms of their housing experiences. The 1946 cohort was born at a time when the development of social housing came to fruition, with the renewal of bombed-out inner cities, the beginning of slum clearance and the building of new towns and new estates. Following the end of the Second World War, the growth of council housing as 'general needs housing' rose dramatically, to reach a peak of almost 250,000 in 1953 (ONS 2000).

Improvements in the quality, as well as the amount, of housing in the postwar period meant that unsatisfactory accommodation was much less common among the 1958 cohort than it had been among their counterparts born 12 years earlier (Essen and Wedge 1982). This was especially reflected in access to basic amenities: whereas one in five of the 1946 cohort had no bathroom at age 15 (1961), this applied to only one in 50 of the 1958 cohort at 16 (1974).

The type and quality of the housing lived in by the members of the three cohorts throughout their childhood, and in adulthood, have been an important topic of data collection in almost every survey from birth onwards. Detailed information has been gathered about the type and tenure of accommodation, and its quality, in terms of access to basic amenities and the amount of space available.

A wealth of investigations during the early lives of the cohorts established an independent association between poor housing and lower school attainment through childhood and adolescence (Douglas 1964; Davie *et al.* 1972; Fogelman 1983; Wedge and Petzing 1970). Such was their importance in accounting for differences in childhood development that living in overcrowded accommodation, and lacking exclusive access to basic amenities such as hot water, were included in a deprivation index derived to identify a sub-group of 'socially disadvantaged' children in the 1958 cohort (Wedge and Prosser 1973; Essen and Wedge 1982; Pilling 1990). A similar 'social index' was devised for the 1970 cohort (Osborn and Morris 1979).

Links were also found between these housing measures and truancy (Tibbenham 1977) and anti-social behaviour (West and Farrington 1973). Somewhat surprisingly, perhaps, the relationship between adverse housing conditions and poor physical health and development appeared less strong among the 1958 cohort. Absence from school due to bronchitis or bilious attacks was more common amongst those living in homes lacking amenities, while bronchitis was also associated with overcrowding (Essen *et al.* 1978). Analysis of the 16-year data found that boys growing up in overcrowded homes were, on average, shorter than their peers in more favourable housing circumstances (Fogelman 1983). Overall, however, there were few significant health differences attributable to accommodation factors, and it was suggested that one reason for this might be that, by the time the 1958 cohort were growing up, only a very small proportion of families were living in conditions so poor as to have a directly adverse affect on health.

By the time the cohorts reached adulthood, the housing situation in Britain was dramatically different to that in which they had grown up – especially for those born in 1946. As a result of the postwar reconstruction programme, a severe housing shortage had turned into a surplus by the 1970s (Holmans 2000). Many of the 1946 cohort would have had access, via the tenure held by their parents, to the social housing in which they had grown up. However, this type of 'council house' accommodation, often seen as a prize by their parental generation, had begun to lose its

attraction by the 1970s – especially that built in the 1960s, which came
to be seen as substituting 'new slums for old' (Holmans 2000). In contrast
to their own parents, many of the economic 'high flyers' in the 1946 cohort
would have been able to move away from social housing and gain a
foothold in the owner-occupied sector, prior to the dramatic rise in house
prices in the early 1970s.

The 1958 cohort, on the other hand, belongs to the first generation for
whom home ownership was likely to be regarded as a natural progression.
They reached adulthood in the late 1970s, a time when buying a home
had become the norm, while the amount of social housing was about to
contract severely. This was in large part due to the policy of selling Local
Authority accommodation to tenants at well below the market value, via
the 'right to buy' scheme introduced by the Thatcher government in 1980.
At the same time, there was a cessation of public funding for new building (local authorities were forbidden to use the proceeds of council house
sales for this purpose), and a large-scale transfer of existing social sector
tenancies from local authorities to Housing Associations.

The total number of owner occupiers rose from 9.9 million (57 per cent
of all households) in 1981 to 13.1 million (68 per cent) in 1991 (DTLR
2001), giving Britain the highest rate of owner occupation in Europe.
However, by the end of the 1980s, when the 1958 cohort had just entered
their 30s, the housing market collapsed. This came at a time when many
of the cohort members would have been making the transition to parenthood and, perhaps, moving up the accommodation ladder in response to
family change. These events in the housing market made them vulnerable
to the resultant problems of negative equity and repossession. High interest rates, combined with falling house prices, meant that many people owed
significantly more on their mortgages than their homes were worth.

The 1970 cohort were just entering adulthood at around this time – the
late 1980s – when the housing market was at a very uncertain point.
Although many of their parents would have been able to take advantage
of the growth in home ownership, for the cohort members themselves the
ability to buy was no longer something to be taken for granted. After the
owner-occupation boom of the 1980s, the 1990s experienced a much slower

growth in home ownership, due in part to economic recession. However, the most important factor affecting the 1970 cohort as they reached their 30s was a further stratospheric rise in the average cost of a home (particularly in the south-east of England) which, for many, blocked off the first step on the home ownership ladder (the average price of a home in the UK approached the £100,000 mark for the first time in 2000). The English Housing Survey 2000 showed that, in households headed by someone aged 25–29, the proportion who were owner occupiers had fallen from 63 per cent in 1991 to 52 per cent in 1999 (DTLR 2001).

Furthermore, the alternatives to buying a home had also become less accessible. The severe reduction in the availability of social housing had barred this route to all but a few: waiting lists were prioritised on the basis of defined categories of need. Combined with the equally sharp rise in the cost of privately rented accommodation, this meant that the transition to independent living was, for many, further constrained. Official statistics reveal that the age at which young people leave home has been rising. Among men born between 1940 and 1954 (thus including the 1946 cohort), 73 per cent had left home by age 25, but the figure was just 61 per cent among those born between 1965 and 1969 (just a year or two younger than the 1970 cohort) (DETR 1997). Of all three cohorts, therefore, those born in 1970 faced the least favourable housing context in which to establish a home for themselves and their families.

In this chapter, we compare the adult housing experiences of the three cohorts, in terms of the tenure of the accommodation they were living in at the time of the surveys in their 30s and 40s. Tenure can be seen as a key indicator of 'success' with regard to the home environment in which they were living as independent adults, and in which those who had become parents were bringing up their own families.

Tenure in early adult life

In the early cohort surveys, information collected on housing circumstances included access to basic amenities, such as an indoor toilet, fixed bath and constant hot water. As described at the beginning of this chapter, these were found to be highly discriminatory measures in relation to developmental outcomes, but, with improvements in housing quality over the years, very few people now do not have sole use of these facilities and such questions are no longer included in adult surveys. Holmans (2000) has pointed out that in the 1980s and 1990s, physically deficient housing was no longer a matter of lack of basic amenities but, far more commonly, disrepair and poor environments. In the most recent surveys, questions have been included on certain aspects of the areas lived in and the cohort members' satisfaction or otherwise with their local neighbourhoods.

Tenure of accommodation, however, remains an important aspect of housing, and this information is updated at each follow-up. Comparing the tenure situation for all three cohorts at or around the age of 30 confirmed that, from the 1980s onwards, home ownership had become the norm. However, there were variations between the experiences of the three cohorts that reflect the impact of the historical trends in the housing market described above.

Levels of home ownership were slightly higher in the 1958 cohort at age 33 (in 1991) than they had been in the 1946 cohort at age 36 (in 1982) (the nearest age at which housing information was collected for this cohort). However, the rates of owner occupation dropped back dramatically for the 1970 cohort at 30 to the lowest figure of all (Figure 7.1). Less than two-thirds of the youngest cohort owned, or were buying, their homes, compared to three-quarters of the 1946 cohort and four-fifths of those born in 1958.

However, this relatively low level of home ownership among the 1970 cohort actually overestimates the extent to which they were established on the housing ladder. We saw in Chapter 4 that fewer of the 1970 cohort (particularly men) had made the transition to independent living by their 30s than either of the other cohorts: 16 per cent of men and 7 per cent of women were living with their parents at 30, compared with only 1 per cent of the men born in 1958 and less than 1 per cent of the women. Further analysis of the 1970 cohort showed that, in the case of 8 per cent of men and 4 per cent of women who were living in owner-occupied accommodation at 30, this was registered in their parents' name. In other words, a proportion

Figure 7.1 *Tenure situation of cohort members in early 30s*

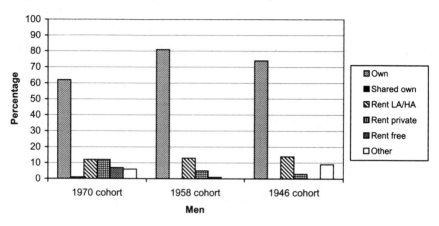

Men

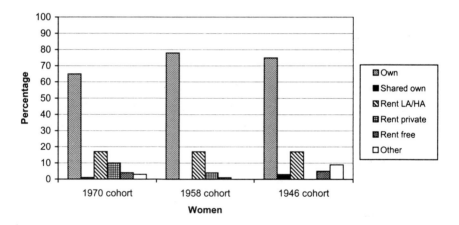

Women

of the 'owner occupiers' in the 1970 cohort included those who had not yet left, or who had returned to, their parents' home.

The proportions in each cohort who were in social housing at age 30 or thereabouts were fairly similar – about one in six women and one in seven men in each case. However, for nearly a fifth of the 1970-born men in Local Authority or Housing Association accommodation, the home was rented in their *parents'* name. These findings confirm the picture of a delayed move to independence among the youngest cohort. It would seem that the later transitions to the labour market linked to the higher proportions going on to tertiary education, and the associated delays in marriage or partnership formation, coincided with a period of rapidly rising housing costs to make owner occupation and/or independent living less attainable goals for the 1970 cohort than it had been for their earlier born peers.

The 1970 cohort contained twice as many as the 1958 cohort living in privately rented accommodation, and three times more than among those born in 1946. It is interesting to note that a resurgence in the previously dwindling privately rented sector in the late 1980s and 1990s was partly based on the purchase for renting out of a large number of repossessed homes, as well as on the deregulation of lettings starting after 1989 (Holmans 2000).

Tenure and partnership status in the early 30s
Not surprisingly, in all three cohorts, the highest rates of home ownership by the early 30s were found amongst those who were married (upwards of 80 per cent in each case). However, there was a marked difference between the 1958 and the other two cohorts in the tenure status of those in other partnership categories. In the 1946 and the 1970 cohorts, married men and women were twice as likely to be home owners as those who were single at the time of the interview in their 30s, regardless of whether the latter group had been partnered in the past (Table 7.1). By contrast, there was little difference in the levels of owner occupation among these groups in the 1958 cohort, except for a lower proportion of owner occupiers among women who had previously lived with a partner. Similarly, the difference in home ownership between the married and the cohabiting was much smaller in the 1958 cohort than in the other cohorts. It would seem, then, that the housing market experienced by the 1958 cohort in their early 30s, combined with their own circumstances, enabled them to acquire, and maintain, a position in the owner-occupied sector, irrespective of their partnership status.

Living in social housing (Local Authority or Housing Association accommodation) was most commonly found among women in all three

Table 7.1 *Tenure and relationship status in 30s*

(a) Men

Tenure	1970 cohort Age 30 in 2000				1958 cohort Age 33 in 1991				1946 cohort Age 36 in 1982			
	No partner by 30 %	Previously partnered, none at 30 %	Married %	Cohabiting %	No partner by 33 %	Previously partnered, none at 33 %	Married %	Cohabiting %	No partner by 36 %	Previously partnered, none at 36 %	Married %	Cohabiting %
Owned	43	41	81	65	77	75	84	79	34	37	80	63
Rented (LA/HA)	12	12	10	15	12	14	12	16	28	16	12	14
Rented (private)	16	21	5	14	10	10	3	4	0	17	2	5
Rent-free	15	13	3	4	<1	1	1	1	8	0	0	0
Other	14	13	1	3	1	<1	<1	<1	30	30	5	18
N (100%)	1,093	848	2,010	1,431	526	323	2,290	1,756	245	135	2,572	78

(b) Women

Tenure	1970 cohort Age 30 in 2000				1958 cohort Age 33 in 1991				1946 cohort Age 36 in 1982			
	No partner by 30 %	Previously partnered, none at 30 %	Married %	Cohabiting %	No partner by 33 %	Previously partnered, none at 33 %	Married %	Cohabiting %	No partner by 36 %	Previously partnered, none at 36 %	Married %	Cohabiting %
Owned	44	37	83	65	74	57	84	77	42	42	79	62
Rented (LA/HA)	20	32	10	18	15	36	12	18	19	44	15	18
Rented (private)	14	19	4	12	10	7	3	4	20	9	2	13
Rent-free	12	6	2	3	<1	0	1	1	0	0	0	0
Other	10	6	1	2	1	0	<1	<1	19	5	4	8
N (100%)	701	985	2,714	1,344	346	489	2,653	1,853	122	199	2,737	107

cohorts who had previously lived in a partnership but were no longer doing so at the time of survey. Nearly half (44 per cent) of the 1970-born women who had formerly been partnered were in this type of accommodation. The most likely explanation for this is that the women concerned were mothers who had retained their tenancy after separation or divorce. By contrast, previously partnered men were as, or more, likely to be living in privately rented accommodation. Further analysis of the housing history data collected for the 1958 and 1970 studies will enable the sequence of partnership and housing experiences to be disentangled.

Tenure and highest qualification by early 30s

Among those whose home was being bought or rented by the cohort (member and/or their partner only), it was evident that, in all three cohorts, levels of home ownership rose in line with qualifications. However, it is worth noting that, despite the overall higher levels of owner occupation among the 1958 cohort, the largest proportion of home owners among the group without any qualifications was in the 1946 cohort. As noted in other chapters, members of the 1946 cohort were the last who could expect to enter the labour market at a young age, without qualifications, obtain a relatively well paid job and achieve financial independence. For the sizeable number in this position in the 1946 cohort, who were also likely to have married relatively young (see Chapter 4), it would have been possible to gain a foothold on the housing ladder before prices rocketed in the early 1970s.

It was also, predictably, the case that, in each cohort, the groups with no qualifications contained the highest number of respondents living in homes rented from a Local Authority or Housing Association. What was more noteworthy was that, among the relatively high proportion of the 1970 cohort living in the *privately* rented sector, this was most common in those with *highest* qualifications. This suggests that the privately rented sector has become a type of accommodation oriented towards more affluent groups. It is likely to be a transitional phase of living among young single professionals who, compared with their earlier born peers, have delayed settling down with partners and starting their own families.

The above patterns were repeated when tenure was compared in terms of the cohort members' social class of occupation in their early 30s. There was very little variation between the three cohorts; those in managerial or professional occupations were far more likely to own their home than those in semi- or unskilled jobs, who, in turn, contained the highest numbers renting from local authorities or Housing Associations. As with qualifications, those in professional or managerial positions were the most likely to be living in the privately rented sector.

Tenure in early middle life

By the time individuals reach their 40s, most are married or in stable relationships, and have established families of their own. Others, however, will have been through more turbulence in their personal lives, having experienced relationship breakdown, lone parenthood and/or the formation of second or third families. The housing situation of the members of the two earlier cohorts by the time they reached their early 40s is likely to reflect these relationship histories.

Figures on tenure status showed that the great majority (over eight out of ten) of men and women in both the 1946 and 1958 cohorts owned their homes by age 42/3. This was similar to the figure for 33-year-olds in the 1958 cohort, but represented an increase for those born in 1946. However, it also appeared that owner occupation, although the most common situation among all groups, was concentrated very much among the married (Table 7.2a and b). This had also been the case among the 1946 cohort at 36, but, as noted earlier, there had been little variation according to partnership status, especially among men in the 1958 cohort at 33. By 42, however, men, as well as women, born in 1958 who had never had a partner, or who had experienced a relationship breakdown, were, like their counterparts in the 1946 cohort, much less likely than the married to own their homes. The pattern at the older age may well reflect the aftermath of separation or divorce involving children, and the consequent loss of owner-occupied homes. In both cohorts, women who had previously been partnered were more likely to be in social housing at 42/3 than renting privately, while

Table 7.2 *Tenure and relationship status in early 40s*

(a) Men

Tenure	1958 cohort Age 42 in 2000				1946 cohort Age 43 in 1989			
	No partner by 42 %	Previously partnered, none at 42 %	Married %	Cohabiting %	No partner by 43 %	Previously partnered, none at 43 %	Married %	Cohabiting %
Owned	59	60	90	71	45	69	88	67
Rented (LA/HA)	18	16	7	16	31	14	6	15
Rented (private)	10	15	2	8	6	15	2	12
Rent-free	7	5	1	3	–	–	–	–
Other	7	5	1	3	17	3	3	6
N (100%)	572	503	3,855	644	193	184	2,612	118

(b) Women

Tenure	1958 cohort Age 42 in 2000				1946 cohort Age 43 in 1989			
	No partner by 42 %	Previously partnered, none at 42 %	Married %	Cohabiting %	No partner by 43 %	Previously partnered, none at 43 %	Married %	Cohabiting %
Owned	58	61	87	74	51	66	87	64
Rented (LA/HA)	28	28	9	18	23	20	9	29
Rented (private)	7	8	2	5	14	7	2	5
Rent-free	5	3	1	2	–	–	–	–
Other	3	1	1	1	12	7	2	2
N (100%)	557	545	3,988	663	112	371	2,686	91

men were equally divided between the two. Previously partnered men were twice as likely as their female counterparts to be living in privately rented accommodation. These differences probably reflect the fact that mothers are most likely to retain care of children following partnership breakdown, and thus receive greater priority for Local Authority accommodation.

Tenure, highest qualification and social class

As had been the case for both cohorts in their early 30s, lack of qualifications appeared to be less of an impediment to achieving home ownership by the early 40s for the 1946 cohort than for those born in 1958. Although both cohorts again showed the expected gradient, with owner occupation rising with qualifications, three-quarters of men and women born in 1946 with no qualifications were home owners at 43, compared with just over a half of their counterparts in the 1958 cohort.

Again, too, being in a lower social class occupation was less of an inhibitor to home ownership for men born in 1946 than for those in the 1958 cohort. Nearly three-quarters of 1946 cohort men in semi- or unskilled manual occupations were home owners at 43 compared to under two-thirds of men born in 1958 at the age of 42. These findings would seem to confirm the proposition that a lack of qualifications and occupational status had not inhibited home ownership in the 1946 cohort in the way that they would among their later born peers.

Conclusion

Looking at the adult housing experiences of our three cohorts in terms of tenure of accommodation, we can see variations as marked as the differences in housing circumstances in which they each grew up. The steady increase in owner occupation, most prevalent among the 1958 cohort, appeared to have stalled among those born in 1970, a generation which, as this chapter has shown, faced a more challenging situation in the housing market.

The apparent difficulties faced by the 1970 cohort in taking the first step towards owner occupation lie partly within the vicissitudes of the housing market itself, in particular the huge rise in prices. Such changes may account to a large extent for the non-linear rise on owner occupation among the three cohorts, with the highest level at age 30 or so found among those born in 1958. However, the type of accommodation lived in at any particular time is also closely linked to other life events and circumstances, and it may be that the relatively low level of owner occupation among the latest born cohort reflects other delays reported in this book – in gaining qualifications and position in the labour market, in forming partnerships and starting a family. It may be, therefore, that subsequent surveys will show the 1970 cohort to have 'caught up' with their earlier born peers in terms of their housing 'success'. Alternatively, a continuation in rising housing costs, plus other debts and demands on financial resources (e.g. pension provision) may prove to be real obstacles in the way of house purchase. All of these phenomena may also be traceable in the households of the 1946 and 1958 cohorts, through the delayed transitions to independent living of their own children (see Chapter 4).

With the massive selling of the most desirable Local Authority accommodation, social housing is now concentrated in the least salubrious areas and among the most economically and socially disadvantaged groups. We have seen some evidence of this in the relatively high proportions of previously partnered women (mostly lone mothers) in all three cohorts who were living in this sector. This could be seen as indicative of a 'polarisation' in the field of housing, comparable to that which has been highlighted in the other major life domains covered in this book.

Further analysis will reveal the other characteristics of groups in different categories of tenure, and with other different housing experiences. More important for longitudinal research are the detailed housing histories, which have recorded the dates of, and reasons for, each move made by the cohort members as adults. These can be investigated in conjunction with the equally rich event history data collected in the areas of employment and occupation, partnerships and fertility, in order to sequence the changes in these major life domains and to understand the processes by which they impinge upon each other. The cohort studies provide an unparalleled source of longitudinal, multidisciplinary information for studying the concomitants of housing change in the latter decades of the twentieth century.

8 Health

Michael Wadsworth, Suzie Butterworth, Scott Montgomery, Anna Ehlin and Mel Bartley

Introduction

Fundamental changes occurred in all aspects of health during the 24 years between the start of the 1946 cohort study and the beginning of the 1970 study, and they have continued in the years since. Extensive developments took place in curative health practice, in knowledge of risks to health, in public perception of health and, as described in Chapters 1, 3 (paid work) and 6 (income and living standards), in material circumstances. These changes brought great differences in health for our three birth cohorts, that can be described in a number of ways. They include how health was cared for, how understanding of the nature of health and of risks to health developed, new perspectives on the health of the individual over long periods of time, and public knowledge about health.

The National Health Service began in 1948, two years after the birth of the 1946 cohort. Antibiotics were scarce at that time, and infectious illnesses were of far higher prevalence and posed a far greater risk to life than they were even by 1958, when our second cohort was born. Surgery, anaesthesia, and treatment of injuries were much less well developed than they had become by the time of birth of the 1970 cohort. The early detection of disease and disability through biochemistry and microbiology, for example, in the form of screening babies for vitamin K deficiency, and screening adults for diabetes and various cancers, only became common practice when members of the 1946 cohort were in their 20s. The pharmaceutical control of fertility first became widely available in the 1960s, at about the same time, and the pharmacological management of raised blood pressure, and later of other aspects of cardiovascular disease risk, began to be available when members of the oldest cohort were in their late 30s.

Understanding of the causes and nature of ill-health also changed greatly between 1946 and 1970. Differences in states of health were very little differentiated in the 1940s and 1950s, other than in terms of physical fitness. Although knowledge of environmental risks to health from infectious disease agents and from atmospheric pollution was well advanced at the beginning of the period, understanding of individual vulnerability to health risks was much less considered. The question of why some individuals seemed more vulnerable than others began to be addressed (Fletcher *et al.* 1976), and, in important respects, thinking of that kind began to develop with the emerging proof during the late 1950s and 1960s of the toxicity of smoking. Before then smoking was scarcely considered a health hazard, and had been widely used as a form of easily accessible relaxant during the war years. New knowledge about the risks to the health of the individual became increasingly concerned with other aspects of everyday life, including diet, exercise and alcohol consumption. Knowledge about risk development through lifestyles brought new concepts of individual responsibility for health, which have since been promoted by governments anxious to reduce the costs of health care.

New knowledge about health has also been developed in two other kinds of study. The first seeks to discover why risks to health, and the risk of premature death, continue to be so much greater among those in adverse socio-economic circumstances, despite the great increases in the efficacy of curative and preventive care (Acheson 1998). Acheson's report on inequalities in health summarised the work that shows the steep gradients in health in relation to social class and education. Work on that topic has also shown the relationship of social cohesion and health, by studying changes in populations over time, and by comparing mortality rates in countries with differing distributions of wealth and opportunity (Wilkinson 1996). Those findings emphasise the need for new research into the question of how social experience influences health, particularly how adverse socio-economic circumstances cause damage to health. Measures have been developed of the individual's satisfaction with life, of stress, anxiety and depression, of anger, and of perception of reward in relation to effort, in order to understand how they relate to health (Stansfeld and Marmot 2002).

At the same time, biological ideas are being developed about how chronic adversities of these kinds may gradually erode health (Brunner 2000).

A further source of new knowledge about health comes from studies of long periods of life. By relating indicators of development before birth (e.g. growth before birth as reflected in birth weight) and in infancy (e.g. height and weight gain) to adult health, they show that development early in life influences adult health. This is explained by the fact that growth in the early months and years is unique; most elements of organ growth are completed before or soon after birth and the essential elements of height growth are completed in infancy. So, it is argued, growth and development in early life are a form of biological programming, providing the individual with lifetime capacity of most, if not all, kinds of vital function, including cardiovascular, respiratory and cognitive function (Barker 1998). Not all aspects of the biological programming hypothesis are accepted as sufficiently proven (Paneth and Susser 1995; Huxley *et al.* 2002), but essentially and intuitively it seems likely to be broadly correct. Current work is concerned with the extent of influence of early life programming effects after account is taken of all the other influences on health in adulthood (Kuh and Ben Shlomo 1997; Wadsworth 2002). In addition to biological programming, there are also much older and well established hypotheses about the influence of mental development and social experience in early life on the development of temperament and behaviour, and there are also biological components in these pathways (Robins and Rutter 1990).

Public knowledge about health increased during the same period, probably as much through improvements in communications and in the general level of education, as through the gradual demystification of medicine and the greater willingness of health-care practitioners to discuss disease and its care and prevention with patients.

Health studies in the three cohorts

The three national birth cohort studies that are the subject of this book have each contributed to many aspects of research on health, and the interaction of health with social and economic circumstances. Their particular strength lies not only in their lifetime collections of data, but also in their breadth of information, which includes data on health, growth and the environment, and which allows them to examine the interactions of a wide range of influences. For example, the 1946 study has been particularly focused on health and on how health risk develops throughout life. It has shown the contribution that early life development makes to many aspects of physical and mental health in adulthood, in addition to biological effects and the effects from the social context and health-related habits throughout life (Kuh and Ben Shlomo 1997; Wadsworth 1999). A study of development of risk of schizophrenia in the 1946 cohort described how problems with physical development initiated a 'cascade of problems' of many kinds before the emergence of the illness (Jones *et al.* 1994). The 1958 study has been similarly concerned with how health risk develops, and has proposed different kinds of pathways along which risk may be accumulated, diminished or augmented (Power and Hertzman 1997; Montgomery *et al.* 1998). That study has also contributed to understanding why health risk is so much greater in adverse socio-economic circumstances (Power *et al.* 1991; Hope *et al.* 1999). The 1970 study has been concerned with similar questions (Montgomery and Schoon 1997), and with studies of development of risk in specific disorders (Shaheen *et al.* 1999; Bennett and Haggard 1999; Montgomery *et al.* 1999). In both the 1970 and the 1946 studies, adverse negative emotional experience in childhood has been shown to have a retarding effect on height growth (Montgomery *et al.* 1997; Wadsworth *et al.* 2002), as Widdowson (1951) predicted.

However, the work on health has been so far almost entirely *within* each of these three cohorts. Comparative work *between* cohorts has been limited because of funds, and also because the studies have pursued rather different approaches to collecting data about health and to the measurement of health. However, in a new phase of work currently beginning, health measurement is being made as similar as possible in each study. The advantages of comparing health in these studies are twofold. Each has the benefit of information on health from birth over long periods of life, and the benefit of such information over a period of historic time, during which many kinds of social and economic change occur. The information on long periods of life has made it possible to study individual development and change with age; these kinds of change are called age effects. Differences in the social context of the lives of our three study populations are called cohort effects. Such effects may also be seen as period effects, since they are specific to a particular historical time, but which, when seen in terms of their impact on the population, have a cohort-specific effect. The postwar epidemics of poliomyelitis (Martyn 1997) are an example of a period effect.

The three cohorts described here offer the opportunity to explore period effects in two ways. The first is by comparison of physical and mental development at different social times. So, for example, the developmental years of members of the 1946 cohort coincided with postwar austerity, when smoking was acceptable and not proven to affect health adversely, and when food was rationed. By contrast, their adult years have been times of much greater abundance of income, food and alcohol, and when smoking has been shown to be harmful. The opportunity to analyse both age and cohort effects simultaneously is a particularly valuable asset in the studies of health-related behaviour such as smoking, nutrition and exercise, where ideas about their effects on health have changed greatly, as described in the following chapter. The population of the 1970 study, by contrast, grew up in times of quite different extents of risks associated with smoking and drinking, and in times of relative affluence, although there was a continuing strong element of poverty in childhood. Comparison of the effects of these differences would be valuable, particularly for evaluation of the biological programming hypothesis, which was developed mostly using data on births that occurred in quite different social and economic circumstances in the first half of the twentieth century (Barker 1998).

The second way in which the interrelationship of age and historically specific effects may be explored using the populations of these studies is through their experience of cohort effects. For example, members of the 1958 cohort encountered the period of national high risk of unemployment early in their working life, at age 23 years. That provided an opportunity to study the effects of unemployment on health. A series of analyses showed that prolonged unemployment of men in their early years on the labour market was associated with raised risks of smoking, problems with drinking, and symptoms of anxiety and depression (Montgomery *et al.* 1998), even after taking account of risk factors that existed before school leaving (Montgomery *et al.* 1996). It was also shown that prolonged unemployment had an adverse effect on indicators of future potential in socio-economic and health terms (Wadsworth *et al.* 1999). Members of the 1946 cohort encountered this kind of risk much later in their careers. Other kinds of historically specific events that are likely to affect the health of each cohort differently or uniquely are, for example, the early postwar epidemics of poliomyelitis, the Clean Air Act of 1956, the great rise in parental separation, and the very considerable changes in health care and in public understanding of health that have taken place since the end of the Second World War.

The purpose of this chapter is to compare and discuss cohort differences in health in early adulthood. These differences also illustrate the studies' potential value for analyses of health data from all of them used together, that is meta analysis. First, some comparisons are made of growth and nutrition in childhood, because of their fundamental role in health throughout life. Then aspects of health and illness in early middle life are described. We have selected information that shows potential for future health, as well as showing current health at the times of the most recent data collections, and we describe differences in health in relation to age, social class of the cohort members' family of origin and of their own social class, and educational attainment. Results from the 1946 cohort have been weighted to take account of the sampling procedure, which is described in Appendix 1.

Health in childhood

Weight at birth
Although at most ages children are bigger now than ever before, the average weight at birth in these three study populations shows a downward trend (Figure 8.1). This reflects the improvements in health care and in

Figure 8.1 *Mean birth weight (kg) in the three cohorts*

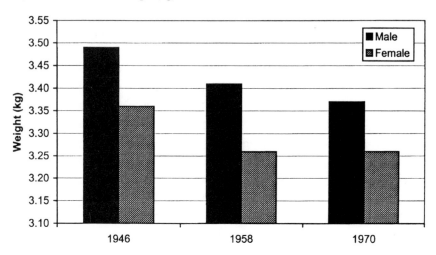

the environment that have made it possible for low-birth-weight babies to survive. These improvements include reduced maternal smoking (Butler *et al.* 1971), reduced atmospheric pollution from coal burning (Bobak *et al.* 2000), and better prenatal care with improved nutrition (Barker 1998). Despite these positive trends, a significant social class gradient in birth weight was found in all three studies, with social class I and II babies being of higher average weight than that of babies in social classes IV and V .

The most important question that arises from these birth-weight differences is whether they will bring an associated increased prevalence of problems arising from the causes of low weight. Low weight at birth may be the result of genetic factors, or environmental factors such as raised maternal blood pressure, and maternal smoking or alcohol misuse. The baby may be of low weight because of slow growth before birth, even though the pregnancy has been of the appropriate period (small for gestational age babies), or the cause may be birth before the due date (pre-term delivery). Follow-up studies show that babies that have experienced the longest periods of growth restriction are at the greatest risk of subsequent childhood neurological problems, such as low IQ, poor reading attainment (Hutton *et al.* 1997), poor educational attainment and increased risk of social behaviour problems (Larroque *et al.* 2001; Paz *et al.* 2001; Lundgren *et al.* 2001). In the 1958 cohort, low weight at birth was associated with socio-economic disadvantage in later life (Bartley *et al.* 1994). The three studies reviewed here are in a strong position to examine outcomes of low birth weight, and each has done so in relation to a range of outcomes. For example, in the longest running of these studies (the 1946 cohort), in which survival of low birth weight was at its lowest, it was shown that weight at birth was positively associated with cognitive function in childhood, adolescence and adult life, even after taking account of social factors, such as social class (Richards *et al.* 2002). Low birth weight is implicated in other aspects of adult health, including physical health, in the three cohorts (Power and Hertzman 1997; Wadsworth 1999; Kuh and Ben Shlomo 1997), as well as in other studies (Barker 1998).

New studies of adult health in all three cohorts will be concerned to see whether survival to adulthood of low-birth-weight babies is associated with any kind of raised risk in terms of mental and physical function.

Height

Average height varied between the three cohorts. Table 8.1 shows that boys, in comparison with girls, made greater gains in height, and that average heights of 7-year-olds increased in the 1958 cohort in comparison with the 1946. Table 8.1 also shows the decline in social class variation in average height between the successive cohorts, indicating the effects of improvements in child health and in nutrition, and in the material circumstances of childhood in all social classes.

Social class differences in height at age 7 years (i.e. before puberty) were greatly reduced between the 1946 and the 1958 births, because of 'catching up' by the children of the lowest classes. For instance, differences in means of heights, comparing social class I with social class V, were 6 cm in boys and 5 cm in girls in the 1946 cohort. These had been reduced in the 1958 cohort to 3 cm in both boys and girls, and in the 1970

Table 8.1 *Average (mean) childhood height (cm) in relation to father's social class*

	1946 cohort Age 7 in 1953	1958 cohort Age 7 in 1965	1970 cohort Age 10 in 1980
Boys			
Father's social class			
I	123	124	140
II	121	124	140
III nm	121	123	140
III m	119	123	138
IV	119	123	138
V	117	121	138
All classes	120	123	139
No. of cases	2,856	3,886	3,524
Girls			
Father's social class			
I	122	124	139
II	121	123	139
III nm	120	123	139
III m	118	122	138
IV	118	122	138
V	117	121	137
All classes	119	122	139
No. of cases	3,020	4,175	3,718

cohort to 2 cm in both sexes at age 10 years. In this respect, too, boys in the oldest cohort made greater gains than girls.

The study of height growth in childhood provides some of the best evidence about the interrelationship of social, psychological and biological factors, which is important, because height growth in childhood is a good indicator of adult height, which is in turn strongly associated with health. Studies of the interrelationships of these kinds show why height growth is a sensitive indicator of the social, economic and emotional circumstances of the child's life. For example, in a study carried out in two German orphanages in 1948, Widdowson (1951) measured the growth in height and weight of children whose ages ranged from 4 to 14 years; their average age was 8 years and 8 months. She found that, despite similar diets, children grew faster in one orphanage than the other. The slow growing children lived in a much stricter regime than the others, and the person in charge of that institution often chose the times when children were at their meals to administer public rebukes, and would single out individual children for special ridicule. 'The children had to sit in silence while this was going on' (Widdowson 1951: 1317). When the strict director transferred from one orphanage to another, the poor growth that was associated with her regime was then seen at the institution that she joined, even though additional food was provided. Under the strict regime, only the director's favourites grew at the expected rate.

Height growth is a product of two components, namely leg growth, and upper body or trunk growth. Leg growth is fastest in infancy, and is sensitive to circumstances at that time. For example, a study in Mexico showed that leg growth was strikingly greater in children who lived in the most favourable social and economic circumstances and had the best diet (Buschang *et al.* 1986). In Japan and Norway, where there have been opportunities to study the increase in population height over 20 years and more, it was found that by far the largest element of that increase was accounted for by growth in leg length (Udjus 1964; Tanner *et al.* 1982). By contrast, trunk growth is known to be sensitive to emotional circumstances (Montgomery *et al.* 1997; Wadsworth *et al.* 2002).

The importance for adult health of poor height growth in childhood is illustrated by findings of its association with increased risk of death from cardiovascular disease and some cancers (Davey Smith *et al.* 2001). The reasons for these associations are not fully understood, and possible explanations suggested by the authors include (a) that these conditions have common social pathways (e.g. mother's smoking reduces the child's height growth and increases the likelihood of the child smoking); (b) that poor height growth reflects poor organ growth, including the growth and development of coronary arteries; (c) that metabolic influences on growth are also associated with risk of some cancers; and (d) that there is a common, but so far unknown, genetic element.

Body mass index

Body mass index (BMI) is an indicator of body shape that takes account of both height and weight. High BMI indicates that weight is high in relation to height. Conventionally, obesity is indicated by a BMI of 30 or more. Nowadays one of the concerns about childhood growth is with fatness. Comparison of BMI in these three studies shows that at age 11 years (Table 8.2) it was very similar in the 1946 and 1958 studies, but children in the 1970 study were, by contrast, considerably larger even when a year younger at age 10 years.

Table 8.2 *Cohort differences in childhood body mass index: mean body mass by father's social class*

	Mean BMI (kg/m^2)		
	1946 cohort Age 15 in 1961	1958 cohort Age 16 in 1974	1970 cohort Age 16 in 1986
Boys			
Father's social class			
I	19.7	19.4	20.6
II	19.7	19.6	21.1
III nm	19.7	19.3	21.4
III m	19.5	19.6	21.0
IV	19.6	19.7	21.2
V	19.3	19.8	21.1
% BMI $\geqslant$ 30	0.3%	0.9%	1.6%
No. of cases	4,192	3,992	1,698
Girls			
Father's social class			
I	20.8	19.4	20.9
II	20.7	21.0	21.4
III nm	20.2	19.9	21.2
III m	20.7	20.6	21.6
IV	20.9	20.7	21.6
V	20.8	20.9	22.1
% BMI $\geqslant$ 30	1.6%	1.3%	2.1%
No. of cases	3,858	4,062	1,945

Nutrition

Although we do not have comparable information on childhood diet in these three birth cohort studies, comparison of diet data from the 1946 study at age 4 years with data on diets of children of the same age in the early 1990s, illustrates the kinds of changes that have taken place. Children born in 1946 lived for their first eight years with food rationing. A study that contrasted diet in the 1946 children at age 4 years in 1950 with diet in 4-year-olds in 1992/3, showed marked differences in total nutrient intake and sources of nutrient supply. Compared to 1992/3, the diet of children in 1950 included substantially more bread, fruit and vegetables, and less sugar and soft drinks, giving it a higher starch and fibre content, although with a higher fat intake (Prynne *et al.* 1999). Nevertheless, despite food rationing in 1950, there was a notably lower intake of fruit and vegetables among the socially disadvantaged compared with others (Prynne *et al.* 2002).

The only data on childhood diet common to all three studies concerns breast-feeding. Comparison of the cohorts shows a great falling off in proportions of babies who were ever breast-fed (Table 8.3). The trend is sharply differentiated by social class, with the proportion never breast-fed being consistently much higher in social class V than social class I. For example, 33 per cent of girls were never breast-fed in social class V in the

Table 8.3 *Cohort differences in breast-feeding*

	1946 cohort		1958 cohort		1970 cohort	
	Men %	Women %	Men %	Women %	Men %	Women %
Never breast-fed	24	25	31	30	62	62
Breast-fed for less than one month	14	12	24	25	17	16
Breast-fed for one month or more	61	63	44	44	21	22
N (100%)	5,841	5,426	4,862	5,049	4,325	4,557

1946 cohort, compared with 18 per cent in social class I. Comparable figures in the 1970 cohort are 77 per cent never breast-fed in social class V and 44 per cent in social class I. Although breast-feeding became more widespread at times after these cohorts were born, the fact remains that for these three cohorts there are great social inequalities in the potentially beneficial legacy that some carry as a result of breast-feeding, and in the potentially adverse legacy that others carry as a result of not having been breast-fed.

Mental health
Although these three cohort studies have not consistently investigated mental health in childhood, each has collected information on some of the circumstances thought to present risks to adult mental health, for example early life physical development (Jones *et al.* 1994; Richards *et al.* 2002), mild retardation of mental function (Maughan *et al.* 1999; Richards *et al.* 2001), adolescent pyschological problems (Maughan and Taylor 2001), and parental separation (Rodgers 1994). As already noted, physical development differs between the three cohorts, at least in terms of weight at birth, and Chapters 1 and 4 describe the steep increase in marital separations that occurred between 1946 and 1970.

Health in adulthood

Height
Adult height is achieved by the late teenage years, and so comparison of heights measured in these three cohorts at different ages in their 30s presents no problem. Figure 8.2 shows that adult average height was least in the 1946 cohort (175 cm in men and 162 cm in women), was greater by 2 cm in men, and 1 cm in women, in the 1958 study, and increased again by 2 cm in men and 1 cm in women in the 1970 study. The greater proportion of those in the lower range of measured heights in the 1958 and 1970 cohorts, compared with the 1946 cohort, is likely to be accounted for by the improved chances of survival to adulthood in the later born cohorts.

Figure 8.2 *Average (mean) and range of height in adulthood*

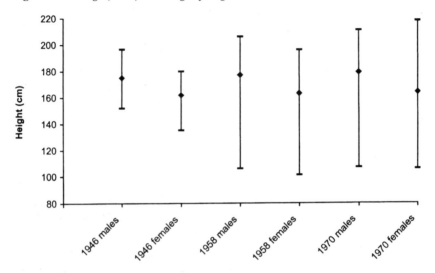

Since height growth potential is established in childhood and early life, Table 8.4 shows adult height in relation to the socio-economic circumstances of childhood, described here by father's social class. Those who grew up in the most advantaged socio-economic circumstances were consistently taller than others in each cohort, although the differences in average heights between the top and bottom two social classes were less in the 1958 and the 1970 cohorts than in the 1946 population. Comparing across cohorts within social classes shows that differences in average heights were slightly greater in men than in women, implying that there was greater growth among men than women.

Body mass index

The relevance of body mass index (BMI) to health is well known. A high BMI at the level that indicates obesity (30 and more) is associated with increased risk in a number of disorders, including diabetes and heart disease, and also with a raised risk of premature death. Comparisons of adult BMI (Table 8.5) are difficult because information was collected at different ages in the three studies. Nevertheless, the trend is evidently

Table 8.4 *Average (mean) adult height (cm) in relation to father's social class*

	1946 cohort Age 36 in 1982	1958 cohort Age 42 in 2000	1970 cohort Age 30 in 2000
Men			
Father's social class			
I	177	179	180
II	177	179	180
III nm	176	178	180
III m	175	177	178
IV	174	177	177
V	173	176	177
All classes	175	177	179
No. of cases	3,513	4,032	4,097
Women			
Father's social class			
I	165	164	166
II	163	164	165
III nm	163	164	165
III m	161	162	164
IV	161	162	164
V	160	161	163
All classes	162	163	164
No. of cases	3,536	4,367	4,294

towards higher body mass at younger ages in the more recently born cohorts. Men at age 33 years in the 1958 cohort, and at 30 years in the 1970 study, already had higher average BMIs than men aged 36 years in the 1946 cohort, and prevalences of obesity that were greater than those in men in the 1946 cohort at age 43 years. Similarly, women in the two later born cohorts had higher average BMI at 33 and 30 years than women in the 1946 study at 36 years, and prevalences of obesity were only slightly lower than those in women in the 1946 cohort at age 43 years. If the 1958 and 1970 populations follow the same trend as the 1946 of increasing body mass as they get older, then the proportion of obese individuals in middle life will be greater than ever.

Table 8.5 *Average (mean) body mass of men and women in adulthood (per cent obese (body mass index ⩾30) given in brackets)*

(a) Men

Age	1946 cohort	1958 cohort	1970 cohort
30 in 2000			25.6 (12%)
33 in 1991		26.4 (12%)	
36 in 1982	24.7 (5%)		
43 in 1989	25.6 (10%)		
53 in 1999	27.6 (23%)		

(b) Women

Age	1946 cohort	1958 cohort	1970 cohort
30 in 2000			24.3 (11%)
33 in 1991		25.1 (12%)	
36 in 1982	23.6 (7%)		
43 in 1989	25.2 (14%)		
53 in 1999	27.6 (27%)		

In each of these studies average BMI is highest in those with no educational qualifications, and lowest in those with university and comparable level qualifications and training (Table 8.6). It varies similarly with social class, being highest among those in classes IV and V and lowest among those in social classes I and II.

Evidence from the 1946 study shows that, although obesity in childhood was rare because of food rationing, adult obesity was not unusual. Evidently, therefore, obesity in childhood was not a necessary precursor of adult obesity. However, social factors in childhood and adulthood seem to be an essential part of the development of risk of adult obesity. In a comparison of the relationship of BMI with father's social class and with own social class in the 1946 cohort, it was shown that men and women who moved from the high-risk situation of manual social class in childhood

Table 8.6 *Adult mean body mass index in men and women by level of attained educational qualification*

Level of attained educational qualification	Mean BMI (kg/m^2)						
	1946 cohort Age 36 in 1982	1946 cohort Age 43 in 1989	1946 cohort Age 53 in 1999	1958 cohort Age 33 in 1991	1958 cohort Age 42 in 2000	1970 cohort Age 30 in 2000
Men						
No qualifications	27.0	26.2	27.9	27.9	27.0	26.0
NVQ 1	25.8	26.6	28.2	27.0	27.2	25.9
NVQ 2	27.2	25.7	27.2	26.3	26.6	25.8
NVQ 3	24.8	25.7	27.6	26.6	26.6	25.8
NVQ 4–5	25.1	25.4	27.2	26.0	26.1	25.2
No. of cases	3,609	3,521	3,165	4,701	5,495	4,896
Women						
No qualifications	26.3	26.2	28.3	33.4	26.5	24.8
NVQ 1	26.8	24.5	26.8	25.9	26.1	24.7
NVQ 2	23.7	25.2	27.7	25.3	25.4	24.4
NVQ 3	22.7	24.3	26.8	24.9	25.0	24.5
NVQ 4–5	23.6	24.3	26.4	25.0	24.7	23.7
No. of cases	3,672	3,523	3,281	5,051	5,589	5,154

to the low-risk situation of non-manual class in adulthood, had reduced chances of being overweight or obese as adults (Langenberg *et al.* in press). In the 1958 cohort, maternal smoking during pregnancy was shown to increase the risk not only of obesity in the child but also of type 2 diabetes. This may be because smoking during pregnancy is associated with fetal malnutrition resulting in reduced expression or sensitivity of insulin (Montgomery and Ekbom 2002).

Ill-health in adulthood
Ill-health and disability have been measured in a number of ways in the three cohorts, and one that is common to all is self-reported health. Table 8.7 shows reports of illnesses and disabilities selected, for present purposes, for their likelihood of having chronic or long-term effects.

Physical health
Compared across the three cohorts, reports of asthma have risen sharply in men and women and reports of bronchitis show a consistent fall (Table 8.7). There may be some overlap of these categories, because asthma was a disease label used much more by the non-manual social classes at the time of the childhood of the 1946 cohort. In that study, reports of asthma are notably higher in the non-manual social class than in the manual, and bronchitis is more common in the manual than the non-manual. Social class differences in asthma are shown in Figures 8.3 and 8.4. In future, when adult respiratory function has been measured in the 1958 and 1970 cohorts, it will be possible to examine differences in respiratory function and pulmonary illness in all three cohorts. Our hypothesis is that they will differ considerably because:

• increased survival of low birth weight in the 1970 cohort compared with the 1958 and 1946 cohorts (Figure 8.1) is likely to be associated with lower respiratory function in adulthood (Barker 1998);

• a diet lower in fruit and vegetables in the 1970 cohort compared with the 1946 cohort is likely to be a raised risk for pulmonary illness (Strachan *et al.* 1991);

Table 8.7 *Reports (per cent) of physical illnesses ever experienced, or experienced over the period indicated, by the given age*

	1946 cohort Age 36 in 1982 %	1946 cohort Age 43 in 1989 %	1958 cohort Age 33 in 1991 %	1958 cohort Age 42 in 2000 %	1970 cohort Age 30 in 2000 %
Men					
Asthma	3	6	8	10	13
Bronchitis	7	19	9	8	6
Back pain	17	32	50	22	13
Diabetes	0.6	1	0.7	2	0.9
High blood pressure	3	9	5	11	5
Cancer	–	1	0.6	1	0.7
Problem with hearing	–	7	–	10	7
Problem with vision	–	–	–	20	23
Illness limiting everyday life	–	–	6	12	8
Women					
Asthma	3	6	10	12	14
Bronchitis	6	22	13	13	8
Back pain	19	34	44	23	16
Diabetes	0.4	1	0.6	2	1
High blood pressure	5	13	6	12	10
Cancer	–	3	2	4	2
Problem with hearing	–	7	–	8	5
Problem with vision	–	–	–	20	29
Illness limiting everyday life	–	–	6	15	10

– No comparable question

• the reduction in own and parents' smoking in the 1970 compared with the 1946 cohort (see Chapter 9) will be associated with improved respiratory function and reduced illness; and

• the opportunity of growing up without atmospheric pollution caused by coal burning that was available to the 1958 and 1970 cohorts because of the Clean Air Act of 1956, will be associated with improved adult respiratory function in those two cohorts.

Other studies show increases over time in forms of allergy other than asthma, and in biological indicators of risk of allergy, which suggests that some of the risks of poor regulation of the immune system associated with asthma are becoming more common (Taylor *et al.* 1984; Nakagomi *et al.* 1994). The inter-cohort differences in breast-feeding practice (Table 8.3) may be of relevance to differences in rates of reporting these illnesses, since breast-feeding is generally found to be protective of these conditions.

Reports of back pain rose across calendar time from 1982 (when the 1946 cohort were aged 36) to 1991 (when those born in 1958 were 33), and were lower again in 2000 (when the 1970 cohort were 30) (Table 8.7). There was a notably higher prevalence of reports of back pain (almost a trebling for men) among members of the 1958 cohort at age 33 years compared with the 1946 cohort at age 36 years. However, while back pain reports increased with age in the 1946 cohort, they *decreased* markedly with age among those born in 1958. At all ages and times, back pain was reported more often among manual social classes than in the non-manual.

Reports of diabetes may be unreliable, because of the small numbers, but this is known to be a disease that is currently rising in prevalence, and that also rises with age. The figures from the three cohort studies conform to this pattern, with increases in reported levels for both men and women in each successive cohort, and also a rise between the 30s and 40s, especially for the 1958 cohort.

Reported high blood pressure also rose with age (Table 8.7, and Figures 8.5 and 8.6). It was less often reported by men than by women in the 1946 cohort, but was of similar prevalence among men and women in the 1958

Figure 8.3 *Percentage reporting asthma in adulthood in relation to own social class:* men

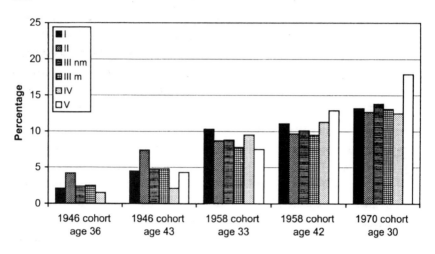

Figure 8.4 *Percentage reporting asthma in adulthood in relation to own social class:* women

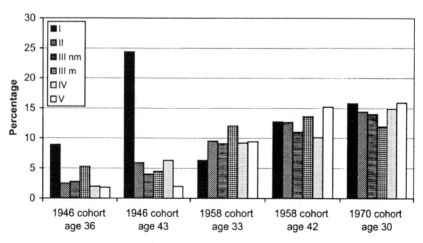

Note: The small number of women in social class 1 employment in the 1946 cohort (n=45 at age 36 and 43 years) is probably responsible for the unusual rate of reporting.

cohort (Table 8.7). In the 1970 study, reports of this problem were much higher at 30 years than at 33 years in the 1958 cohort, or at 36 years in the 1946 cohort. It may be that the higher prevalence of obesity and over-weight that occurs at earlier ages in the later born cohorts (Table 8.5) is associated with the cohort differences in prevalence of high blood pressure. The sex differences in each cohort in reported high blood pressure are likely to be the result of frequent checks made on blood pressure in women during pregnancy and in consultations about contraception. There is a slightly greater risk of reports of high blood pressure in the manual compared with the non-manual social classes in each of the three cohorts (Figures 8.5 and 8.6).

The small number of reports of cancer were made more often by women than by men, as expected in early adulthood (Table 8.7). Among men and women in the 1946 and 1958 cohorts the percentages of reported cases increased considerably between their early 30s and their early 40s, and were a little higher among the 1970 cohort at age 30 years than in the two earlier born cohorts at slightly older ages. It must be noted that these are reports made by survivors, and deaths are not included.

Comparison of reports of hearing problems show a somewhat higher rate at younger ages in the 1958 and 1970 populations compared with those born in 1946 (Table 8.7). However, questions about such problems in general are not the best way to collect information about hearing, and each of these studies is currently seeking more accurate methods of mea-suring hearing and its change with age. Similarly, problems with vision have so far not been measured in adulthood, and reports of difficulties have problems of interpretation similar to those of hearing.

Mental health

In the USA, large population studies have generally, but not universally, reported greater prevalence of lifetime major depression in more recently born populations as compared with those born at earlier times (Fombonne 1993). Although depression, anxiety and feelings of sadness have so far been measured differently in the three cohort studies, comparisons of the findings (Table 8.8) are of interest, although not easy to interpret.

Figure 8.5 *Percentage reporting raised blood pressure in relation to own social class:* men

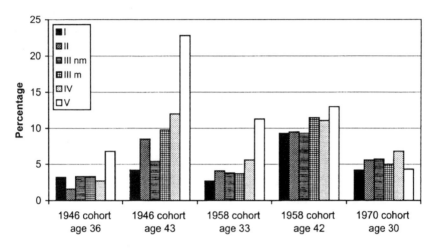

Figure 8.6 *Percentage reporting raised blood pressure in relation to own social class:* women

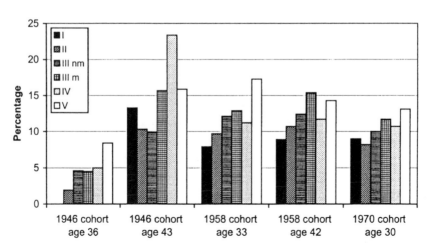

In the 1946 sample, comparison of rates of anxiety and depression at 36 and 43 years shows little difference in the measures made with the mental health questionnaires (the Present State Examination and the Psychiatric Symptom Frequency scale) (Lindelow *et al.* 1997; Paykel *et al.* 2001). In the 1958 cohort there was a considerable rise in depression and anxiety with age in men and women, as rated by the Malaise Inventory. In the 1970 cohort the rate reported from the Malaise Inventory at age 30 years was, in both men and women, as high or almost as high as that reported by the 1958 cohort at age 42 years, and notably higher than that reported by the 1946 cohort at 43 years using the Psychiatric Symptom Frequency scale (Table 8.8). All three cohorts found, especially in women, higher risks of depression among those in manual social classes (Figures 8.7 and 8.8).

Questions asking for self-reporting of trouble with nerves and of feeling low, depressed or sad differed in ways that make the 1946 rates not strictly comparable with the rates in the two later studies; the notes to Table 8.8 explain the differences. The self-reported rates were similar to the inventory prevalences in men, but higher at all except one point in women. Self-reported problems of this kind increased with age among men in a similar way in the 1946 and 1958 cohorts, almost doubling in prevalence between their 30s and their early 40s. But the prevalence in men in the 1970 cohort at age 30 years was nearly as high as in men in the other two studies at later ages. In women, self-reported problems of this kind were, at all except one age, at a higher prevalence than the inventory assessments, and increased considerably in the 1946 and 1958 cohorts between their 30s and 40s. As among men, the rates reported by women in the 1970 cohort were already, at age 30 years, as high as rates reported by the older cohorts in their early 40s. In men and women in all three cohorts, rates of reported troubles with nerves were highest in the manual classes (Figures 8.9 and 8.10).

Conclusions

Earlier work in each of the cohorts described here has shown how adult health can usefully be regarded as the end point of a pathway that begins

Table 8.8 *Reports (per cent) of mental illnesses ever experienced, or experienced over the period indicated, by the given age*

	1946 cohort Age 36 in 1982 %	1946 cohort Age 43 in 1989 %	1958 cohort Age 33 in 1991 %	1958 cohort Age 42 in 2000 %	1970 cohort Age 30 in 2000 %
Men					
Depression and anxiety[a]	8[a]	10[a]	7[b]	14[b]	14[b]
Trouble with nerves,[c] feeling low, depressed or sad[d]	8[c]	15[c]	7[d]	15[d]	13[d]
Women					
Depression and anxiety[a]	18[a]	16[a]	12[b]	21	20[b]
Trouble with nerves,[c] feeling low, depressed or sad[d]	16	28	19	29	29

a   The 1946 study data come from the Present State Examination at age 36 years (score ≥4) and the Psychiatric Symptom Frequency Scale at 43 years (score ≥23) to establish a definition of caseness (Paykel *et al.* 2001).

b   The 1958 and the 1970 data come from the Malaise Inventory in which a score ≥8 indicates caseness (Grant *et al.* 1990).

c   In the 1946 study the question at age 36 years was 'Do you have nervous or emotional trouble or persistent depression?' and at 43 years the question was 'Have you ever had nervous or emotional trouble or depression?'

d   In the 1958 study the question at age 33 years (in 1991) was 'Which of the problems (feeling low, depressed, sad) have you been to see a GP or specialist about since March 1981?' and at age 42 years in the 1958 cohort and age 30 years in the 1970 cohort the question was 'Since the last contact have you seen a specialist, been to a hospital or seen a doctor because of feeling low, depressed or sad?'

Figure 8.7 *Percentage reporting depression in relation to own social class: men*

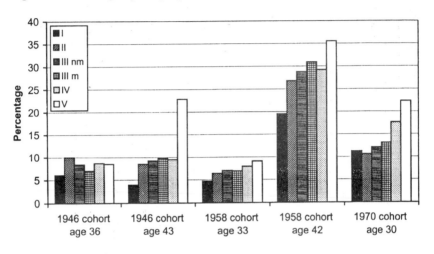

Figure 8.8 *Percentage reporting depression in relation to own social class: women*

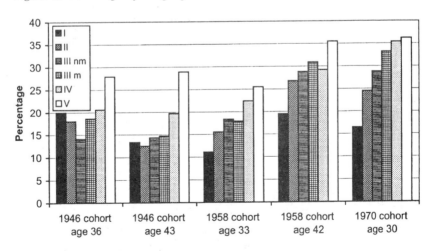

Figure 8.9 *Percentage reporting troubles with nerves: men*

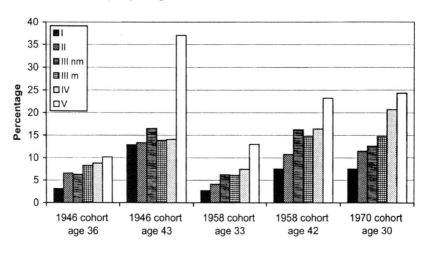

Figure 8.10 *Percentage reporting troubles with nerves: women*

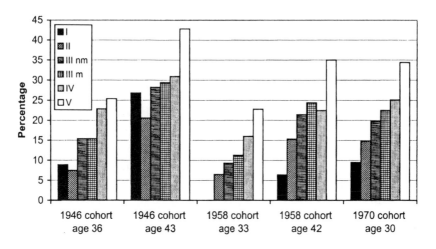

in early life, even before birth. Such pathways have been seen as processes of accumulation of different kinds of risk from the earliest time of life onwards, and as interactions of risks from early life with risks in adulthood (Power and Hertzman 1997; Kuh and Ben Shlomo 1997; Wadsworth 1999; Wadsworth 2002), showing in each case the effects of protective factors.

In this chapter we have mostly compared health between, rather than within, cohorts. By doing so we raise the question of how much the pathways to adult health differ between the cohorts because of the effects of differences in some key aspects of health and factors associated with health: for example, periods of economic depression and high risk of unemployment; poverty and plenty; the changing conventions of social acceptability of such practices as breast-feeding and smoking; childhood obesity; and health-related behaviour such as diet choice and smoking.

Growth and development in childhood were described in the three cohorts because they are in many respects the bases for health in adulthood. Clearly, the inter-cohort trends are towards improved chances of survival of low birth weight, greater height growth before puberty, and reduced social class differences in childhood height. Nevertheless, these trends must be seen in the context of increased body mass index, particularly among children in the most disadvantaged social circumstances, of reduced likelihood of breast-feeding in these three cohorts, and greater likelihood of a poorer diet. Some childhood factors thought likely to be risks to adult mental health, namely low weight at birth and parental separation, have also increased in prevalence.

Height and body mass index were used as indicators of adult health in the early 30s and 40s. Despite the advantage of the inter-cohort increase in mean adult height, those whose fathers were in manual social classes were shorter than others. However, the social class differences in height were less in the later born cohorts. Body mass index is clearly increasing across the cohorts, and the risk of obesity is greatest in those with no or low educational attainment, and in those in the most disadvantaged socio-economic circumstances.

Adult ill-health has so far been assessed in rather different ways in the three studies. In so far as that restriction permits, comparison of self-reports shows increasing prevalences across the cohorts of asthma, raised blood pressure, problems with hearing, and feelings of anxiety. Generally, there was a higher prevalence of these reports among those in the least advantaged circumstances. Inter-cohort comparisons of measures of depression and anxiety also show a tendency to increase, and for prevalence to be higher in social classes IV and V.

Current data collection in the 1958 and 1970 cohorts is concerned with new measurements of such sensitive health indicators as blood pressure, respiratory and cognitive function, and function and health of muscle and bone, vision and hearing, which have mostly been collected already in the 1946 study. These new measures will allow us to continue to evaluate the legacy of health risks and protective factors accumulated throughout life in the form, for example, of physical growth and development, the extent of exposure to parental and own tobacco smoke, and the quality of nutrition throughout life, all of which are known to differ notably between the cohorts.

Future research on health in the three studies will investigate social, psychological and biological interactions of risk and protective factors throughout life, in order to further our understanding of how they influence health (Brunner 2000). Within the cohorts, this work is likely to be concerned, for example, with the effects on physical and mental health, and cognitive function, of the cohort members' occupation and the physical and psychological nature of their work, the effects of family change and psychological factors, and the effects of diet, especially on respiratory and on cognitive function, and their change with age. New sources of genetic information in each cohort will make it possible to compare the relative power of genetic and environmental information.

New work of inter-cohort comparison is proposed, in order to study the health effects of known differences in exposure to risk and protective factors, such as atmospheric pollution, prolonged unemployment, and dietary change. The inter-cohort research will be concerned also with differences in cohort experiences of community and family cohesion, social participation, and concepts of citizenship (see Chapter 10), and their effects on mental and physical health, through the study of interactions between genes and environment. The opportunity for meta analyses offered by the use of data from all three of these studies will be of great value in studies of conditions where prevalence is not very high (for example diabetes and many cancers), and for the investigation of gene/environment interactions.

Each of these kinds of research will be of policy relevance, by showing the impact of actual policy change (for example the Clean Air Act, and the changes in the provision of educational opportunities) and of broader societal changes on the health of the cohort members, and by describing the state of health of these future generations of the elderly. As noted in Chapter 1, these three studies began as policy-related investigations of health, and this will no doubt continue to be a prominent feature of future surveys.

9 Lifestyle and health-related behaviour

Ingrid Schoon and Samantha Parsons

Introduction

The second half of the twentieth century has been described as a time when 'personal liberation and social liberation ... went hand in hand', so that 'the cultural revolution of the later 20th century can best be understood as the triumph of the individual over society, or rather, the breaking of the threads which in the past had woven human beings into social textures' (Hobsbawm 1995: 334). The personal liberation associated with these changes was seen particularly in the growing desire for self-expression. Three other contemporary social changes are of relevance to the study of health-related habits. First is the increasing independence of women, as seen in education and employment (see Chapters 2 and 3). Second is the increase in purchasing power available to the majority, although not all, of the population (see Chapter 6). This gave easier access to alcohol, drugs, cigarettes, and foods rich in sugars and fats as means of celebration, relaxation and recuperation. The third change is the rise of an independent youth culture, which has strong economic muscle and an overwhelming concern with image.

Over the same period, the pattern of prevalent illness gradually changed from acute, infectious diseases, prominent in the years before the Second World War and for a period afterwards, to chronic diseases that tend to begin insidiously and become a permanent feature of life, such as cardiovascular disease, chronic obstructive pulmonary disease, and diabetes. Ideas about causes of chronic disease were discussed in the preceding chapter, which showed how cause is multifactorial, takes place throughout life, and is in important respects associated with the health habits discussed in this chapter. Ideas about prevention of physical illness have changed from those based on hygiene, appropriate for infectious illness, to concern with the need for regular exercise, for restraint in diet, recreational drug use, alcohol consumption, and for abstinence in smoking.

Rich foods, intoxicants, and stimulants are considered as important aspects of relaxation, recuperation and celebration, as well as being 'fashion statements' and markers of prestige, image and social position. It has been argued that their increasing availability has made life more comfortable, and more tolerable in times of stress (Graham 1987). As a result, warnings about their long-term potential for adverse effects on health can easily be disregarded. Pressures for conformity to everyday norms are usually greater than pressures to conform to long-term health advice. Health education thus has the difficult task of trying to reconcile the pressures for freedom of expression with those for health-associated restraint and control. It was initially thought that change in health-related habits could be brought about through 'education' of individuals, based on reasoned explanation of risk. However, the history of education of this kind, for example, to stop smoking, shows that it has not been greatly successful (Jarvis *et al.* 1984). More recently, ideas about changing habits have been concerned with action at the population level, by means, for example, of taxation on cigarettes, banning cigarette advertising, increased sports facilities, and campaigns to encourage better dietary choice. The argument for health education concern at the population level was expressed by Rose (1992: 101) in these terms: 'A 10 per cent lowering of the population's levels of blood cholesterol ... can be expected to reduce coronary heart disease by 20–30 per cent, and such a reduction of a condition that now kills one quarter of the population would be a benefit indeed.'

In practice, some aspects of the many social changes that have taken place since the end of the Second World War have favoured the direction required by health education. High levels of educational attainment, for long known to be asssociated with receptivity to health education ideas, are being achieved by an increasing proportion of the population (see Chapter 2). Being physically fit has become fashionable, and smoking is becoming increasingly unfashionable. Studies of what is associated with taking up, and quitting, the smoking habit, and with the ability or otherwise to control adverse dietary habits, are therefore increasingly concerned with the importance of public image in the development of habits associated with health. Further investigation of these concepts requires information on changes in images of and fashions in these health-related habits, as well as on individual health beliefs (Pitts 1996). Our three cohorts have encountered historical periods of great change in health-related habits, and in the social acceptability of these practices. They thus each offer opportunities to study such changes within their historical context.

However, there are barriers to the achievement of health education goals that operate in other ways. Poverty is the primary problem, since it restricts access, for example, to healthy dietary choice, through expense and restricted local availability (Mooney 1990), as well as restricting opportunities for educational attainment. Poverty, unemployment and despair increase the need for readily affordable, and available, comforting habits such as smoking and consumption of fatty foods (Graham 1989; Montgomery *et al.* 1998).

This chapter describes the adult health habits of smoking, alcohol consumption, recreational drug use, exercise and diet in the three birth cohorts. We look in particular at the extent of differences between them in terms of these behaviours, and at the patterning of habits by sex, socio-economic and family factors, as well as educational attainment. Our aim is to describe the types and ranges of information available on health-related behaviour in the three cohorts, and to compare cohort- and age-related differences in these habits in early and middle adult life.

Smoking

Smoking was not clearly demonstrated as a health risk until the mid-1950s. The peaks in men's smoking occurred during the world wars in the last century, and the highest was in 1944 (Todd 1975). During the 1940s and 1950s, the level of smoking among men reached almost 80 per cent (Wald *et al.* 1988). Social acceptability of women smoking came later than for men, and women 'caught up' with men's smoking only in the 1980s (McNeill *et al.* 1988). Although the proportion of people who smoked then began to fall (Wald *et al.* 1988), the 'downstream effects' of earlier higher rates are reflected in lung cancer incidence, which rose in women later than in men, and which are highest in the lowest socio-economic groups, since smoking was, and is still, highest in that part of the population. In addition to the risk of death associated with smoking, it is known also, because of pioneering work in the 1958 cohort, that smoking in pregnancy decreases the weight, and chances of survival, of the baby at birth (Butler *et al.* 1971). Maternal smoking increases the risk of poor lung function in the child (Tager *et al.* 1983), and it is therefore particularly unfortunate that those currently most inclined to take up smoking are young women (Jarvis and Wardle 1999). The 1946 cohort grew up at the time of maximum smoking among fathers, and heavy smoking in mothers, and so carries the greatest associated risk. However, the burden was not a great deal less in the later born cohorts.

A comparison of smoking in all three cohorts of cohort members in their 30s showed little difference in the proportions of men who were smokers (36 per cent of the 1946 cohort, 33 per cent of those born in 1958, and 35 per cent among the 1970 cohort). Among the women, however, there was a slight, though consistent downward trend, from 38 per cent of the 1946-born women, through 33 per cent of their counterparts born in 1958, to 29 per cent of the women in the 1970 cohort (Figure 9.1).

In the 1946 and 1958 cohorts, the proportion of those who smoked declined with age. Thus, although in the 1970 cohort the proportion of men who smoked was relatively high at age 30 years, both they, and the women smokers in that cohort, may yet follow the age-related decline of the two earlier born groups.

The Acheson Report (Acheson 1998) showed that smoking was strongly related to social class background. This pattern was echoed in the cohort studies, with smoking much more prevalent amongst those from manual than non-manual social classes (Table 9.1). This pattern persisted at all ages and in all three cohorts. In the 1958 cohort, the overall tendency for smoking rates to decline with age was also apparent in all social classes, but for men and women in the 1946 cohort, the trend was much less consistent.

Figure 9.1 *Percentage of men and women who currently smoke cigarettes*

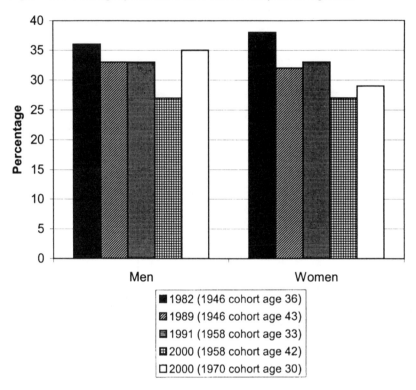

Among the smokers there was a tendency for women to smoke less than men (Table 9.2). In all cohorts, and at all ages, the heaviest smokers were those in unskilled manual occupations.

In all three cohorts, too, there was an association between economic status and smoking. Couples in which one or both partners were employed were least likely to smoke, while couples in households in which no one worked were most likely to be smokers. Smoking was also relatively high among those with no, or only low level, qualifications. For example, just 20 per cent of men with degree-level qualifications in the 1970 cohort were smokers, compared with 47 per cent of men with no qualifications.

Table 9.1 *Percentage of men and women who currently smoke cigarettes by own social class*

Social class	Men					Women				
	1946 cohort Age 36 in 1982	1946 cohort Age 43 in 1989	1958 cohort Age 33 in 1991	1958 cohort Age 42 in 2000	1970 cohort Age 30 in 2000	1946 cohort Age 36 in 1982	1946 cohort Age 43 in 1989	1958 cohort Age 33 in 1991	1958 cohort Age 42 in 2000	1970 cohort Age 30 in 2000
I	20	15	19	9	14	22	28	14	13	11
II	30	26	25	18	25	34	25	26	20	22
III nm	29	34	25	17	26	33	27	29	25	25
III m	44	43	41	35	43	36	41	41	32	42
IV	45	36	45	33	41	47	45	43	32	37
V	49	59	53	44	51	53	42	51	46	45
All	36	33	33	27	35	38	32	33	27	29
No. of cases	1,356	1,192	5,151	5,212	4,926	1,067	1,133	5,355	5,043	5,216

Table 9.2 Mean number of cigarettes smoked daily by men and women (who smoke) by own social class

Social class	Men					Women				
	1946 cohort Age 36 in 1982	1946 cohort Age 43 in 1989	1958 cohort Age 33 in 1991	1958 cohort Age 42 in 2000	1970 cohort Age 30 in 2000	1946 cohort Age 36 in 1982	1946 cohort Age 43 in 1989	1958 cohort Age 33 in 1991	1958 cohort Age 42 in 2000	1970 cohort Age 30 in 2000
I	19	20	14	16	15	11	12	10	16	14
II	22	22	15	18	15	14	16	14	16	12
III nm	16	18	16	17	15	16	17	14	15	12
III m	20	22	18	19	16	17	17	16	16	14
IV	19	21	20	18	15	18	18	17	16	14
V	26	23	20	18	18	18	17	17	19	15
All	20	22	18	18	16	16	17	15	16	13
No. of cases	3,846	1,180	1,758	1,362	1,693	3,838	1,057	1,703	1,341	1,492

For women in the same cohort, the comparable figures were 14 per cent and 42 per cent. Similar sex differences were found in the other two cohorts. When family status was examined, it was found that in all three cohorts, those living alone, or as single parents, were the most likely to smoke.

Alcohol consumption

Consumption of alcohol, by contrast with smoking habits, has increased throughout most years since 1946, and sales of alcohol rose particularly strongly in the 1960s. This was followed by a plateau in sales during the high unemployment years of the 1980s, just as it had been during the Depression years of the 1930s (Williams and Brake 1980). Consumption of alcohol has thus changed greatly during the lives of our three cohorts. Although alcohol consumption now differs very little by social class, alcohol drinking among women is considerably higher in the non-manual classes and among those with higher educational attainment (ONS 1998; Ely *et al.* 1999b). Whilst there is some dispute about the health effects of moderate drinking, there is none about the risks associated with heavy consumption at any stage in life, including pregnancy.

Information on the quantities of alcohol drunk by members of the 1946 cohort was obtained with the question 'In the last seven days have you had any of the following drinks? *(a) Spirits or liqueurs: answered in measures; (b) Wine, sherry, martini or port: answered in glasses; (c) Beer, lager, cider or stout: answered in half pints.* A near identical question was put to the 1958 and 1970 cohorts, but they were additionally asked about their consumption of bottles of alcopops.

The Acheson report on inequalities in health showed that an increasing proportion of women drank alcohol regularly and above the recommended limits (Acheson 1998). We found a similar inter-cohort trend in quantities of alcohol drunk, particularly by women (Figure 9.2).

Although men drank considerably more than women (between two and three times as much overall) there was little change over time in the quantity drunk by men.

Figure 9.2 *Mean number of alcohol units consumed by men and women in one week*

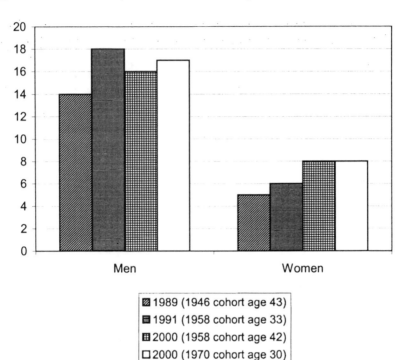

Men in the 1958 cohort tended to drink less as they got older, particularly men in unskilled occupations, who were the heaviest drinkers of all at age 33 (Table 9.3). This may reflect the inhibiting costs of drinking among relatively low paid men, most of whom would have dependent children at age 42. Financial factors may also underlie the relatively low levels of alcohol consumption in 2000 among the 30-year-old men in the 1970 cohort who were in unskilled jobs.

By contrast, in all three cohorts, women in non-manual occupations drank the most, and women in unskilled employment drank the least (Table 9.3). Unlike the men, too, women drank more as they got older, particularly those in the 1958 cohort who were in the lowest social class.

Table 9.3 *Mean number of alcohol units consumed by men and women in a week by own social class*

Social class	Men				Women			
	1946 cohort Age 43 in 1989	1958 cohort Age 33 in 1991	1958 cohort Age 42 in 2000	1970 cohort Age 30 in 2000	1946 cohort Age 43 in 1989	1958 cohort Age 33 in 1991	1958 cohort Age 42 in 2000	1970 cohort Age 30 in 2000
I	13	16	15	17	6	7	8	9
II	15	17	15	18	5	6	8	9
III nm	14	15	14	16	5	5	8	7
III m	15	18	16	17	4	6	8	9
IV	11	19	16	17	3	5	7	7
V	15	23	17	15	3	4	7	6
All	14	17	16	17	5	5	8	8
No. of cases	2,427	5,212	4,783	4,696	2,337	5,402	4,068	4,173

There were differences in drinking patterns according to family status. Couples with children drank the least, while the heaviest drinkers were single men and women of all age groups with no children, as well as men and women living in households where there were no earners.

Information on problems with alcohol was collected in all three cohorts using the CAGE questions, which are given in a note to Table 9.4. The proportion of men and women who reported alcohol problems almost doubled across time. Although the proportion did not change much with age in men, it did rather more so in women, in the cohort (1958) in which that comparison was possible at these ages. In the 1946 cohort, drink problems were more often reported by men in non-manual occupations. In the two later born cohorts, however, they tended to be more often reported by men in manual jobs. By contrast, women in the non-manual occupational groups in all three cohorts reported more drink problems than other women. These results do not necessarily imply that excessive quantities of alcohol were drunk by women in the three cohorts (Ely *et al.* 1999b). As noted above, women generally drank considerably less than men.

Problems with alcohol were most often reported by men and women with higher qualifications, by single men and women of all age groups with no children, and men and women living in households where no one was working, with the exception of single working men in the 1946 cohort. Couples with children were the least likely to indicate that they had such problems. In the 1958 and the 1970 cohort there were also regional variations, with men living in Greater London containing the highest proportion reporting drink problems.

Drug use

Access to recreational drugs was very limited in the adolescence and early adulthood of the 1946 cohort, but became gradually more widespread during those stages in the lives of the two later born cohorts, and for the 1946 cohort in middle adulthood. Although recreational drug use is evidently associated with risk of criminal behaviour, its association with

Table 9.4 *Percentage of men and women who have ever had a drink problem (CAGE) by own social class*

Social class	Men				Women			
	1946 cohort Age 43 in 1989	1958 cohort Age 33 in 1991	1958 cohort Age 42 in 2000	1970 cohort Age 30 in 2000	1946 cohort Age 43 in 1989	1958 cohort Age 33 in 1991	1958 cohort Age 42 in 2000	1970 cohort Age 30 in 2000
I	12	13	15	18	13	12	7	6
II	12	18	17	20	7	10	9	11
III nm	9	15	16	20	5	7	8	7
III m	13	18	15	20	6	9	7	7
IV	4	18	14	20	6	7	7	7
V	7	19	20	22	2	6	9	0
All	11	17	17	21	5	8	9	8
No. of cases	526	5,241	5,406	5,258	224	5,253	5,172	5,512

Note: A drink problem was defined as a 'yes' answer to one or more of the CAGE questions, which are:

Have you ever felt that you ought to cut down on your drinking? Yes/No.

Have people ever annoyed you by criticising your drinking? Yes/No.

Have you ever felt bad or guilty about your drinking? Yes/No.

Have you ever had a drink first thing in the morning to steady your nerves or to get rid of a hangover? Yes/No.

physical and mental health is not yet understood, except in the case of abuse and overdose.

Reports of drug use for purposes other than medication at age 36 years in the 1946 cohort were so few (36 men and 3 women) that we report drug use only in the two later born cohorts. Cohort members in the 1958 and 1970 cohorts were asked in 2000 about *current* use of illegal drugs and whether they had *ever* used illegal drugs. Cannabis was classed as an illegal drug.

There were dramatic differences between the 1958 cohort and the 1970 cohort in the proportion of those reporting drug use (Figure 9.3), even in the same year (2000), but at different ages (42 and 30).

Figure 9.3 *Percentage prevalence of drug use by men and women*

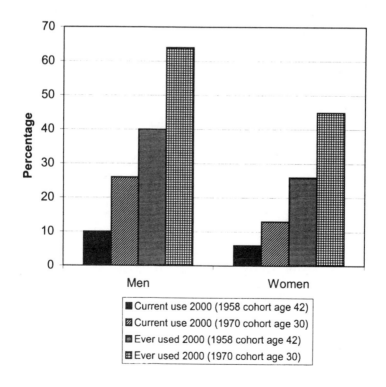

Legend:
- ■ Current use 2000 (1958 cohort age 42)
- ▨ Current use 2000 (1970 cohort age 30)
- ▤ Ever used 2000 (1958 cohort age 42)
- ⊞ Ever used 2000 (1970 cohort age 30)

Clearly, experience of drugs, especially current use, was much more common among the later cohort. In both cohorts, a greater proportion of men than women reported using drugs. Cannabis was the most frequently reported drug ever, or currently, used, and there was a wider range of drugs reported by the 1970 cohort members than by those in the older cohort (Table 9.5).

Among men in the 1958 cohort, current drug use was not strongly associated with social class. Among women, 7 per cent of those in managerial positions reported current drug use, compared with 5 per cent of women in unskilled jobs. There was a tendency for a greater proportion of higher status individuals to report ever taking drugs; 45 per cent of men and 34 per cent of women in managerial positions said that they had at some time used drugs, compared with 35 per cent of men and 25 per cent of women in unskilled occupations.

In the 1970 cohort there were no social class differences in reports of ever using drugs. However, men in managerial positions showed less current drug use at 30 years than men in unskilled occupations (21 per cent as compared with 34 per cent). By contrast, current drug use was *more* often reported by professional women than by women in unskilled occupations (14 per cent versus 9 per cent).

Although current drug use did not vary by educational attainment, reports of previous experience were greater among men and women with higher qualifications, compared with those with few or no qualifications. Both previous and current drug use was more commonly reported among those living as couples in which neither partner worked, followed by single parents, and working singles. Couples with children, in which either one or both partners were employed were least likely to have ever used, or to be currently using, drugs. Drug use was highest in Greater London and lowest in the North, Yorkshire and the East Midlands.

Exercise

Physical exertion has been increasingly less necessary at work and at home throughout the period covered by the three studies, as the nature of

Table 9.5 *Percentage of men and women using drugs, by type of drug*

Drug type	Men				Women			
	Current use		Ever used		Current use		Ever used	
	1958 cohort Age 42 in 2000	1970 cohort Age 30 in 2000	1958 cohort Age 42 in 2000	1970 cohort Age 30 in 2000	1958 cohort Age 42 in 2000	1970 cohort Age 30 in 2000	1958 cohort Age 42 in 2000	1970 cohort Age 30 in 2000
Any drug	10	26	40	64	6	13	26	45
Cannabis	9	23	38	60	4	11	23	42
Amphetamines	1	6	11	30	0	2	6	16
Poppers	1	3	7	28	0	1	3	13
Ecstasy	1	6	4	22	0	2	2	11
LSD	0	1	7	20	0	1	3	11
Magic mushrooms	1	1	9	20	0	0	4	8
Cocaine	2	8	7	19	1	4	3	9
Temazepan	1	1	3	7	1	1	4	9
Ketamine	0	1	1	4	0	0	4	4
Crack	0	1	1	3	0	0	0	1
Heroin	0	1	2	3	0	0	1	1
Methadone	0	0	1	2	0	0	1	1
No. of cases	5,461	5,302	5,461	5,302	5,253	5,581	5,253	5,581

employment has become predominantly less manual (75 per cent of fathers of the 1946 cohort were in manual employment compared with 45 per cent of their sons and 22 per cent of their daughters), and as labour-saving domestic devices and access to personal transport increased. However, frequency of exercise in leisure time has shown an overall increase, although it is much more common among those in favourable socio-economic circumstances (Colhoun and Prescott-Clarke 1996), and in childhood it is more common in boys than in girls (Power 1995). Although leisure time physical activity is known to be good for both physical and mental health (Glenister 1996), its increasing popularity is not keeping pace with adverse trends in diet and alcohol consumption, as shown by the steeply rising rates of obesity in both adults (Prentice and Jebb 1995, and see Chapter 8) and in children (Chinn and Rona 1994), and, possibly too, by the apparently increasing prevalence of depression and anxiety (Chapter 8). Both infrequent exercise in leisure time, and obesity, are associated with increased risk of cardiovascular disease and non-insulin dependent diabetes mellitus (NIH Consensus Panel 1996; Brunner and Marmot 1999).

Exercise habits in leisure time were reported in quite different ways in the three studies. For the 1946 cohort, an extensive self-completion questionnaire was used at 36 years to collect information on frequency and intensity of many different types of exercise, but at 43 years, three simple questions were asked. Information on exercise in the 1958 and 1970 cohorts was gathered by asking how often they took exercise in an average week, with answers ranging across a five-point scale from 'never' to 'most/every day'.

It was not surprising to find those in their 40s reported taking less exercise in leisure time than those in their 30s (Figure 9.4). However, those born in 1946 were much less likely to exercise than those in both the later born cohorts when in their 30s, and the difference between them and the 1958 cohort in their 40s was even more striking. There was also a marked sex difference in the 1946 cohort: at both 36 and 43 years, women were less likely than men to take exercise. Six out of ten 43-year-old women in the 1946 cohort said that they never exercised, more than twice the

Figure 9.4 *Percentage of men and women who never exercised*

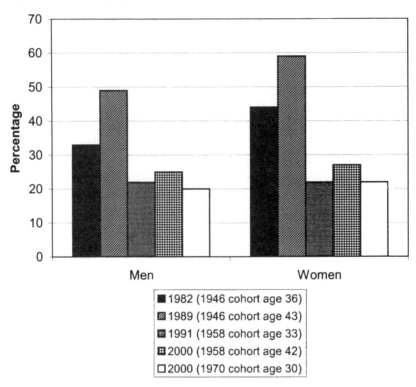

proportion among 42-year-old women born in 1958. Interestingly, there were only small sex differences in exercise habits in the 1958 cohort at ages 33 and 42, and the prevalence of exercise at these ages was similar to that in the 1970 cohort at age 30.

In all three cohorts, those in professional and managerial jobs were more likely to report taking leisure time exercise, compared with those in semi-skilled and unskilled occupations, but the social class differences tended to be smaller at more recent calendar times. In all three cohorts, too, those with higher qualifications were the most likely to report taking regular exercise compared with those with no qualifications, and these differences changed very little over time. Uptake of leisure time physical activity was not strongly differentiated by family status, but was strikingly lower among those living in households in which no one was employed.

Diet

Diet for the 1946 cohort moved from the stringencies of wartime food rationing, which they lived with until the age of 8, to increasing plenty in their adolescent and early adult years. By contrast, the two later born cohorts lived in periods of increasing availability and choice of food. All three cohorts experienced the trends towards increasing sugar, fat and salt intake. There has been some reduction in fat intake during the last decade (Stephen and Gieber 1994). Nevertheless, despite the increases in quantities and varieties of foods available, people in lower socio-economic circumstances have been shown in many studies to have a comparatively poor diet, particularly in terms of the antioxidants, vitamins and minerals which are mostly derived from fruit and vegetables (Prynne *et al.* 2002). Women are at greater risk of poor diet than are men, and this is of concern in those of childbearing age, since poor nutrition in pregnancy is likely to be a source of long-term health risk to both the child and the mother (Ravelli *et al.* 1998; Forsen *et al.* 1997). Poor diet is partly a matter of expense, as well as accessibility of shops that provide fresh food. The Acheson Report (Acheson 1998) on the health of the public concluded that 'access to a cheaper and wider range of food is most restricted for some of the groups who need it most', and quoted King's (1997) finding that 'households in the bottom tenth of the income distribution spend an average of 29 per cent of their income on food compared to 18 per cent for those in the top tenth'.

Information on diet was collected using diet diaries in the 1946 cohort, and by questions asking about frequency of consumption of specified foods along a seven-point scale from 'more than once a day' to 'never' in the two later born cohorts. In this analysis, we use three negative indicators of the healthiness of the cohort members' diets, namely: not eating fresh fruit, eating chips and not eating wholemeal bread, each on a weekly basis.

Fresh fruit

Reports of not eating fresh fruit were highest by far in the 1946 cohort, especially among men, half of whom, at age 43, did not eat fresh fruit at all in an average week (Figure 9.5). The proportion of those not eating fruit was more than twice as high in the 1946 cohort at 43 years as among the 1958-born men and women at age 42. Interestingly, there was a rising trend towards less fruit eating in the 1970 cohort compared with the 1958 cohort. Although the proportion of those born in 1958 who did not eat fruit rose with increasing age, more so among women than men, fruit-eating was less common among the 30-year-olds in the 1970 cohort than among the 1958 cohort members at either age.

Figure 9.5 *Percentage of men and women who did not eat any fruit in an average week*

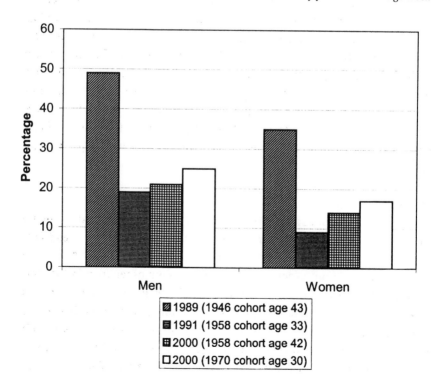

In all three cohorts those in manual jobs were less likely than those in non-manual jobs to report that they ate fresh fruit on a weekly basis. Within each class men were more likely than women not to eat fruit. The association with education was similar, in that the lower the educational attainment, the greater the likelihood of not eating fresh fruit. In terms of family status, the highest proportions of those who did not eat fruit weekly were found among single mothers, and couples living in households where no one was gainfully employed. Couples with children were the most likely to eat fruit.

Fatty foods

Consumption of fatty foods is summarised here using reports of whether chips were eaten in an average week. In each cohort and at each age, more men than women reported that they ate chips (Figure 9.6). Men and women in the 1958 cohort were less likely to be regular eaters of chips as they got older. Comparison of the three cohorts shows that in both sexes, chip consumption was at its lowest in the 1946 cohort. In each cohort, eating chips was most frequent in the manual social classes and in those with no, or only low, educational qualifications. Most likely to eat chips were single parents, and couples living in households in which no one was gainfully employed, and least likely to consume fatty foods were single, employed women with no children, and men living with a partner and without children.

Wholemeal bread

Consumption of wholemeal bread was regarded as an indicator of intake of dietary fibre content. Clearly, there was more wholemeal bread consumption in the 1958 and 1970 cohorts compared with the 1946 (Figure 9.7). Whereas six out of ten women and seven out of ten men in the 1946 cohort did not eat wholemeal bread in 1989 when they were 43, by the year 2000, this figure had dropped to three out of ten for both sexes in both the later born cohorts. Those in non-manual jobs were more likely than others to report that they ate wholemeal bread, and so were those with highest levels of educational attainment. In terms of family status,

Figure 9.6 *Percentage of men and women who ate chips in an average week*

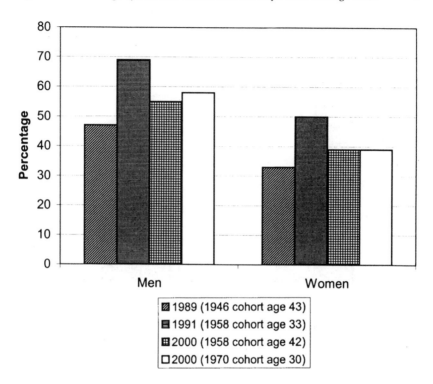

those least likely to eat bread with high fibre content were single parents, and couples living in households where no one was gainfully employed.

Conclusions

There is evidence from these three studies of a degree of favourable differences between cohorts in exercise and smoking habits, and in two of the three dietary indicators. The proportion of people who smoke has decreased, more people have taken up exercise, and the consumption of fresh fruit and wholemeal bread has increased, suggesting that men and women born in 1958 and 1970 have increased their fibre intake in comparison

Figure 9.7 *Percentage of men and women who did not eat wholemeal bread in an average week*

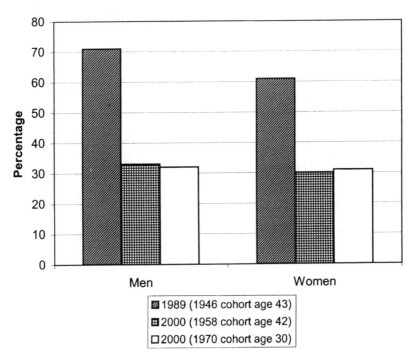

to the generation born in 1946. On the other hand, we have seen a dramatic increase in the consumption of drugs in the 1970 cohort when compared with the 1958 cohort. The proportion of women who drink alcohol nearly doubled in the last decade of the twentieth century, and there was a notable increase in drink-related problems in men and women in their early 40s. There is furthermore an increase in the consumption of fatty food, as indicated by the consumption of chips. Generally, men drank more than women, they were more likely than women to take drugs, and they ate less healthily, in terms of less fruit, more fatty foods, and less wholemeal bread. In the 1946 cohort, men took more exercise by comparison with women, but there was no great gender difference in this habit in the two later born cohorts. Current smoking was very little differenti-ated by gender in the 1946 and 1958 cohorts, but in the youngest cohort, smoking was more common in men than in women. Thus, our findings suggest that men at these ages have, for the most part, less healthy lifestyles than women.

Our findings have also revealed striking inequalities in health behav-iour by socio-economic group across a range of measures. The social class differences were especially marked for smoking, uptake of exercise, and healthy diet (in particular fatty foods). This is important since smoking, physical inactivity, high cholesterol and poor diet are among the main risk factors associated with sickness and death (OECD 2001). The findings show that the most excluded and most vulnerable members of society, that is, those living in households in which no one was an earner, those living alone, and those who were single parents, were most at risk of living 'unhealthy' lifestyles. Each of these vulnerable groups is increasing proportionately in the national population.

Smoking in the 1946 and 1958 cohorts, alcohol consumption, and eating fatty foods in the 1958 cohort have declined with age, but we do not explore here how far that is the result of losses through death, or other reasons. Although problems with alcohol have not changed with age, physical inactivity increased in the 1946 and 1958 cohorts as they grew older, and not eating fruit increased with age in the 1958 population, particularly among women. We are not yet able to say whether there may be a decline with age in drug taking in the 1970 cohort, or whether, with increasing availability and access, particularly to cannabis, the following generation will, at 30 years, be greater drug users than the 1970 cohort.

Differences between cohorts in some aspects of these habits is to be expected, because of differences in educational opportunities and in earn-ing power in early adulthood (see Chapters 2 and 6). Striking differences between cohorts, when those of similar age were compared, were evident in the increased consumption of alcohol by women in their early 40s, and women in non-manual occupations. There was also a greatly increased likelihood in both sexes of taking leisure time exercise in the 30s and 40s when the 1946 and 1958 cohorts were compared, and of eating fruit and wholemeal bread in their early 40s. Chip eating, by contrast, was lowest in the 1958 cohort among cohort members in their early 30s, but increased among men and women in the 1970 cohort in their 30s.

Although some of the changes with age and successive cohorts show trends favourable to health, these are not yet reflected in most aspects of physical wellbeing; for example, as the trends in obesity show (see Chapter 8). This may change, however, and the public health benefits of increased awareness about diet and exercise may have a gradually beneficial effect.

How beneficial changes in these health-related habits can be achieved is a matter of considerable debate. It has been argued that health behaviours such as smoking, drinking, diet and exercise involve a degree of personal choice. Such a victim-blaming approach, however, is unhelpful, as it fails to address underlying questions of why unhealthy behaviours are maintained. Targeting interventions appropriately requires understanding of the settings and the context in which behaviours take place. It is clear from the differences between the cohorts reported here that socio-economic factors are of considerable importance in influencing health behaviours and lifestyles. The data have shown that the most excluded and most vulnerable members of society – cohort members living in a household where no one works or single parents – are most at risk of living 'unhealthy' lifestyles. Knowledge of patterns and trends in health behaviours should be used for the development of effective interventions targeting, in particular, the social and economic causes of ill-health behaviours, and aiming to achieve behaviour change among disadvantaged groups (Lupton 1995; Marks *et al.* 2000). In addition, it is being argued that social images of these behaviours are important, and that these have changed notably during the years covered by these three cohorts. Future research will show how these changed images will influence health beliefs and health behaviours.

10 Social participation, values and crime

John Bynner and Samantha Parsons

Introduction

Much has been made in recent years of the collapse of civic society as shown in declining memberships of organisations and lack of political interest. Building on earlier conceptions about the social basis of education advance in the US context by James Coleman (1988), a major line of explanation has been devoted to the decline of *social capital* (Baron *et al.* 2001). The American political scientist, Robert Putnam, whose work and ideas have been particularly influential, has developed a whole thesis, based mainly on American experience, to suggest that the 'bridges' and 'bonds' that cemented communities in the past are no longer present (Putnam 2000). Community values have given way to individualistic orientations and cynicism about the capability of local institutions to meet individual needs. The social capital vested in associational life is under threat.

The data presented by Putnam relate to evidence of change in relatively self-contained communities in the United States and the country as a whole, which compare unfavourably with those of other countries. For example, comparable communities in Italy display the formal bonding between individuals and a community that Putnam claims prevailed in the United States 20 years ago. Scandinavian countries generally show higher level of cohesion than others and so on. He also rather downplays the differentiation between different kinds of communities in the United States, for example those of the inner city and those in the middle-west and the different ethnic and cultural basis of the identity that defines them as communities (Fevre 2001). Fractured communities are more common in the former and display much more of the alienation that Putnam identifies as part of all areas. His emphasis on the importance of trust, in neighbours and strangers, is also seen as central to a healthy society, but some analyses suggest that this element of social cohesion may work quite differently in relation to socio-economic consequences from those elements to do with memberships and participation (e.g. Norris 2001).

In the European context, though there are concerns about social and political participation and growing recognition of the need to foster social capital under modern conditions (OECD 2001), the policy agenda has tended to focus more on *social exclusion* as a growing phenomenon in European states (Atkinson 1998; Room 1998). The agenda to promote *social cohesion* is less concerned with differences in mean levels of activities and values in communities across time than with the evidence of disparities between groups within communities identified as having various kinds of success and failure. Emanating from original concerns in France about the problems faced by disabled people in modern society, the social exclusion concept focuses attention on 'disenfranchisement' related to poor qualifications, lack of skills or capacity for employment, together with poverty (Evans 2000). These constitute the bottom (disadvantaged) end of the distribution of employability attributes – the defining feature of social exclusion. Failure to engage with the labour market extends to general disengagement at the society level. Non-participation in community and civic activities may have psychological consequences manifested in a sense of personal isolation, low self-esteem, the foundations of mental illness and, in the extreme case, suicide. Social consequences may include rising levels of alcoholism, drug abuse and crime (Bynner 2001a).

The Putnam hypothesis concerned with declining social capital, and the European agenda to combat social exclusion, share in common a focus on the impact of social change. If what they say is correct, then different cohorts, assessed around the same age, will show outcomes reflecting the impact of a changing social situation on individual lives. The 1946, 1958 and 1970 birth cohorts, separated by intervals of 12 years, can offer important evidence on the validity of these claims. The 1970 cohort faced a more uncertain occupational future than the 1946 cohort, virtually all of whom stepped straight into jobs on leaving school at the minimum age. As we saw from Chapter 3, the 1958 cohort also obtained jobs relatively easily after leaving school. Their difficulties came later with the recession of the early 1980s. With the collapse of the youth labour market in the mid-1980s, the 1970 cohort faced a difficult transition from education into any kind of job. Their response was to stay on in education beyond the minimum age of 16 in greater numbers – a rise from one-third to one-half by the middle of the 1980s. The early leavers were likely to face the prospect of training schemes rather than jobs with full pay. Successful completion of a youth training scheme (YTS) was, moreover, not the sure path to employment, as apprenticeships had tended to be previously. The quality of the YTS varied enormously, with many young men and women experiencing unemployment shortly after leaving their scheme (Banks *et al.* 1992; Roberts and Parsell 1989; Bynner 2001b).

Such changing experience has been characterised in terms of greater *risk* and *uncertainty* in the life course for the more recent generations (Beck 1986; Beck *et al.* 1994). In the 'late modern' world, as Giddens terms it, occupational destinies are no longer the foregone conclusion based on family background as they were in the past, but require much more flexible and fluid occupational identities as a basis for the 'navigation' through the modern labour market that is now required (Evans and Furlong 1996). As we have seen in earlier chapters, social class continues to maintain a strong connection with later life chances. What remains unclear is whether the more complex challenges faced by recent generations add another layer of difficulty in entering adult life. From the point of view of this chapter, our interest lies in whether such difficulty translates into the kinds of shifts in behaviour and attitude that Putnam on the one hand, and the advocates of the social exclusion thesis on the other, predict.

Comparisons in this chapter largely focus on the 1958 and the 1970 cohort, and where data are available, the 1946 cohort as well. We examine community involvement, trade union activity, church attendance, political participation and interest, self-concept, a selection of community oriented values and evidence of misconduct at school and criminal activity as revealed by contact with the law, arrests and court appearances. A number of the questions put to the 1958 cohort and the 1970 cohort members asked if they were *currently* or had *ever been* a member [of a particular organisation]. Attitudes and values of the 1958 and 1970 cohort members were measured from single questions in the case of self-concept, and from a battery of opinion items using a five-point scale of opinion ranging from 'strongly agree' to 'strongly disagree' for the social and political attitudes. Many questions asked in 1991, when the 1958 cohort members were age 33, were identical to those asked in 2000 when they had reached age 42 and the 1970 cohort had reached age 30. Relevant questions put to the 1946 cohort, although similar, were not always identical. Differences in question design are highlighted through the chapter.

We look for evidence of breakdown, or at least changes, in community and political participation when compared with that of an earlier time; and changes in self-concept and values. As in previous chapters, we also examine differences by gender, family and own social class (as assessed from occupation), highest qualification, family status and family economic status (combined employment status of the cohort member and partner). Depending upon the availability of data, we are able to examine *cohort effects* by comparing 30-year-olds in the 1970 cohort with 33-year-olds in the 1958 cohort and 26-year-olds or 36-year-olds or 43-year-olds in the 1946 cohort. We are also able to see if participation changed with age by comparing information given by 33-year-olds with that given by 42-year-olds in the 1958 cohort and between 26-year-olds, 36-year-olds and 43-year-olds in the 1946 study. If there is no change between 33 and 42 in the 1958 cohort, for example, then the data are free of age effects, at least when the cohort members have passed the age of 30. By taking a close look at gender differences throughout, we are able to gain an idea of how the changing experience of women with respect to employment and family life, highlighted in earlier chapters, may also be reflected in changes in their social and political participation.

Social and community participation

A striking feature of these comparisons was the marked decline in social participation between the cohorts both with respect to current membership of community organisations and reports of ever having been members of one of them (Tables 10.1a and 10.1b). In the 1946 cohort at age 36, 59 per cent of men and 46 per cent of women were currently members of an organisation. For the 1958 or the 1970 cohort the complete list of organisations[1] was not as comprehensive, but apart from this, current membership in the later cohorts was substantially lower. In the 1958 cohort at age 33, current membership was 14 per cent for men and 25 per cent for women – figures that had barely changed by the time the cohort members had reached the later age of 42. For 30-year-olds in the 1970 cohort, current membership dropped further to only 8 per cent for men and 12 per cent for women.

Membership was strongly related to social class and was qualifications-dependent in all three cohorts, particularly among women. Over 40 per cent of the 1958 cohort women with a professional occupation (social class I) were currently members of at least one organisation, compared with 17 per cent of women with an unskilled occupation (social class V). Figures 10.1a and 10.1b show the pattern by occupational group for men and women across the three cohorts. For women, substantial gradients were evident for the 1946 and 1958 cohort. There were much weaker gradients for the 1970 cohort dropping from 18 per cent for professional women (social class I) down to 6 per cent for those currently in unskilled work (social class V). These kinds of gradients and differences were repeated across the qualifications groups, with those having the highest qualifications participating at much the same level as social class I, and those without any qualifications participating least.

In the 1958 and 1970 cohorts, participation differed very little by family status or the economic status of the household, except that there was a tendency in both cohorts for those that were part of a non-working household – particularly women – to be the *least* likely to be actively involved in any organisation.

Perhaps surprisingly, there were only modest increases in the reports of *ever* having been a member of an organisation between ages 33 years and 42 years for the 1958 cohort members. In the 1970 cohort at age 30, the percentage that had *ever* participated was again far lower.[2] There

Table 10.1a *Overall levels of social participation (percentage) for men in the 1946, 1958 and 1970 cohorts*

	1946 cohort		1958 cohort		1970 cohort
	Age 36	Age 26	Age 42	Age 33	Age 30
Current membership	59		15	14	8
Ever membership			27	22	15
Current membership of a Trade Union		43	27	31	18
Attending a religious service in a month	21		10	10	6
Voting in a General Election		66	76	75	60
No political interest			18	12	26
N (100%)	3,713	4,215	5,596	5,580	5,433

Table 10.1b *Overall levels of social participation (percentage) for women in the 1946, 1958 and 1970 cohorts*

	1946 cohort		1958 cohort		1970 cohort
	Age 36	Age 26	Age 42	Age 33	Age 30
Current membership	46		22	25	12
Ever membership			43	36	21
Current membership of a Trade Union		14	22	18	17
Attending a religious service in a month	19		17	20	10
Voting in a General Election		69	78	78	65
No political interest			24	18	33
N (100%)	2,981	4,089	5,766	5,776	5,762

Figure 10.1a *Current membership of an organisation in three cohorts by occupation group: men*

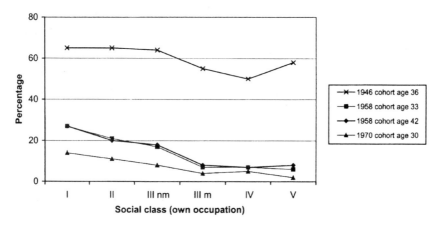

Figure 10.1b *Current membership of an organisation in three cohorts by occupation group: women*

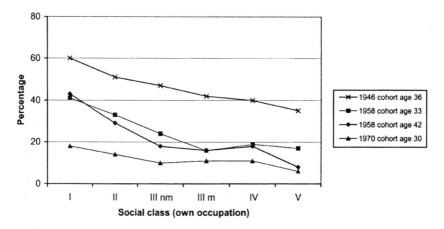

were also massive social class and qualification gradients though, most notably in the 1958 cohort and particularly among women. We find a clear drop in membership across cohorts, and across all occupational groups. For example, with respect to qualifications, whereas over half of 33-year-old women in the 1958 cohort with at least a degree-level qualification had at some time in their lives been a member of an organisation, this dropped to below one-third among similarly qualified women in the 1970 cohort. Among women without any qualifications, comparable figures were 18 per cent in the 1958 cohort and 12 per cent in the 1970 cohort.

Trade union activity

The 1979 Conservative government curtailed the powers of trade unions. The consequence was a reduction in trade union membership that was evident across the three cohorts. Among men, current membership was highest back in 1972 among 26-year-olds in the 1946 cohort at over 40 per cent. This compared with 18 per cent of 30-year-olds in the 1970 cohort in 2000.

Figure 10.2a shows that current trade union membership among men was highest in all cohorts among partly skilled or skilled manual workers (social class IIIm or IV), although greatly reduced in the 1970 cohort. Membership had also declined most among these groups of workers in the 1958 cohort between age 33 (1991) and age 42 (2000), for example falling from 41 per cent at age 33 to 33 per cent at age 42 for men in partly skilled manual occupations (social class IV).

Among women, differences between cohorts in overall membership were smaller, perhaps reflecting a much lower level of involvement in unions by women in general (Figure 10.2b). However, in contrast to men, women in the 1946 cohort were *least* likely of all the cohorts to have been members of a Trade Union, reflecting the more limited engagement of women in the 1946 cohort with the labour market. Comparison by social class of occupation and by highest qualification showed little difference between cohorts. In fact, only for women in managerial occupations was membership substantially enhanced. Similarly, at the highest qualification

Figure 10.2a *Current membership of a trade union in three cohorts by occupation group: men*

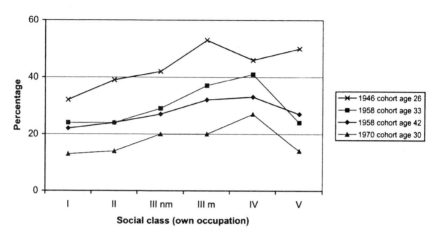

Figure 10.2b *Current membership of a trade union in three cohorts by occupation group: women*

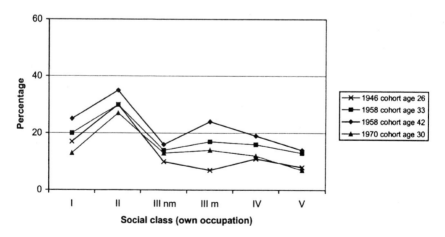

levels, women's membership rose. In fact at degree level, more women were members of trade unions than were similarly qualified men.

In the 1958 and 1970 cohorts, family status bore little connection with union membership among men, though there were reduced rates among women with children, most probably as a reflection of childcare responsibilities and the non-unionised part-time employment that often goes with it. Economic status, on the other hand, did show a participation difference, with men and women who were part of a non-working household being far less likely to be members of trade unions than were those who were working – as few as 5 per cent of men and 3 per cent of women in both the 1958 and 1970 cohorts. This compares with 36 per cent membership among 1958 cohort men in households where both partners were working.

Questions on whether the respondent had *ever* been a trade union member (restricted to the 1958 and 1970 cohorts) showed a considerable boost in these figures, but again membership was massively lower in the more recent cohort. Across all social class levels, and at all levels of qualification, experience of membership never exceeded two-fifths for the men or women born in 1970 and in most cases, was a long way below that, at one-third or one-quarter. In contrast, at the upper levels of the occupational scale in the 1958 cohort, two-thirds had been members of a trade union at some time, and the proportion barely dropped below two-fifths in any occupational group. These figures also showed a levelling off between economic status groups. Thus, those who were currently not working were only marginally behind the others in their experience of trade union membership. This suggests that current unemployment status usually meant absence of union membership, even though there had been membership of a union in the past.

Religion

The declining importance of religion, and in particular the Church of England, has been well documented (Wadsworth and Freeman 1983). No more than 10 per cent of the population regularly attended church on a

Sunday in 1989, a figure that declined to 8 per cent in 1998. People attending church were also more likely to be older members of the community, better educated and better off financially (Berkeley 1999).

In our surveys, 8 per cent of 42-year-olds and 5 per cent of 30-year-olds reported they attended a religious service every week. Taking a more generous definition of church attendance – those who followed any kind of religion and attended services within each month – figures still showed signs of declining participation over time, particularly among men and in the younger cohort. Among the 36-year-olds in the 1946 cohort, 21 per cent of men and 19 per cent of women attended a religious service at least once a month. For the 33-year-olds in the 1958 cohort, just 10 per cent of men and 20 per cent of women attended religious services at least once a month. Attendance by 30-year-olds in the 1970 cohort was lowest, at just 6 per cent of men and 10 per cent of women. Social class and qualification gradients were again apparent. Figures 10.3a and 10.3b show that the professionally skilled were the most likely to attend church, particularly in the 1958 cohort, and those in unskilled manual occupations were the least likely to attend. The most qualified were similarly the most likely to attend church. In the 1970 cohort, men with degrees showed the highest prevalence of all the qualification groups. Differences across family status and economic status groups showed no clear pattern in either the 1958 or 1970 cohort.

Political interest and participation

Political engagement, perhaps more than any other civic action, signifies the rights and responsibilities of citizenship. Most people, whatever their social background have in the past considered it a civic duty to vote – the exercising of a hard won right. This does not mean that their action is backed by strong interest in politics. Feelings of inability to change things and cynicism about motives of politicians are widespread, and, unlike voting, are likely to be strongly related to social class and education (Bynner and Ashford 1994). The interest here in comparing our three cohorts is whether these well-established relationships are breaking down.

Figure 10.3a *Attending religious services in a month in three cohorts by occupation group: men*

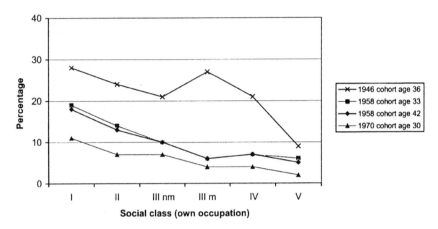

Figure 10.3b *Attending religious services in a month in three cohorts by occupation group: women*

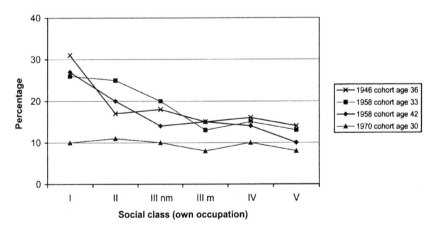

A number of questions were asked about political involvement. We first considered voting in the General Elections of 1997 (the 1970 cohort age 30, the 1958 cohort age 42), 1987 (the 1958 cohort age 33) and 1970 (the 1946 cohort age 26).[3] The second question concerned expressed 'political interest' measured at comparable ages, and the third, membership of a political party.

Confirming the heightened trends towards not voting in the 2000 General Election (too late to be covered by the survey) and especially among younger voters, voting in the election of 1997 was lower among 1970 cohort men and women, than among 1958 cohort men and women in either of the elections in 1997 or 1987. This points to a higher level of commitment to political participation among the earlier (1958) cohort than among the later (1970) cohort. However, against this conclusion, 26-year-olds in the 1946 cohort were more likely to report staying away from the voting booth in the 1970 election than were 33-year-olds in the 1958 cohort in the 1987 election. Surprisingly, gender differences were not apparent in these results.

There were marked social class and qualification gradients with respect to political involvement, particularly among the 1970 cohort at age 30. Figures 10.4a and 10.4b show that voting in the most recent election was substantially more common among the professional occupational groups than among the unskilled manual groups, with 77 per cent of 1970 cohort professional women and 71 per cent of professional men voting compared with 47 per cent of unskilled women and 41 per cent of unskilled men. Notably, professional men and women in the 1946 cohort at age 26 were *less likely* to have voted than professionals in either the 1958 cohort at ages 33 and 42, or the 1970 cohort at age 30.

Similar differences were apparent between the highly qualified and those without qualifications. Smaller gradients for the 1946 and 1958 cohorts suggested a more common commitment to voting across all classes and qualification levels in these generations than subsequently. The political voice of men and women who were part of a non-working household was also the least likely to be heard, with a third of this group in the 1958 cohort at both 33 and 42 not voting, and one half of the men and women in the 1970 cohort at age 30.

Figure 10.4a *Voting in a general election in three cohorts by occupation group: men*

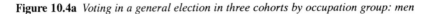

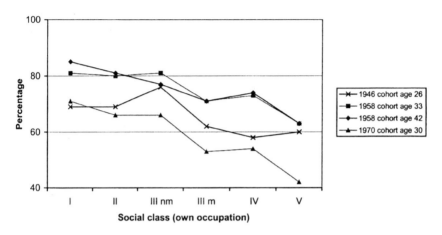

Figure 10.4b *Voting in a general election in three cohorts by occupation group: women*

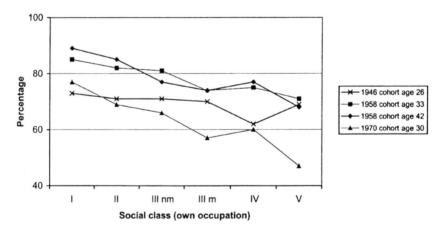

Political apathy, as shown by the increased proportions not voting, particularly in the latest cohort, was reflected further with respect to an interest in politics. 1958 and 1970 cohort members were asked to grade their political interest as 'very interested', 'fairly interested', 'not very interested' or 'not at all interested' in politics. A big difference was again apparent between cohorts when comparing the 33-year-olds in the 1958 cohort with the 30-year-olds in the 1970 cohort. In the 1958 cohort only 12 per cent of men and 18 per cent of women reported they were 'not at all interested' in politics compared with 26 per cent of men and 33 per cent of women in the 1970 cohort. Political interest also declined between ages 33 and 42 in the 1958 cohort, but remained above the level of the 1970 cohort (see Tables 10.1a and 10.1b).

Political interest was highest among professionals and least evident among the unskilled workers of both cohorts (Figures 10.5a and 10.5b). Just 2 per cent of professional men and women in the 1958 cohort at age 33 were 'not at all interested' in politics compared with a third of men and women in the unskilled occupational group. Comparable figures for lack of political interest in the 1970 cohort were 12 per cent for professional men, 18 per cent for professional women and over 50 per cent for unskilled men and women. There was much the same pattern across qualification levels with low interest concentrated in the groups without qualifications. With respect to family and economic status, female single parents and men and women who were part of a non-working household were the groups with the *least* interest in politics.

Even among the men and women who do vote and express an interest in politics, membership of a political party is very rare. In line with their increased disenchantment with the political process, this was lowest among men and women born in 1970. Just 3 per cent of men and 1 per cent of women had ever been a member of a political party. This compared to 6 per cent of 33-year-old men and 4 per cent of 33-year-old women born in 1958. By the time they were aged 42, membership had only increased among men to 8 per cent and to 5 per cent for women. Membership was highest among professionals and the most qualified.

Figure 10.5a *No political interest in two cohorts by occupation group: men*

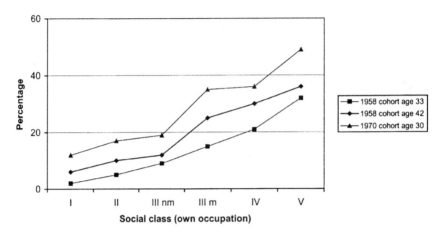

Figure 10.5b *No political interest in two cohorts by occupation group: women*

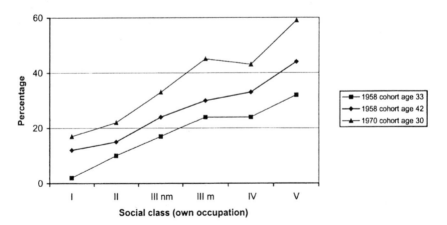

Self-image

The signs of increased disenchantment with politics and community participation appear to support Putnam's thesis of a decline in associational life and civic values across the generations. Perhaps even more notable, however, is the concentration of this breakdown in particular groups. Those without qualifications and those in unskilled or semi-skilled manual occupations were disengaging to the greatest extent. This offers support to the social exclusion thesis about the negative impact on active citizenship in a world dominated so much by the drive for skills and qualifications.

We followed these findings a stage further by examining cohort members' own views of what their lives were like. The 1958 and 1970 cohort were asked to indicate on a scale of 1 to 10 how 'satisfied they were with the way their life had turned out', and to answer three more specific questions on how they felt about their life. Each question had two options, as shown in Table 10.2.

Those at the highest occupational levels and those with degree-level qualifications consistently viewed their lives the most positively. Figures 10.6a and 10.6b show the differences for occupational status. Those in

Table 10.2 *Self-concept questions*

A. *I never really seem to get what I want out of life*
or
I usually get what I want out of life.

Also asked in the 1946 cohort at age 36 as,

Would you say that, on the whole, life has been good to you? Yes or No.

B. *I usually have free choice and control over my life*
or
Whatever I do has no real effect on what happens to me.

C. *Usually I can run my life more or less as I want to*
or
I usually find life's problems just too much for me.

Figure 10.6a *Belief that 'I never really seem to get what I want out of life' in three cohorts by occupation group: men*

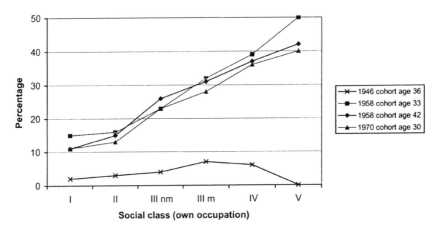

Figure 10.6b *Belief that 'I never really seem to get what I want out of life' in three cohorts by occupation group: women*

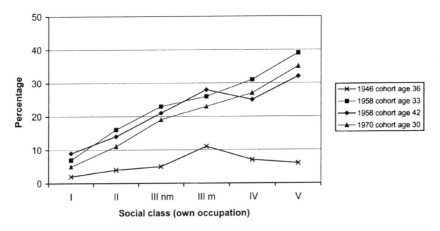

unskilled manual occupations or without qualifications viewed their lives the least positively. Women in the 1958 cohort at age 33 seemed particularly disenchanted with their lot. Men and women in the 1946 cohort seemed much more satisfied, though this may have been due to a difference in question wording.

Those members in the lowest social status groups in the 1958 and 1970 cohorts were also most likely to say 'whatever I do has no real effect on what happens to me' – around one-fifth with an unskilled occupation or without qualifications – compared with around one-twentieth of the professional classes. Even for the question 'I usually find life's problems just too much for me', around one in ten men and women with an unskilled occupation or without qualifications held this view about their own lives. For those with a degree or a professional occupation, figures ranged between 2 per cent and 5 per cent.

With respect to family status, couples without children seemed the most satisfied and content with their lives; single men, with or without children, and single women with children were the least happy. There was also a marked difference between those who were part of a non-working household and the rest, with half of men in either cohort and at each age belonging to a non-working household saying 'I never really seem to get what I want out of life'.

Attitudes and values

The figures for memberships and political engagement point to a startling degree of disengagement and alienation among certain groups and across cohorts suggesting a generational shift. A sense of personal alienation seems to be less cohort-specific and driven more by social and educational status. To what extent are these differences also reflected in differences in social and political values between the cohorts and across statuses? We are able to compare the 33-year and 42-year age group in the 1958 cohort with the 30-year-olds in the 1970 cohort. As in previous studies of cohort members' attitudes (Ferri 1993; Bynner *et al.* 1997), batteries of opinion statements were included in a self-completion questionnaire to tap different aspects of the same topic. In this section we examine six of these scales that reflect views about community and roles and relationships within it: political cynicism, left–right beliefs, support for authority, anti-racism, the work ethic and support for the environment. Table 10.3 shows the opinion items comprising each scale,[4] and Table 10.4 compares mean scores and variability around the means (standard deviations) on these scales across cohorts and across age groups for the 1970 and the 1958 cohorts. Full details of the research behind the scales are given in Bynner *et al.* (1997).

Cohort differences were again less evident in the values expressed in these scales than the reported changes in civic participation might have led us to expect, though there were some realignments of political positions. Thus, political cynicism was slightly higher among the 1970 cohort 30-year-olds, compared with the 1958 cohort 33-year-olds and at much the same level as the 1958 cohort 42-year-olds, i.e. cynicism appeared to be increasing across the generations, but was also growing with age. On the left–right scale of political beliefs there was a shift marginally towards the 'right' among the 1970 cohort members compared with those born in 1958. The 1970 cohort members at age 30 were also more supportive of authority than the 1958 cohort members had been at age 33, and showed most support for the work ethic. However, they were also the most anti-racist. There was virtually no difference for attitudes to the environment.

As in previous surveys, there were substantial gradients across social class, occupational and other status groups. Political cynicism was highest among the least qualified and least skilled groups, but only in the 1970 cohort. Cynicism was generally strongest among the lowest status groups, i.e. among single parents and among those in families where neither partner was working. Gender differences were marked, with women showing less cynicism than men.

Left–right political beliefs are typically associated with economic status. Those in the strongest economic position tending to be the most right wing; though women have also tended to lean more to the right than have men. The surveys confirmed these tendencies. Women tended to be

Table 10.3 *Opinion statements included in the attitude scales*

Political cynicism

None of the political parties would do anything to benefit me.

Politicians are mainly in politics for their own benefit and not for the benefit of the community.

It does not really make much difference which political party is in power in Britain.

Left–Right political beliefs

Big business benefits owners at the expense of the workers.

Private schools should be abolished.

Ordinary working people do not get their fair share of the nation's wealth.

Government should redistribute income from the better off to those who are less well off.

Management will always try to get the better of employees if it gets the chance.

The time has come for everyone to arrange their own private health care and stop relying on the National Health Service.

There is one law for the rich and one for the poor.

Support for authority

The law should be obeyed, even if a particular law is wrong.

People who break the law should be given stiffer sentences.

Young people today don't have enough respect for traditional British values.

For some crimes the death penalty is the most appropriate sentence.

Censorship of films and magazines is necessary to uphold moral standards.

Schools should teach children to obey authority.

Anti-racism

It is alright for people from different races to get married.

I would not mind working with people from other races.

I would not mind if a family from another race moved in next door to me.

I would not mind if my child went to a school where half the children were of another race.

Work ethic

Having almost any job is better than being unemployed.

If I didn't like a job I'd pack it in, even if there was no other job to go to.

Once you've got a job it's important to hang on to it even if you don't really like it.

Support for environmentalism

Problems in the environment are not as serious as people claim.

We should tackle problems in the environment even if this means slower economic growth.

Preserving the environment is more important than any other political issue today.

Note: Each statement was rated on a 5-point continuum from 'strongly agree' to 'strongly disagree'.

Table 10.4 *Attitudes to community roles and relationships: mean scores for men and women in the 1958 and 1970 cohorts*

		Men			Women		
		1958 cohort		1970 cohort	1958 cohort		1970 cohort
		Age 42	Age 33	Age 30	Age 42	Age 33	Age 30
Political cynicism	mean	3.23	2.85	3.25	3.12	2.81	3.08
	s.d.	(.85)	(.82)	(.80)	(.74)	(.74)	(.69)
Left–Right beliefs	mean	2.65	2.62	2.70	2.72	2.72	2.78
	s.d.	(.65)	(.72)	(.59)	(.56)	(.62)	(.51)
Support for authority	mean	3.71	3.54	3.63	3.74	3.60	3.71
	s.d.	(.66)	(.65)	(.61)	(.59)	(.58)	(.59)
Anti-racism	mean	3.87	3.72	4.01	3.95	3.84	4.17
	s.d.	(.71)	(.74)	(.73)	(.62)	(.63)	(.61)
Support for the work ethic	mean	3.39	3.31	3.46	3.30	3.14	3.40
	s.d.	(.79)	(.82)	(.81)	(.74)	(.76)	(.73)
Support for the environment	mean	3.64	3.66	3.60	3.63	3.67	3.56
	s.d.	(.66)	(.68)	(.66)	(.60)	(.61)	(.59)
N (100%)		5,537	5,142	5,389	5,744	5,406	5,727

Notes: All attitudes scores range between 1 to 5; s.d. = standard deviation; overall 'n' for the 1958 cohort at age 33 is the average number to answer all questions.

more right wing than men in both cohorts. Strong gradients were also evident across social class and qualification levels, with right-wing beliefs being more common at the top end of the social class scale and at the highest qualification levels. There were also signs of a widening gap between the top and bottom groups with respect to this attitude dimension in the more recent 1970 cohort, but only among the men. As we might expect, couples without children in both cohorts were likely to be more right wing than the others; single parents were the most left wing. Similarly, cohort members in the non-working households were more left wing than those in households where both partners were working. More notably, the ideological gap between these groups appeared to be widening across cohorts – but this time particularly among women.

We have noted signs of attitudes hardening against transgression particularly among those who have traditionally had the strongest commitment to 'law and order'. Mean scores on the support for authority scale were higher in 2000 than they had been in 1991. Those aged 42 in the 1958 cohort showed the strongest support for authority, followed by the 1970 cohort at 30 and the 1958 cohort at 33. Across the social class and qualification groups however, the relationships were not quite what might have been expected. At the higher occupational and qualification levels, men and women in both cohorts showed *least* support for authority. This may have been because of the 'authoritarianism' expressed through some of the scale items referring to obedience to authority, for example: 'The law should be obeyed even if a particular law is wrong'. The most educated were most questioning of obedience to authority on any terms.

Parents showed more respect for authority than those without children, particularly single men and women. With respect to economic status, single employed men and women showed the weakest support for authority, alongside men who were part of a non-working household.

Attitudes about race reflect more than anything views about community relations in the 'bridging' sense that Putnam (2000) considered so important as a defining factor of social capital. Overall women tended to be marginally less racist than men. The really large gradients occurred for social class and education, with the most qualified and the most occupationally successful having the strongest anti-racist attitudes. Couples with children were more racist in comparison to other groups; as were men with children and men with no partner in the 1958 cohort at ages 33 or 42.

In this case, there was no sign of increasing polarisation within cohorts, nor of rising racism across the generations as revealed by the overall mean scores. This tends to challenge the commonly held view that the potential for inter-racial conflict in Britain is increasing.

The work ethic showed a small gender difference in the 1958 cohort, with men having the stronger commitment to work, but this difference had almost disappeared in the 1970 cohort. With respect to social class and education, there was a similar result to one found earlier for 26-year-olds in the 1970 cohort (Bynner and Parsons 2000b). There was a marginally lower commitment to work for those with the *highest* qualifications and those with the *lowest* qualifications. In other words, relatively more of these two groups shared in common the rejection of work as being the most important thing in life. This 'u-shaped' relationship was not found for the 1958 cohort, where moving *down* through the occupational classes and qualification levels, the work ethic scores rose consistently. In other words those in unskilled occupations, and with the lowest qualifications, were the most committed to work. This suggests, for the more recent (1970) cohort, a possible turning away from work as the central feature of identity among some of those with the poorest opportunities for it. Such a conclusion can be seen as lending support to those who claim the emergence of an 'underclass' rejecting work values among the most socially excluded (e.g. Macdonald 1997).

The really large difference, however, related to the economic status of the family. Notably in families where no one was working, the work ethic was substantially lower than it was for any other group. This suggests that people in such families had reconciled themselves to a life of not working by shifting their values to reject the need for it. This gives more striking evidence for the 'emergent underclass' thesis. In other words, people who are most economically excluded will come, after time, to reject work as the basis of economic activity.

Finally, attitudes to the environment showed a more marked gender difference with women showing more environmentally friendly attitudes than men. The most notable finding, however, was a clear reversal in the relationship between environmental attitudes and the social class and qualification comparisons for men and women. The higher the social class of occupation and the higher the qualification level achieved, the *less* likely were men to express pro-environment attitudes. For women, the reverse was the case. Those in the highest social classes and at the highest qualification levels had the *top* environmentalist scores.

Crime and misconduct

An expected consequence of the decline in civic participation and the increasing evidence of polarisation and social exclusion is a rising crime rate. Twenty-seven per cent of the British population reported being a victim of crime in 2000 (Simmons 2002), and at the time of the British Crime Survey, just over one in 1,000 of the total population were currently serving a prison sentence (Home Office 2001). There have been numerous studies documenting the factors associated with offending, all of which point to disadvantage early in life as a critical factor (Wadsworth 1979; Farrington *et al.* 1996; Graham and Bowling 1995). A major theme running through this work is that accumulating risk factors, some possibly biologically based and others rooted in the adverse circumstances and experiences of early childhood, underpin the tendency to commit offences – supplying the foundations of the criminal career. Protective factors are to be found in the relationships between the growing child, the family and the school (Bynner 2001a).

The question arises as to whether the signs of disengagement in certain groups we have been observing are reflected in evidence of increased misconduct and law breaking, as social exclusion theorists would predict. We are limited to information collected up to age 21 for the 1946 cohort. Questions about crime were avoided for the 1958 cohort until the most recent survey, when both cohorts were asked about misconduct at school and *any* involvement cohort members had had with the police and the courts. Many of our comparisons are, therefore, restricted to the 1970 cohort members at age 30 and the 1958 cohort members at age 42. As such, any emerging cohort differences will need to be treated with a degree of caution, because of the possible confounding of age effects with cohort effects.

Age effects are, however, minimised when questions refer to behaviour at an earlier age, for example truanting when at school, or when questions start with '*have you ever*' ... [been arrested]? Since they were older, men and women in the 1958 cohort had more years to experience an event – (with the obvious exception of misconduct at school) and so they were, if anything, more likely to have had the experience. Notably, the substantial differences between cohorts in reported contact with the police or conflict with the law are in the opposite direction: far more men and women in the 1970 cohort reported experience of *each and every one of these measures of transgression* included in the survey. Given that most brushes with the law happen in the teenage years, or in the early 20s (Farrington 1996), even if the 1958 cohort had difficulties recalling events that happened further back in time, the differences between the cohorts were so large that this could not be the sole reason for them.

We need to acknowledge the well rehearsed criticism of self-reported methods for collecting information about offending. As is true of all self-report measures, there is a risk that respondents will adjust their answers to what they think is expected of them, which in this instance leaves only court records of actual offences to provide reliable data. However, Farrington (2001) challenges this view, demonstrating across a number of studies a remarkably high correlation between recorded and self-reported offences. He and other researchers also believe that self-report studies provide a more accurate estimate of crime than do official crime statistics, as they reveal large numbers who admit to committing some crime that has gone unrecorded, and that the amount of such 'hidden crime' is substantial (Bartol 1999; Youth Survey 2000). As an example, self-reported offending from a random sample of 14–25-year-olds in England and Wales showed that as many as 50 per cent of young men and 33 per cent of young women admitted to ever having committed an offence and 23 per cent of young men and 4 per cent of young women admitted to being found guilty of a crime by a court of law (Graham and Bowling 1995). Accordingly, we feel justified in placing confidence in the striking figures presented here.

Earlier signs of misconduct and alienation
The 1946 cohort finished compulsory full-time education in 1961, the 1958 cohort in 1974 and the 1970 cohort in 1986. Few members of the 1946 cohort admitted to 'sometimes' truanting from school, just 7 per cent of men and 4 per cent of women, whereas truanting was far more frequently reported, and equally common, in the 1958 and 1970 cohorts. Half of men

and two-fifths of women admitted they had 'sometimes' truanted. A social class and qualification gradient again emerged in all three cohorts, with truanting being more common among those from unskilled family backgrounds, in the lower occupational groups and among those at the lowest qualification levels. For example, in the 1958 and 1970 cohorts, a third of women who had a degree had truanted at some time compared with half of those without any formal qualification. No women with a degree in the 1946 cohort had truanted, compared with 8 per cent without qualifications. No real differences emerged between family status groups, but men and women in the 1958 and 1970 cohorts who were part of a non-working household were more likely to have truanted when they were at school compared to other economic status groups.

Twice as many of the 1970 cohort members acknowledged temporary suspension from school in comparison to those in the 1958 cohort: 15 per cent and 7 per cent respectively for men, 6 per cent and 3 per cent for women. Once again, the experience of temporary suspensions *increased* going down the social class scale (Figure 10.7) and qualifications ladder. Differences were much smaller among women, though again, insofar as there was experience of temporary suspension from school, it was

Figure 10.7 *Experience of temporary suspension from school in two cohorts by occupation group: men and women*

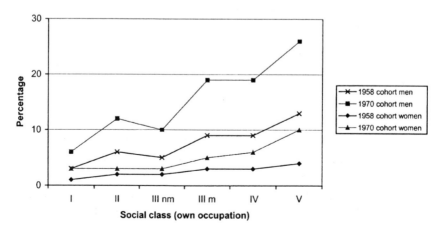

concentrated in the lowest social class and qualification groups. As with truanting, cohort members in both studies who were part of a non-working household were more likely to have experienced temporary suspension, as were single parents in the 1970 cohort (22 per cent men and 12 per cent women). Such figures should not be interpreted to mean that conduct problems at school *led* to a particular economic status and family status later. Rather, the social exclusion route was more common in these groups of adults, starting typically with an impoverished family background and poor educational achievements at school. Consequently, they tended on average to show more of the risk factors associated with offending.

Trouble with the police during adolescence and adulthood
Substantial cohort differences occurred in relation to reports of conflict with the law in adolescence and adulthood. The 1958 and 1970 cohorts were asked if they had ever been 'moved on by the police', 'stopped and questioned', 'let off with a warning', 'arrested', 'formally cautioned' or 'found guilty by a court of law', although the reason why, or the type of crime committed, was not asked. Figures 10.8a and 10.8b highlight the cohort differences occurring for men and women in the two more recent cohorts. As many as one in three men in the 1970 cohort said they had been moved on by the police at least once in their lives compared with just 6 per cent of the men in the 1958 cohort. These differences were repeated in answers to all the other questions. For example, one in three men in the 1970 cohort had been arrested, while one in four had received a formal caution or been found guilty in a court of law. No more than 8 per cent of men in the 1958 cohort reported ever having such contact with the law. In the 1946 cohort, figures for men reporting being convicted *or* formally cautioned for a criminal offence by the time they were age 21 were higher at 18 per cent.

As we might expect, the figures for women were much lower, but were still by far the highest among the 1970 cohort. For example, the police had moved on 6 per cent of women in the 1970 cohort at some time, compared with 1 per cent of women in the 1958 cohort. In the 1970 cohort 5 per cent of women had been formally cautioned while 4 per cent had

Figure 10.8a *Type of contact with the police in three cohorts: men*

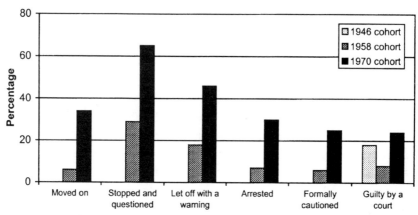

Type of police contact (data for 1946 cohort combines those
formally cautioned and found guilty by court of law)

Figure 10.8b *Type of contact with the police in three cohorts: women*

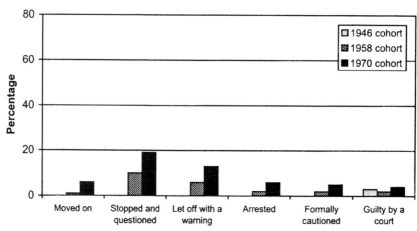

Type of police contact (data for 1946 cohort combines those
formally cautioned and found guilty by court of law)

been found guilty of a crime by a court of law. Comparable figures for women in the 1958 cohort were 2 per cent for either offence, while 3 per cent of women in the 1946 cohort reported they had been convicted of, or formally cautioned for, a criminal offence by the time they were aged 21.

The familiar social class and qualification gradients were apparent for men, but not so much for women. In the 1946 cohort, 10 per cent of men from a non-manual background had been convicted of or formally cautioned for a criminal offence by the time they were aged 21, in comparison to 19 per cent of men with a manual background. Examining social class in more detail, the gradient was much steeper among men in the 1970 cohort, with a heavy concentration of crime and police contact being evident among the least educated and most poorly skilled and disadvantaged groups. For example, four-fifths of unskilled male workers in the 1970 cohort acknowledged being stopped and questioned by the police, compared with half of men in professional occupations. The comparable proportions for the 1958 cohort were one-third of men with an unskilled manual job and one-quarter of professionals. In Figure 10.9, we can see a similar picture for men without qualifications. Far more of the 1970 cohort men than the 1958 cohort men had been arrested at some time in their lives – a gap which widened with lower qualification levels.

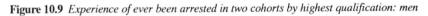

Figure 10.9 *Experience of ever been arrested in two cohorts by highest qualification: men*

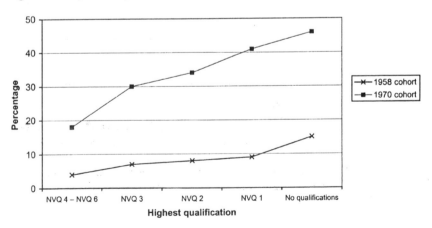

Reflecting the point made earlier about routes to socially excluded statuses, family and economic status were also associated with police contact. Brushes with the law, being arrested, receiving a formal caution or being found guilty in court, had all been more commonly experienced by men and women who were currently part of a non-working household. For example, in the 1970 cohort, 53 per cent of men and 16 per cent of women who were currently part of a non-working household had been arrested compared with 26 per cent of men and 3 per cent of women who were currently part of a double income household. These percentages were halved in the 1958 cohort. There was also a tendency for single parents in the 1970 cohort more frequently to report experience of early law breaking.

Conclusions

The figures presented in this chapter reveal a shift across the generations, which tends to support writers like Putnam (2000), who has claimed a dramatic collapse in social capital, and Atkinson (1998), who has stressed the increasing polarisation of society, with those in certain economic and social categories increasingly socially excluded. The overall decline in community activity, voting and other signs of civic participation, such as religious attendance, is clearly demonstrated by these data.

Putnam puts the 'generational shift' down to the pressures on families driven by the need for both partners to earn money, the expansion of the single lifestyle, the growth of what he calls 'suburbanisation', the replacement of live entertainment by television and most of all the generational shift away from civic values. Such conclusions reflect changes in the mean values for indicators of engagement across whole populations. Putnam makes less of the shifts in the distributional aspect of power and influence in society as reflected in such attributes as social class, education and gender. We have been at pains to stress the gradients in participation across groups defined by such attributes, with particularly low participation levels among the unskilled and the unqualified. As opportunities continue to diverge between those with the human capital that extended education bestows and those lacking it, we may expect the disengagement of the latter to become even more accentuated.

Lower levels of apparent satisfaction with life and expression of difficulties at these more disadvantaged levels, suggests that this disengagement does not lead to the positive benefits that membership of a distinct underclass might bestow. The poorly educated respondents, those in unskilled work, and those in households where both partners were unemployed, had clearly not come to terms with their disadvantaged position by shifting their feelings about themselves in positive directions as underclass theory would predict. Such individuals appear to be located in an excluded category of citizenship – which is under growing pressure as the increasingly globalised economy continues to transform at an ever-accelerating rate.

The signs of 'post-materialistic' rejection of work values among the professional classes, as Inglehart (1990) would describe it, and continuing and growing rejection of them among the disenfranchised, suggest a shift in these values – the long-term consequences of which are difficult to see. It may well be, of course, that a more relaxed and sceptical view of a mainstream value such as the work ethic is an essential part of engaging with a modern economy. If there is no certainty of an occupational future, whatever your educational level, then it is perhaps best not to sign up too heavily to work values. With respect to other kinds of value orientation towards the political system and in political beliefs, the modest shifts suggest that mainstream values are, by and large, standing up over the 12 years separating the two recent cohorts. The well-established gradients for them, however, across social class and education, do show signs of increasing in the more recent cohort. The 'excluded groups' do also appear to be farther apart from the others in their views than they were in the past. In one case, that of attitudes to the environment, there was also a major difference in the relationship of the value with class and education between women and men. The most educated women were the most environmentally aware, but the opposite was the case for men. The more educated the men, the less likely they were to be 'environmentalist'.

These relationships generally support the social exclusion argument by pointing to growing polarisation between the educational and occupational haves and have-nots. The only encouraging sign is that in the area where conflict is often assumed to be increasing, that of race, there is no sign of this happening. Anti-racist attitudes were, if anything, stronger among the most recent cohort and there is no sign of a growing divide between social groups in their expression. Social capital may be declining in one sense as Putnam defined it, but lack of social cohesion overall is not accompanying it, at least in this vital respect.

The most disturbing of our findings remain, however, the cohort shift in offending behaviour, including trouble with the law and court appearances. There is a much higher prevalence of these activities in the more recent cohort and a concentration in the most potentially excluded groups. Such experiences that were rarely reported in the past, especially among women, are now becoming increasingly common. It is as if a substantial and, perhaps, growing minority of the population is in conflict with mainstream society norms, or at least no longer cares if it appears to be. This might lead us to expect increasing support for authority among the best off. Notably, it is those at the bottom of the social scale who are the strongest advocates of 'law and order'.

The findings we have reviewed here leave as many questions unanswered as answered. The striking differences between the earlier and later cohorts in social participation, memberships and voting, and the trend towards offending, need to be pursued much further in more wide ranging analysis. They are reflected in national figures, which have led to the all-embracing policy response engineered by the Social Exclusion Unit to deal with problem of disadvantaged communities and disengaged youth (Social Exclusion Unit 1999a, b; 2000a, b, c, d). However, we still need to find out though which groups are losing interest in association most and what characterises those who continue to be interested in it. Who are rejecting the traditional values associated with work and community and who are retaining them? Most of all, we need to know more about the origins, mechanisms and consequences of social exclusion processes, their relation to offending, and how many people are able to resist them whatever their circumstances. The datasets provide an excellent vehicle for finding out.

Notes

1   Includes membership of a Charity/Voluntary Group (environment), Charity/ Voluntary Group (other), Women's Groups, Townswomen's Guild/Women's Institute etc., Parents/School Organisations, Tenants/Residents Associations.

2   Includes membership of a Charity/Voluntary Group (environment), Charity/ Voluntary Group (other), Women's Groups, Townswomen's Guild/Women's Institute etc., Parents/School Organisations, Tenants/Residents Associations.

3   'Ever' membership figures were not available for the 1946 cohort.

4   The 1958 and 1970 cohorts were aged 42 and 30 when surveyed in 2000, but were aged 39 and 27 when the 1997 General Election took place. Similarly, the 1958 cohort were aged 33 when surveyed in 1991, but aged 29 when the 1987 General Election took place. The 1946 cohort were aged 26 when surveyed in 1972, but aged 24 at the time of the 1970 General Election.

5   We used the statistical technique of factor analysis to test whether groups of items could be considered to relate to a particular attitude dimension and also whether there were sufficient numbers of them to measure this dimension reliably, i.e. to form an attitude scale.

11 Changing lives?

John Bynner, Elsa Ferri and Michael Wadsworth

We introduced this book reporting findings from the first three British birth cohort studies by considering the main features of 'half a century of change'. Since the end of the Second World War, Britain has undergone a series of transformations, each of which impacted on the economic and social context in which our cohort members grew up. The 1944 Education Act, and the establishment of the National Health Service in 1948, provided the underpinnings of a welfare state, in which opportunities were to be available for all and the stultifying effects of poverty, so prevalent before the war, would finally be eliminated. These optimistic hopes supplied some of the foundations of later affluence, echoed in Harold Macmillan's famous phrase – 'You've never had it so good'.

But the path to sustained economic achievement and improved quality of life for all was never an easy one. Economic upswings were followed by economic downturns – 'boom and bust' – and a growing belief that some of Britain's most long-standing institutions in the public and the private sector were inhibiting progress to the kind of world-class economy that technological transformation and globalisation were demanding. By the end of the 1970s, large areas of traditional industry were collapsing. The impact of the technological revolution that transformed employment in the 1970s and 1980s challenged fundamentally the social structures and institutions that had served Britain effectively in the past. Over the period covered by our cohorts, what had earlier been clear pathways to adult life dictated by gender, social class and local labour market prospects, were becoming increasingly blurred. The 'job for life', which had been the aspiration and expectation of so many, disappeared, to be replaced by the much more fluid notion of a 'portfolio career' in a labour market characterised by insecurity and uncertainty (Gershuny and Pahl 1994).

One consequence of the increasing risk and 'individualisation' of life chances was the growing problem of alienation and social exclusion of some individuals and groups unwilling, or, more typically, unable, to take advantage of new opportunities. Social capital was in decline and social cohesion was under threat. Government attention therefore moved increasingly towards improving the life chances of marginalised groups.

The findings we have presented in this book need to be viewed against this backcloth of social, political and economic change. Different governments bring new policy scenarios, which form an important part of the context of people's lives. New solutions are offered for old problems and new policy is shaped in response to new problems as they emerge. In interpreting our results, we have drawn attention to the role of these contextual features as factors in some of the striking continuities and discontinuities across the era embraced by the studies that our analysis has revealed.

Our approach has been to compare the situations of our cohort members at comparable ages to establish *cohort* effects that might be attributed to socio-economic change impacting differentially on people born at different times. These need to be set against *age* differences reflecting the different changes between the stages of life. The time when follow-ups took place added the third factor accounting for differences, that to do with the prevailing socio-economic context at the time of data collection – the *period* effect. At each age and stage when comparisons have been made we have also drawn attention to differentiation identified with key demographic factors. We examined, particularly, evidence of differences identified with gender, social class of origin and destination, family structure and family economic status. Such differences lie at the heart of the differential life chances to which a major part of the scientific and policy research agenda using the birth cohort studies is directed.

We have been able to demonstrate societal trends by comparing the lives of our cohorts across the 24-year gap separating their births. The striking differences between their experiences, as manifested in their adult lives, can be attributed in large part to the effects of social change. But there are also continuities. The effects of such social structural factors as social class, gender, education and family background, though waning in some areas of life, are as strong as ever in others. Their effects on people's life chances interact with the effects of social change, as revealed by our findings. Our analysis enables us to see the extent to which these sources of disadvantage and opportunity continue to prevail.

Throughout the book there have been certain recurring themes, coalescing around our findings. They include:

• Continuities and discontinuities across cohorts associated with socioeconomic change at different ages;

• The extension of the transition to adult life;

• Polarisation identified with gender, education, social class, family composition and economic position;

• The persistence of family social class as a driver of life chances;

• The growing importance of educational achievement and qualifications;

• Changes in the impact of gender;

• The growing role of risk, uncertainty and insecurity.

These feature strongly in the overview of findings that this chapter provides. We also set out some key elements of the research agenda that the cohort studies, enriched by the new data, enable us to address, and end by considering whether British lives are really changing and what this tells us about their likely shape in the new century.

Qualifications and opportunity

Over the decades covered by our cohorts, qualifications have increasingly been seen as the key to successful adult life. They carry a growing premium with employers in the modern labour market, so that without them, opportunities can be limited. Governments since the last war have invested increasingly in raising the levels of human capital in the population. This has meant expanding educational opportunities and, more recently, redirecting resources to ensure that previously excluded sections of society are able to take advantage of them.

The findings reported in Chapters 2 and 3 demonstrate the impact of these changes on our cohort members' lives and show how much their experience differed from that of their parents. From 1961 when the 1946 cohort reached the statutory minimum school leaving age of 15, to 1986 when the 1970 cohort reached the comparable transition point, one year older, there was a massive rise in staying on in education. The 40 per cent of the 1946 cohort who left without qualifications gave way to a proportion of close to 10 per cent in the later cohorts and, at the other end of the scale, the proportion gaining a degree quadrupled.

But these achievements were not evenly distributed. Those from the higher social classes were the most likely to be staying on to gain the highest qualifications. And those who had shown the most promise at the end of primary school were tending to monopolise the best qualification routes. These patterns were reasonably constant across cohorts and in the case of the 1958 cohort showed wider disparities later on. The best educated were those who continued taking courses, increasing their human capital even further. The big difference across cohorts was in the demographic profile related to gender. Women, whose qualification rates were substantially below those of men in the 1946 cohort, not only stayed on in education in higher numbers than men in the 1970 cohort, but had overtaken them with respect to gaining the highest level qualifications.

These changes reflected labour market shifts, which were leading to increasing spells of unemployment among men – due to changes in the nature of employment and economic cycles – and rising labour market participation by women. The employment career in women's case, however, was likely to embrace periods out of the labour market to have children and re-entry, often into part-time jobs. Such movement, however, was progressively postponed across the cohorts, as qualifications and career took precedence over family for larger numbers of women.

The jobs entered by our cohort members also reflected the wider labour market transformations. The manual work in manufacturing that dominated the employment prospects of men in the 1946 cohort had declined dramatically by the time the later cohorts were seeking jobs. But, again, the opportunities available were not evenly distributed: family background and qualifications were major factors, not only in getting the best jobs, but also in retaining them at times of unemployment. Again, women appeared relatively better protected against the vicissitudes of the changing labour market.

Affluence and polarisation

The findings for standards of living parallel those for qualifications and employment. Rising incomes and increased home ownership – at least between the 1946 and 1958 cohorts – were coupled with increasing disparity between those with the most, and the least, access to the educational and economic resources that are central to gaining them. In Chapters 2 and 3 we see rising skills levels reflected in the changing occupational structure and in the ever-higher qualifications required for entry into them. At the same time, those whose achievements were most limited – the 12 per cent who left education without qualifications and the further 10 per cent who left with only minimal qualifications – were increasingly left behind.

Those at the bottom end of the socio-economic scale manifested little evidence of the rising standards enjoyed by the majority. Their route to adulthood was still very much based on the tradition of early school leaving, entry into unskilled or semi-skilled employment and a patchy employment career. Their labour market participation tended to be characterised by low-grade jobs interspersed with unemployment. Poverty and disadvantage was the likely life experience throughout life for many, while the rising affluence of the majority passed them by.

Our findings give few grounds for optimism that these disparities are disappearing, or even diminishing. Despite rising education levels and rising affluence across the three cohorts, as reflected in earnings, better housing and home ownership, and improved prospects for women, the old polarities based on social class appear, if anything, to be strengthening. In one area of previously improving standards, the latest cohort as a whole is showing signs of a reverse. As Chapter 7 shows, the massive inflation in house prices was making the goal of owner occupation increasingly difficult to achieve. Chapter 6 shows even more starkly that relative poverty, defined as less than 60 per cent of median earnings was actually increasing across our cohorts.

This 'polarising effect' is particularly evident in connection with women's career opportunities and achievements. Across our three cohorts, there is evidence of a reducing gender gap in the levels of qualifications gained, the status of occupations entered and the earnings received. But at the same time the 'glass ceiling' remains in place, preventing women from achieving full labour market equality. Significantly, too, the improving opportunities for women were mainly evident among those at the top end of the education scale. Those at the bottom remained relatively more disadvantaged, tied to traditional female roles and responsibilities, and gaining little in terms of improved life chances. They were often taking the 'fast route' to adulthood, substituting early parenthood for labour market participation. Britain continues to have the highest teenage pregnancy rates in Western Europe (Social Exclusion Unit 1999a).

But such polarisation is not restricted to women. Chapter 2 reports that in all three cohorts boys left education at the minimum age in greater numbers than girls. Half of the boys in the 1970 cohort left education at age 16 and half of these left with minimal or no qualifications. The prospects for these young men could be in many cases as bleak, if not bleaker, than those of young women. The changing nature of the labour market that the three cohorts encountered meant a steady contraction in unskilled manual work and increasing insecurity in the jobs obtained.

One notable phenomenon associated with the reducing opportunities for these young men was the single lifestyle, driven more by poverty and insecurity than rational choice. As Chapter 4 shows, there were rising numbers of young men staying on in the family home and increasing numbers who had not formed partnerships and started their own families by age 30. In fact, the growing diversity of domestic patterns was one of the most striking features of the whole period from the late 1970s onwards that was in part a reflection of growing difficulties for the educationally disadvantaged in making the transition to adult life.

As we have seen, underpinning much of this increasing differentiation and polarisation is the ever-present influence of social class. Though 'social class of origin', based on the classification of parents' occupations, is, in many respects, an inadequate indicator of the distribution of power and achievement in society, the comparisons across its categories in the findings we have presented reveal widening gaps. Our findings on employment and earnings (Chapters 2, 3 and 6) demonstrate the role of education as a mediator of the effects of family background on later adult outcomes, while at the same time education serves to ameliorate adverse family effects. Thus, although social class and later earnings maintained much the same linkage in all three cohorts, in successive cohorts the links with educational achievement were strengthening.

Education thus provides the human capital resources for navigating the best possible pathway to adult life, as the lifelong learning policy agenda recognises. But the underlying class-based continuities remain. As our findings demonstrate, the family one is born into, and its location in the social structure, are as pervasive influences as ever in shaping individual lives. The conclusion we draw from the analysis of cohort differences is that with rising affluence generally, and the decline in unskilled and semi-skilled jobs, the gap in opportunities continues to widen. In this sense, social class, which at one time reflected an inclusive occupational structure, is now one of the main drivers of social exclusion.

The 'demise of the family'?

A prominent theme in social commentary and social policy over the last three decades of the twentieth century has been the widely reported breakdown in traditional family structures. In particular, this has centred on the supposed demise of the traditional 'nuclear' family, comprising a married mother and father and their biological offspring, living in a unit that remains intact until the children leave home to form families of their own. A further source of popular concern has been the fragmentation of the extended family, with the mutual support and obligations characterising relations between various kin and generations being eroded through increasing geographical and social distance.

The picture of partnership relations and parenthood experiences of our three cohorts, as reported in Chapters 4 and 5, strikingly demonstrates the increasing diversity and impermanence of family structure and family life. The relatively youthful marriages entered into by a high proportion of the 1946 cohort had been replaced in those born 12 or 24 years after by cohabiting partnerships, which tend to be established at later ages, and which may or may not lead to subsequent marriage. The age of cohort members when they had their first child also rose dramatically across the cohorts; and although women born in 1970 are still a long way from ending their period of fertility, it is likely that a higher proportion than in earlier cohorts will remain childless, or, for those consciously rejecting parenthood, child-free.

The other major change we demonstrate in the partnership and family arrangements of the three cohorts is their increasing fragility. Just as the 'job for life' has vanished from the labour market, so, too, the notion of a lifelong relationship has come to seem archaic. Partnership breakdown was a more frequent experience among successive cohorts, as was lone parenthood – predominantly involving mothers raising children on their own. However, the failure of one relationship appeared not to be a deterrent to re-partnership, and another increasingly common feature of family life in the younger cohorts was 'social parenting', in which children were being raised in homes in which one adult, usually the father figure, was not their biological parent.

The findings in other areas of the analysis contained in the book help to throw light on what underlies some of these trends in family life and personal relationships. What is most striking, perhaps, is the extent to which they are rooted in the changing position of women. For example, the delays in partnership formation and the transition to parenthood are strongly linked to the striking increase in the proportions of women entering higher education, obtaining qualifications and establishing themselves in the labour market. For these women, career paths do not fit easily with early partnership and parenthood. For those born in 1946, early marriage and motherhood were common, and expected for a large section of society. Relatively few women proceeded to higher education and a continuing professional career in place of marriage and childbearing was the exception rather than the norm. Discrimination in the workplace and subtle pressures from family and friends typically combined together to discourage ambition and to lock women into a primarily domestic role (Griffin 1985). However, among their sisters born just over two decades later early parenthood, rather than being socially sanctioned, became increasingly concentrated among the least advantaged. Those who were not successful in the education system, and who had ended up in the least attractive areas of the labour market, were the most likely to be pursuing the 'fast route' to adulthood. Early parenthood, often unsupported by a partner, now became characterised as a major problem category in social policy terms.

The educational and occupational advancement of women, which has been increasingly evident in the three birth cohorts, also offers a partial explanation for the seemingly inexorable rise in partnership breakdown. Unlike the majority of their mothers and grandmothers, the growing financial independence among women in the later cohorts means that economic considerations were less likely to force them to remain in unhappy partnerships. But this is only one element in a complex situation. In the latter half of the twentieth century, the economic and social role of marriage and family gave ground to its emotional aspects. This links with the rise of individualism, in which relationships are seen less in terms of social responsibilities and obligations and more in terms of personal resources and fulfilment. As the emotional dimension becomes more salient, the greater the potential for mismatched expectations and disillusionment. When competing demands of employment and domestic work put the relationship under further strain, break-up may seem the only solution.

Our findings have shown the highest levels of unhappiness and dissatisfaction with partnerships among the most recent of our cohorts and especially among women. One reason for this may lie in the continuing imbalance in the domestic roles of men and women, especially as parents. The move towards more egalitarian arrangements found among the dual earner families in the 1958 cohort in their 30s, appeared to have stalled when the 1970 cohort were compared at the same age. The huge increase in full-time employment among mothers of young children, combined with their continuing responsibility for home life, may well be putting pressure on both their own wellbeing and their relationships. The evidence from the cohort studies on the personal and social effects of the 'work/life balance' (or, more accurately, imbalance) gives strong support for policy measures to support parents and to encourage 'family-friendly' employment practices.

While the information on the cohort members' partnerships and family formation confirms the picture of change and uncertainty which has become familiar in recent years, our findings regarding their relationships with their extended family were rather less predictable. Here, there was more evidence of stability: there was no indication that the more recent cohorts had less contact with their own mothers and fathers, and, indeed, there appeared to be a greater degree of closeness to their parents. In both the 1958 and 1970 cohorts, their own parents were major providers of childcare for those with young children, and also, among the 1970 cohort, a source of financial and housing assistance.

However, the demographic changes in the cohorts' experience revealed in Chapters 4 and 5 also point to a new phenomenon in relation to family life – what might be described as the 'sandwiched generation'. The lengthening period of education and economic dependency means that the later cohorts, who delay having children until their late 30s or early 40s, are likely to have these children at home until they themselves are in late middle age. The analysis of housing circumstances in Chapter 7 indicated that the extended life transitions, combined with the massive rise in the cost of housing, put pressure on young people to remain in the family home for ever-extending periods. At the same time, the cohort members' own parents will be reaching old age and a period in their lives when they are becoming dependent and in need of care and support. These later cohorts are thus increasingly likely to become 'sandwiched' between the demands of the two adjacent generations, and unlikely to enjoy the extended period of freedom from dependency enjoyed by adults in the past.

Health and wellbeing

Comparison of the three cohorts in Chapters 8 and 9 shows that health in childhood improved considerably over the period covered by the studies, particularly in terms of survival of low weight at birth, growth in height and the reduction of social-class differences in growth in height. The improvements are likely to be the outcome of a combination of improvements in education, housing and nutrition, and in the reduction of poverty, as well as the result of improved preventive care and treatment of disease. Nevertheless, some degree of socio-economic gradient remains in childhood growth and in the risk of disease and death in childhood.

Health in adulthood builds on childhood health, and on lifestyles that are themselves a product of childhood behaviour styles, temperament and educational attainment, and peer group and family influences in adolescence and adulthood. Our cohort comparisons of adult health are limited by the measures currently available, but they show the extent of obesity increase, and the greater risk of obesity in those with least educational attainment and in the lowest social classes. Similarly there seems to have been a rise in depression and expressed anxiety from the first to the most recent cohorts, especially among women. As we show in Chapter 8, these problems continue to have highest prevalence in the manual social class and among those with low or no educational attainment. Thus, the economic and social effects manifested in increasing polarisation, are evident also in health, and constitute potential burdens, both for the individual and the state.

Early adult lifestyles in relation to health showed some improvement in comparisons between the three cohorts. Healthy behaviour such as exercise and consumption of wholemeal bread increased, and the proportion smoking fell. Our findings presented in Chapter 9 show that some of these improvements increased with age, for example, in relation to smoking, but others, such as exercise, showed an age-related decline. In health therefore, perhaps more than in any other domain, we see age-related pressures associated with ageing, which may override in negative or positive directions the cohort effects associated with social change.

In the case of some adverse health-related behaviour, there is clear evidence of cohort effects. Consumption of fatty foods appeared to be increasing in the later cohorts. There were also more frequent reports of perceived problems with alcohol, and of greater quantities of alcohol being drunk, particularly by women. Men drank less as they got older but women drank more. Again, the comparisons show that adverse health-related behaviour, such as smoking and heavy drinking, was most prevalent in the most vulnerable and potentially excluded parts of society, namely those in households with no earner, and those living alone, particularly as single parents. The notable exception is in alcohol consumption by women, which was highest in those in non-manual occupations and among those with higher educational qualifications.

Analyses using cohort study data have demonstrated that such outcomes in early adulthood are the product of long-term life course processes, beginning even before birth and reflecting a continuous interaction between individual biology and environment – part physical, part social. The positive benefits of social policy interventions such as the National Health Service, the Clean Air Acts and other means of producing a healthy environment are detectable in our analyses, but need to be set against the stresses of modern living.

These issues illustrate the complexity of formulating health policy. While an increase in educational attainment has been shown to be associated with improvements in health and in health protective lifestyles, our findings suggest that it is not necessarily so, as others have also found. Similarly, while a general reduction in poverty and an increase in non-manual employment were associated with improved conditions at home and at work, they also brought greater risk of a sedentary lifestyle and the kind of malnutrition that results in obesity. And while greater opportunities for social and geographical mobility offer opportunities to improve many aspects of adult life over that of one's parents, they seem not to have greatly reduced the risks associated with perceived and relative social isolation and exclusion.

Continuing work within these cohorts, and comparisons between them, offer health policy the opportunity to see the health profiles and trends in these three future generations of the elderly before they arrive at retirement.

Strains on the social fabric?

The impact of individually pursued affluence and personal lifestyle also helps to explain the other major area in which change of dramatic proportions has been revealed – the decline in civic participation, as reflected in membership of community associations and trade unions, church attendance and voting. As Chapter 10 reports, the later cohorts showed substantial reductions in all these activities and a much lower level of interest in the political process than was the case in the past. Declining levels of involvement were also accompanied by widening differentials *within* cohorts. Thus, again, all indicators of civic activities and interest showed a rise in prevalence across social class and qualification levels. But those with the poorest qualifications showed the least involvement and interest, and their counterparts with the highest educational achievement showed the most engagement.

There are strong signs of a major opting out of civic society by substantial minorities – typically among those most excluded from the rising affluence and achievement which are enjoyed by the rest. Couples living in non-working households, and single parents, showed the strongest signs of alienation from mainstream civic activity. This applied even in relation to activities like voting, which in the past was more readily seen as a public duty accepted by almost everybody.

We pursued this theme of civic breakdown in terms of declining 'social capital', and its impact on identity, as weakening the underpinnings of cohesive societies (Baron *et al.* 2000). Certainly, the findings give some support to social analysts like Robert Putnam (2000) who claim such breakdown is happening. Positive feelings of wellbeing and self-efficacy are declining. But again, it is the inequality and disparity between different groups that is the most striking feature of the changes. Feelings of self-worth were lowest among the most marginalised groups. On the other hand, there were few signs of rising potential for overt social conflict in the attitudes expressed. Racist attitudes have declined, while overall support for law and order has increased.

Finally, the most negative side of social breakdown and individualism is crime. Chapter 10 reveals startling rises in the evidence of conflict with the criminal justice system, beginning early in life and extending into adulthood at higher levels in the most recent cohort than was the case for the earlier ones. Again, these indications of offending were not evenly spread across all social and educational groups, but concentrated among the lowest achievers. Surprisingly, those most concerned about crime, in terms of demanding more support for 'law and order', were not the high achievers – who tended to reject the idea of unquestioning obedience to authority – but those at the bottom of the educational and social class scales. These groups are, of course, in terms of geographical and social location, often the most vulnerable to the effects of crime.

The studies in retrospect

We embarked upon these cohort comparisons knowing that the histories of each study were quite different, driven by different funding criteria and following different design strategies. Although all three cohort studies began as health-policy driven investigations, this has not been the case for all of them subsequently. Since 1962, the Medical Research Council has supported the 1946 cohort study as a study of health and ageing, and support has also been received from a range of funders. The 1958 cohort study has been supported throughout its life on a rather sporadic basis, mainly by government departments and the Economic and Social Research Council. The 1970 cohort has had, until relatively recently, an even more precarious existence, moving between government and research council support and reliance on charitable donations. More recently, the ESRC has taken a responsibility for the continuation of both the 1958 and 1970 cohort studies, and funding has been given by the Medical Research Council for measurements of health in the 1958 cohort study.

The frequency of surveys and their coverage reflect the different funding interests and the different scientific programmes they address. It comes therefore, as quite an achievement that we were able to find so much common ground in attempting to compare them. At one level this success reflects the essential continuities of the critical factors in the construction of the human life course and the way the life course is characterised. At another level, it points to the perennial questions thrown up by the policy process which seeks ways of improving standards of living and of health, and reducing inequalities.

At the same time, we cannot deny that sometimes the data for comparison were missing, or the form of questioning to elicit the required information was different from one study to another. We have drawn attention to these anomalies where they might be important in interpreting a particular finding or findings. Rather in the nature of cross-national research, when data do not exist in precisely the same form for the subject under consideration, we have had to resort to 'functional equivalence' of the variables involved in cohort comparison to justify the conclusion reached.

Apart from these necessary qualifications, we remain confident that our main conclusions regarding continuity and discontinuity are robust. Above all, the three cohorts show the long reach of childhood and early family circumstances into adult life. The nature and experience of childhood changed considerably over the period covered by the studies, and so the comparisons between the cohorts, as described in the preceding chapters, reflect the different effects that those changes brought to subsequent adult life.

But, at the same time, we also confirm that in certain respects the ties with family of origin are weakening. While social class continues to have its pervasive effect on adult life chances, the role of educational achievement appears in certain respects to be overriding it. Moreover the more fluid nature of the life course with respect to employment careers and family life, place much greater emphasis on individual resources and capabilities in determining the way the life course is constructed. This is why continuing opportunities for education through the lifelong learning policy agenda are an important part of reducing social inequalities. Many individuals encounter obstacles to satisfactory life chances. But social exclusion in adulthood is no longer the inevitable consequence; provided that the door to educational opportunities is kept continually open, and the resources are in place to enable everybody, not just the educationally best qualified, to take advantage of them.

The research agenda

The cross-cohort comparisons reported in this book have been primarily descriptive, pointing to socially differentiated effects relating to social change, age and period differences, rather than to the life course processes that underlie them. Gaining understanding of these processes is where the three British birth cohort studies, which have been the subject of this book, have such a major part to play. There are no other longitudinal research resources anywhere else in the world that encompass the lifespan from birth to adulthood and reflect, through their size, geographical coverage and representativeness, a whole society in transformation. The data from the new surveys enhances the potential for analysis even further. We can now trace the course of life from birth to age 54 in the earliest of our cohorts, and can observe the course and outcomes of the transition to adult life in all three. The findings we have reported give pointers to the kind of research agenda that can be pursued.

Life course trajectories
In this book we have compared temporal slices of different trajectories in education, employment, earnings, family life, health and citizenship. A central task for the future is to determine both the full course of these trajectories over the lifespan and how they vary across cohorts in response to societal change. The biographical (event history) information the studies contain on education, employment, housing, partnership and health supply the means of doing this.

Shaping and outcomes of transition
The next tasks, which follow from the first, are to establish the foundations of the trajectories; to show how they are subsequently shaped, and to ask what triggers the different transitions in them and determines their outcomes. Answers to these research questions embrace identification of the biological and social components of life course processes. They also direct attention to interactions between domains, such as the family and health. The breadth of information the studies contain offers exceptional

opportunities for theoretical insights founded on comprehensive modelling of hypothesised causes and effects.

Vulnerable groups

Throughout the book, we have stressed differential life chances for
different groups with evidence of greater polarisation across successive
generations since the last war. There is much to be done in uncovering
more precisely what constitutes disadvantage and vulnerability and identifying those who are able to overcome their effects. The large size of the
birth cohort studies offers opportunities to examine the lives of particular subgroups ranging from children growing up in difficult family circumstances, in different parts of the country, to the physically and men-
tally disabled. There are opportunities to model prospectively the likely
consequences of particular conditions early in life and to model retro-
spectively the pathways of 'risk and protection' leading to particular outcomes in adulthood.

The policy dimension

Finally, a key component of societal change is economic and social
policy. As we have stressed throughout the book, each cohort has experienced, at critical formative stages in their lives, a different policy regime.
The development of the National Health Service improved particularly
the circumstances of birth and early life; the transformations of the welfare
state changed the nature of the safety net designed to protect individuals
and families against the ravages of unemployment and poverty; the reform
of the school curriculum and qualifications system, and the targets for
raising standards and levels of participation, reflected the changing nature
of the labour market that young people were entering and the resources
they needed to make successful transitions to adult life. In experiencing
each of these policy contexts at different stages of life, our cohort studies,
rather in the nature of 'natural experiments', offer the opportunity for gaining powerful insights into the ways the policies were working. They also
offer pointers to gaps in existing provision and the need for new policies
in response to old and emerging problems.

In our survey findings we have seen signs of what life in the new century will be like. Has Britain changed? Is Britain changing? Certainly, the optimism following the last war now rests on much shakier foundations. There is generally a much higher standard of living; but there are no signs of greater equality in our society, rather the reverse. There is more of all forms of capital available – economic, human, and social – but a substantial minority fails to gain full access to them. The consequence, as we have seen, is increasing polarisation and social exclusion.

There are many manifestations of such social exclusion, of which perhaps the most disturbing concerns our evidence on offending. The shadow of rising crime appears to be a highly specific phenomenon associated with the experience of our most recent cohort. Our data suggest that policy makers are right to give so much attention to combating social exclusion and its effects. Its prevalence is likely to continue to grow while inequality under the conditions of the modern world continues to increase. The consequence is a crumbling social fabric, which enlightened policy is in a position to reverse. Maintenance of social cohesion for the coming generations, therefore, presents the major policy challenge.

The government's 'Neighbourhood Renewal' and 'Health of the Nation' agendas already acknowledge the need for intervention (Social Exclusion Unit 2000a). But, in targeting such policies and initiatives at those who need them, it is important not to lose sight of the dynamics of individual lives and the impact of societal change, whereby vulnerability to exclusion can occur at any time and in a variety of forms.

These indications of the required policy scenario rest on the foundations of sound, empirically based descriptions of changing lives in a changing Britain across a 24-year period. As we have argued, to gain a proper understanding of what is likely to be most effective, when, and with whom, we need much more research on the mechanisms and processes of success and failure in an increasingly complex, changing world. Investigation of the interactions of the effects of social change with the development of individual lives will continue to drive research using the cohort study data in the years to come.

Appendix 1: Summary descriptions of the three studies

The MRC National Survey of Health and Development (1946 cohort – NSHD)

The population

The 1946 birth cohort study began as a national study of health, survival, health care, and the cost of having a baby. All the births in one week in England, Wales and Scotland in March 1946 (16,695) were included in the scope of the study, and information was collected on 13,687 (Joint Committee 1948). Dr J.W.B. Douglas, who had designed and carried out the births study, then designed and undertook a follow-up study of a class-stratified sample comprising 5,362 of the births studied. That sample was selected from the single births to the married (12,930, 77 per cent of all the births in the one week). Multiple births were excluded being thought too few for follow-up (180), and since almost all births to the unmarried (672) were adopted they could not be traced for follow-up. From the population in scope a sample was taken comprising a random one in four of those whose fathers were in manual employment, and all those whose fathers were in non-manual or agricultural employment, a total of 5,362. That population forms the sample studied in the MRC National Survey of Health and Development, referred to throughout this book as the 1946 cohort, and it has been studied ever since. Results from analyses reported here that use data from the 1946 cohort are weighted to account for the sampling procedure by multiplication by the denominator (4) of the sampling fraction.

Participation

Information has been collected from the whole follow-up population on 21 occasions, and from cohort members who were parents of first children born between 1965 and 1971, that is at cohort ages 19–25 years. A study of women's health has been undertaken in annual data collections from all women cohort members from 1993–2000. Contacts and topic areas are summarised in Table A1.

Methods and coverage

During childhood and adolescence mothers and cohort members responded to questions and requests for measurement from health professionals (school doctors and nurses, health visitors), educational professionals (teachers), and youth employment officers. In early adulthood (19–25 years) information was collected by health visitors and by postal questionnaire, and at age 26 years professional interviewers employed by Social and Community Planning Research (trained by them and by the research team) collected information. In adulthood at ages 36 and 43 years information was collected by our own team of research nurses who also measured cohort members, and at 53 years by a team of research nurses employed by the National Centre for Social Research (trained by them and the research team). Information for the study of first-born offspring was collected by our own team of interviewers, and was also provided by teachers. Information for the study of women's health was collected by postal questionnaire.

The primary concern is with health. Measures of growth and development, and of cognitive function and educational attainment were made throughout childhood and the school years. From age 36 years onwards measures of physical function (e.g. blood pressure, respiratory function, musculoskeletal function, cognitive function) have been made, together with the use of inventories to measure anxiety and depression and the collection of data on health-related habits (smoking, diet, exercise and alcohol intake). Information on illness and death has been collected throughout. The current concern is with the processes of ageing and with health in middle life, and the study of their precursors. Information on the home and family context, and on occupation and socio-economic circumstances has been collected throughout.

Representativeness

A description of the extent to which the study sample at age 43 years represented the population of England, Wales and Scotland of a similar age is given in Wadsworth *et al.* 1992 and Wadsworth *et al.* in press.

Key publications that describe the study

Douglas, J.W.B. (1964) *The Home and the School*. London: MacGibbon and Kee.

Douglas, J.W.B. and Blomfield, M. (1958) *Children Under Five*. London: Allen and Unwin Ltd.

Douglas, J.W.B., Ross, J.M. and Simpson, M.R. (1968) *All Our Future*. London: Peter Davies.

Joint Committee (1948) *Maternity in Great Britain*. Oxford: Oxford University Press.

Kuh, D.J. and Hardy, R.J. (2002) *A Life Course Approach to Women's Health*. Oxford: Oxford University Press.

Wadsworth, M.E.J. (1991) *The Imprint of Time*. Oxford: Oxford University Press.

Wadsworth, M.E.J. and Kuh, D.J. (1999) 'Childhood influences on adult health: a review of recent work from the British 1946 national birth cohort study, the MRC National Survey of Health and Development'. *Paediatric and Perinatal Epidemiology*, 11, 2–20.

Wadsworth, M.E.J., Mann, S.L., Rodgers, B., Kuh, D.J.L., Hilder, W.S. and Yusuf, E.J. (1992) 'Loss and representativeness in a 43 year follow up of a national birth cohort'. *Journal of Epidemiology and Community Health*, 46, 300–4.

Wadsworth, M.E.J., Butterworth, S., Hardy, R.J., Kuh, D., Richards, M., Langenberg, C., Hilder, W.S. and Connor, M. (in press) 'The life course prospective design: an example of benefits and problems associated with study longevity'. *Social Science and Medicine*.

Our website gives references to all publications and further details of recent and current work.

Website addresses: www.nshd.mrc.ac.uk *and* www.ucl.ac.uk/epidemiology

Table A1 *Follow-up of contacts made with the 1946 cohort after the initial birth survey*

Year	Age in years	Respondent[a]	Data collector[a]	Location	Target sample[b]	Achieved sample (% achieved)	Topic areas[e]
1948	2	Mother	HV	Home	4,993	4,689 (94%)	H M PH
1950	4	Mother	HV	Home	4,900	4,700 (96%)	H M PH
1952	6	Mother & child	SD	School	4,858	4,603 (95%)	H M PH
1953	7	Mother & child	SN or HV	School	4,838	4,480 (93%)	H M
1954	8	Mother & child	SN or HV & T	School	4,826	4,435 (92%)	H M E T
1955	9	Mother & child	SN or HV & T	School	4,807	4,181 (87%)	H M
1956	10	Child	T	School	4,811	4,077 (85%)	E
1957	11	Mother & child	SN or HV SD T	School	4,799	4,281 (89%)	H M E T
1959	13	Child	T	School	4,794	4,127 (86%)	E
1961	15	Mother & child	SN or HV T	School	4,790	4,274 (89%)	H M E T PH
1965	19	All CMs	HV	Home	4,741	3,561 (75%)	H
		Mothers of 1st born	I	Home	c		H E
1966	20	All CMs	P	Home	4,715	3,899 (83%)	H
		Mothers of 1st born	I	Home	c		H E
1967	21	Mothers of 1st born	I	Home	c		H E

Year	Age	Sample	Contact	Location	N	Response	Data
1968	22	All CMs	P		4,634	c	H
		Mothers of 1st born	I	Home		3,885 (84%)	H E
1969	23	All CMs	P		4,518	c	H
		Mothers of 1st born	I	Home		3,026 (67%)	H E
1970	24	Mothers of 1st born	I	Home		c	H E
1971	25	All CMs	P	Home	4,446	c	H
		Mothers of 1st born	I			3,307 (74%)	H E
1972	26	All CMs	I	Home	4,410	3,750 (85%)	H T PH
1977	31	All CMs	P		4,293	3,340 (78%)	H ,
1982	36	All CMs	RN	Home	3,863	3,322 (86%)	H MF PH
1989	43	All CMs	RN	Home	3,839	3,262 (87%)	H MF PH AT
1993–2000	47–54	Women	P			d	H
1999	53	All CMs	RN	Home	3,673	3,035 (83%)	H MF PH AT

a HV = health visitor; SN = school nurse; SD = school doctor; T = teacher; P = postal contact; I = interviewer; RN = research nurse; CM = cohort member

b Excludes the dead, those living abroad, and permanent refusals

c 1,676 mothers were interviewed in the study of 1st born offspring, with a response rate of 94%

d This postal questionnaire was sent annually between 1993 & 2000 to all women cohort members, with response rates of 84–90%

e Demographic information was collected at all contacts. H = health & survival; M = measures of physical growth & development; E = education including behaviour at school; T = cognitive & educational tests; PH = parental health & survival; MF = measures of physical function; AT = adult cognitive tests

National Child Development Study (1958 cohort – NCDS)

Population

This study began with a perinatal mortality study of 17,000 births in a single week in March 1958 directed by Neville Butler. The whole cohort was followed up subsequently at ages 7, 11, 16, 23, 33 and, most recently, 42 (Davie *et al.*, 1972; Ferri 1993; Shepherd 1995). A number of specialised follow-up studies have also been carried out, e.g. of people revealing respiratory illness symptoms in the 23- and 33-year surveys, and of people identified as suffering particular disadvantages in early childhood followed up qualitatively in adulthood. In the age 33 survey the children of a one-third sample of cohort members were selected for a special study sponsored by the US National Institute for Child Health and Development. The children completed a battery of tests adapted for use in Britain from tests used in the US *National Longitudinal Survey of Youth*. Detailed information was collected from their mothers about the children's development. Another subsequent contact with cohort members involved a 10 per cent representative sample survey sponsored by the Basic Skills Agency (a UK Government agency) of 1,700 cohort members, when the cohort members were 37 (Bynner and Parsons 1997; Parsons and Bynner 1998). A medical follow-up of the cohort funded by the Medical Research Council with fieldwork due to start in July 2002 is currently in preparation.

The reference population is defined as those living in Great Britain at the time of each survey born in Great Britain during the reference week in 1958. Tracing of survey members between sweeps 1–3 took place through school records and the National Health Service Central Register. In the first three follow-ups, when the cohort members were all still at school, immigrant children, born in the same week, were added to the survey sample. Through adulthood tracing has been undertaken through existing address records and updated through an annual birthday card.

As Table A2 shows, the participation rate for a longitudinal survey of this kind has remained high, with 11,419 taking part in the most recent survey at age 42. Checking the distribution of birth characteristics, such as family social class in this 'achieved sample' with the distribution of the same characteristics in the sample at birth, shows relatively little bias. There is a small tendency for more women than men to continue to participate and for the most educationally disadvantaged to leave the study.

Participation

Table A2 *NCDS follow-ups and sources of information 1958–2000*

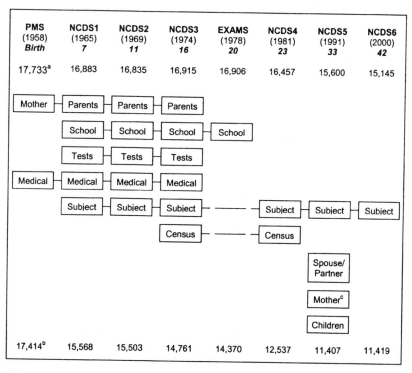

PMS (1958) Birth	NCDS1 (1965) 7	NCDS2 (1969) 11	NCDS3 (1974) 16	EXAMS (1978) 20	NCDS4 (1981) 23	NCDS5 (1991) 33	NCDS6 (2000) 42
17,733[a]	16,883	16,835	16,915	16,906	16,457	15,600	15,145
Mother — Parents — Parents — Parents							
	School — School — School — School						
	Tests — Tests — Tests						
Medical — Medical — Medical — Medical							
	Subject — Subject — Subject ————— Subject — Subject — Subject						
		Census ————— Census					
					Spouse/ Partner		
					Mother[c]		
					Children		
17,414[b]	15,568	15,503	14,761	14,370	12,537	11,407	11,419

Notes:
a: Target sample – immigrants with appropriate date of entry to the study
b: Achieved sample – at least one survey instrument completed
c: This could be the cohort member, their spouse, or partner

Method and coverage

The method and coverage of data collection in each survey depended on the stage of life the cohort members had reached (Table A2). Thus during the cohort members' childhood, parents, teachers and head teachers were the main sources of information and the children were tested. By age 16, cohort members themselves provided much of the information and through adulthood. Partners of cohort members were also questioned at age 33. From age 23 data have been collected by survey interview, most recently at age 42 using Computer Aided Personal Interviewing (CAPI). Family background, cognitive and behavioural development and educational achievement, were the main focus in the school years; vocational education and training, employment, family formation and parenting, health and social and political participation and attitudes, gained prominence in adulthood. Supplementary data from the 1971 census were incorporated in the 16-year follow-up and from the 1981 census in the 23-year follow-up. School leaving examination results were collected from schools at age 21. In the 33- and 42-year surveys, a substantial battery of social attitude and other self-assessment measures was also included.

1970 British Cohort Study (1970 cohort – BCS70)

Population

BCS70 follows a similar pattern to NCDS. It began with a birth survey of the 17,000 babies born in a week in April 1970. Data were collected subsequently at ages 5, 10, 16, 26 and, most recently, 30 (Butler *et al.* 1985; Bynner *et al.* 1997). Paralleling the comparable NCDS basic skills survey, a 10 per cent sample survey of 1,640 cohort members sponsored by the Basic Skills Agency focusing on basic skills, was carried out at age 21 (Ekinsmyth and Bynner 1994; Bynner and Steedman 1995). A postal survey of the cohort was carried out at age 26 and a full interview survey coordinated with the 42-year NCDS survey (using a common CAPI instrument) was carried out at age 30.

Tracing of cohort members was more limited than in NCDS until 1991 when the same procedures were instituted for both cohort studies (annual birthday card between-survey tracing). Though the study was more ambitious in data coverage, in some respects than NCDS, this has to be set against a poorer response rate, particularly in the 1986 (age 16 survey), which took place during a teachers' industrial action and produced much reduced numbers for some instruments (Table A3). With the most recent surveys conducted in 1999/2000, the study has now been restored to much the same response level as NCDS, with 11,261 cohort members responding at age 30. As for NCDS, the biases in this obtained sample are fairly minimal.

Table A3 *BCS70 follow-ups and sources of information 1970–1999*

BBS (1970) Birth	CHES (1975) 5	CHES (1980) 10	Youthscan (1986) 16	BCS70 (1996) 26	BCS70 (2000) 30
Mother	Parents	Parents	Parents		
		School	School		
	Tests	Tests	Tests		
Medical	Medical	Medical	Medical		
		Subject	Subject	Subject	Subject
16,135[a]	13,135	14,875	11,628	9,003	11,261

Note:
a: Achieved sample – at least one survey instrument partially completed

Methods and coverage

During the school years, methods of data collection were similar to those of the NCDS with data collected from parents (by health visitors), teachers and head teachers up to age 10. At ages 10 and 16 there were also medical examinations conducted by doctors. At age 16, dietary and leisure diaries were also used alongside a battery of self-completion questionnaires to assess behavioural and psychological attributes. Coverage was wider than in the NCDS with the medical focus at birth broadening to encompass physical, cognitive and behavioural development at age 5; physical, educational and social development at age 10 and 16; and physical, educational, social and economic development at the age of 26. In adulthood the questioning has largely converged with that of the NCDS, with the study spanning all the main domains of adult life: education, employment, housing, family formation, health, citizenship and values.

Table A4 shows the response rates in the 1999–2000 surveys for both the NCDS and BCS70 cohorts.

Table A4 *BCS70 and NCDS response rates in 1999/2000 surveys*

	BCS70			NCDS		
	No.	Yield (%)	% of those contacted	No.	Yield (%)	% of those contacted
Initial sample	**16,108**	**100**		**15,147**	**100**	
Total contact made with cohort member*	*12,823*	*79.6*	*100*	*12,853*	*84.9*	*100*
Total refusals	*1,178*	*7.3*	*9.2*	*1,196*	*7.9*	*9.3*
Total other reasons for non interview with cohort member**	*384*	*2.4*	*3.0*	*237*	*1.6*	*1.8*
Total interviews achieved	*11,261*	*69.9*	*87.8*	*11,419*	*75.4*	*88.8*
Full interview + self-completion	11,116	69.0	86.7	11,282	74.5	87.8
Full interview, no self-completion	88	0.5	0.7	94	0.6	0.7
Long partial interview	15	0.1	0.1	7	0.0	0.1
Short partial interview	7	0.0	0.1	6	0.0	0.0
Proxy interview	35	0.2	0.3	30	0.2	0.2

* Main category of non-contact was movers who were untraced by the time of the survey.
** Mainly due to absence from home address at the time of the interview.

Key publications that describe the 1958 and 1970 birth cohort studies

Butler, N.R., Golding, J. and Howlett, B.C. (1985) *From Birth to Five: A study of the health and behaviour of a national cohort.* Oxford: Pergamon.

Bynner, J. (1993) *Use of Longitudinal Cohort Studies in the Policy Process.* London: Anglo German Foundation.

Bynner, J., Ferri, E. and Shepherd, P. (1997) *Twenty-something in the 1990s: Getting on, getting by, getting nowhere.* Aldershot: Ashgate.

Bynner, J., Goldstein, H. and Alberman E. (1998) 'Neville Butler and the British Birth Cohort Studies'. *Paediatric and Perinatal Epidemiology,* 12, suppl.1, 1–14.

Bynner, J. and Parsons, S. (1997b) *It Doesn't Get any Better: The impact of poor basic skills on the lives of 37 year olds.* London: Basic Skills Agency.

Bynner, J. and Steedman, J. (1995) *Difficulties with Basic Skills.* London: Basic Skills Agency.

Davie, R., Butler, N.R. and Goldstein, H. (1972) *From Birth to Seven.* London: Longman.

Ekinsmyth, C. and Bynner, J. (1994) *The Basic Skills of Young Adults.* London: Adult Literacy and Basic Skills Unit.

Ekinsmyth, C., Bynner, J., Montgomery, S. and Shepherd, P. (1992) *An integrated approach to the design and analysis of the 1970 British Cohort Study (BCS70) and the National Child Development Study (NCDS),* Inter-Cohort Analysis Working Papers 1, Social Statistics Research Unit, City University.

Falkingham, J. (1993) *Report on the findings of the Consultative Exercise to the Working Group, ESRC Strategic Review of British Birth Cohort Studies.* Swindon: ESRC.

Ferri, E. (ed.) (1993) *Life at 33.* London: National Children's Bureau.

MRC (Medical Research Council) (1992) *Review of Longitudinal Studies.* London: Medical Research Council.

Parsons, S. and Bynner, J. (1998) *Influences on Adult Basic Skills.* London: Basic Skills Agency.

Shepherd, P. (1995) *The National Child Development Study: An introduction to its origins and the methods of data collection*, NCDS User Support Group Working Paper 1 (revised).

Our website gives references to all publications and further details of recent and current work.

Web siteaddress: www.cls.ioe.ac.uk

References

Abel-Smith, B. and Townsend, P. (1965) *The Poor and the Poorest*. London: Bell.

Acheson, D. (1998) *Independent Inquiry into Inequalities in Health*. London: The Stationery Office.

Ainley, P. (1988) *From School to YTS: Education and training in England and Wales 1944–1987*. Milton Keynes: Open University Press.

Ainley, P. and Corney, M. (1990) *Training for the Future*. London: Cassell.

Ashton, D. and Maguire, M. (1983) *The Vanishing Youth Labour Market*. Youthaid Occasional Papers No. 3. London.

Atkinson, A.B. (1998) 'Social exclusion, poverty and unemployment'. In A.B. Atkinson and J. Hills (eds), *Exclusion, Employment and Opportunity*. CASE Paper 4. London: Centre for the Analysis of Social Exclusion, London School of Economics and Political Science, 1–20.

Atkinson, A.B. (2000) 'Distribution of wealth and income'. In A.H. Halsey and J. Webb (eds), *Twentieth Century British Social Trends*. London: Macmillan.

Atkinson, A.B. and Hills, J. (1998) *Exclusion, Employment and Opportunity*. CASE Paper 4. London: Centre for Analysis of Social Exclusion, London School of Economics.

Banks, J., Pistaferri, L. and Smith, Z. (2001) *Accounting for Changes in Household Composition: Evidence from Great Britain, 1968–1999*. Institute for Fiscal Studies, mimeo.

Banks, M., Bates, I., Bynner, J., Breakwell, G., Emler, N., Jamieson, L. and Roberts, K. (1992) *Careers and Identities*. Buckingham: Open University Press.

Barker, D.J.P. (1991) *Fetal and Infant Origins of Adult Disease*. London: BMJ Publishing.

Barker, D.J.P. (1998) *Mothers and Babies and Health in Later Life*. 2nd edition. Edinburgh: Churchill Livingstone.

Baron, S., Field, J. and Schuller, T. (2000) *Social Capital: Critical perspectives*. Oxford: Oxford University Press.

Bartol, C.R. (1999) *Criminal Behaviour – a psychosocial approach*. Fifth Edition. London: Prentice-Hall International (UK) Limited.

Bartley, M., Power, C., Blane, D., Smith, G.D. and Shipley, M. (1994) 'Birth-weight and later socioeconomic disadvantage – evidence from the 1958 British Cohort Study'. *British Medical Journal*, 309 (6967), 1475–8.

Beck, U. (1986) *The Risk Society*, Frankfurt am Main: Suhrkamp Verlag.

Beck, U., Giddens, A. and Lash, S. (1994) *Reflexive Modernization: Politics, traditions and aesthetics in the modern social order.* Cambridge: Polity Press.

Bennett, K.E. and Haggard, M.P. (1999) 'Behaviour and cognitive outcomes from middle ear disease'. *Reprinted from Archives of Disease in Childhood*, 80, 1, 28–35.

Berkeley, P. (1999) *Relious Trends 2000/2001.* No. 2. London: HarperCollins religious/ Christian Research.

Berrington, A. (2001) 'Change and consistency in family formation among young adults in Britain'. Paper presented at the workshop on 'Union formation in interdependent life courses'. Rostock, Germany, 30–31 August.

Berthoud, R. (1998) *Incomes of Ethnic Minorities.* Wivenhoe, Essex: Institute for Social and Economic Research, University of Essex.

Beveridge Report (1942) *Report on Social Insurance and Allied Services.* Cmd 6404. London: HMSO.

Bjornberg, U. (ed.) (1992) *European Parents in the 1990s: Contradictions and comparisons.* New Brunswick and London: Transaction.

Blundell, R., Dearden, L., Goodman, L. and Reed, H. (1997) *Higher Education, Employment and Earnings in Britain.* London: Institute of Fiscal Studies.

Bobak, M., Richards, M. and Wadsworth, M.E.J. (2000) 'Air pollution and birth weight in Britain in 1946'. *Epidemiology*, 16, 358–9.

Bradshaw, J., Kennedy, S., Kilkey, M., Hutton, S., Corden, A., Eardley, T., Holmes, H. and Neale, J. (1996) *The Employment of Lone Parents: A comparison of policy in 20 countries*, London: Family Policy Studies Centre.

Brannen, J. (1992) 'British parenthood in the wake of the New Right: some contradictions and changes'. In U. Bjornberg (ed.), *European Parents in the 1990s: Contradictions and comparisons.* New Brunswick and London: Transaction.

Brannen, J. and Moss, P. (1991) *Managing Mothers: Dual earner households after maternity leave.* London: Macmillan.

Bruhn, J.G. and Wolf, S. (1979) *The Roseto Story.* Norman, OK: University of Oklahoma Press.

Brunner, E. and Marmot, M.G. (1999) 'Social organisation, stress and health'. In M. Marmot and R.G. Wilkinson (eds), *Social Determinants of Health.* Oxford: Oxford University Press.

Brunner, E.J. (2000) 'Toward a new social biology'. In L.P. Berkman and I. Kawachi (eds), *Social Epidemiology.* Oxford: Oxford University Press.

Buchanan, A. and Ten Brinke, J. (1997) *What Happened when they were Grown Up?* York: Joseph Rowntree Foundation.

Buck, N., Gershuny, J., Rose, D. and Scott, J. (1994) *Changing Households: The British Household Panel Study 1990–1992*. ESRC Centre on Micro-social Change, University of Essex.

Buschang, P.H., Malina, R.M. and Little, B.B. (1986) 'Linear growth of Zatopec schoolchildren: growth status and yearly velocity for leg length and sitting height'. *Annals of Human Biology*, 13, 225–33.

Butler, N.R. and Alberman, E.D. (1969) *Perinatal Problems*. Edinburgh: E & S Livingstone.

Butler, N.R. and Bonham, D.G. (1963) *Perinatal Mortality*. Edinburgh: E and S Livingstone.

Butler, N.R., Goldstein, H. and Ross, E.M. (1971) 'Cigarette smoking in pregnancy: influence on birth and perinatal mortality'. *British Medical Journal*, i, 127–30.

Bynner, J. (1998) 'Education and family components of identity in the transition from school to work'. *International Journal of Behavioral Development*, 22, 29–53.

Bynner, J. (2001a) 'Childhood risks and protective factors in social exclusion'. *Children and Society*, 15, 285–301.

Bynner, J. (2001b) 'British youth transitions in comparative perspective', *Journal of Youth Studies*, 4, 5–23.

Bynner, J. and Ashford, S. (1994) 'Politics and participation: some antecedents of young people's attitudes to the political system and political activity'. *European Journal of Social Psychology*, 24, 223–36.

Bynner, J. and Egerton, M. (2001) *The Wider Benefits of Higher Education*. London: Higher Education Funding Council.

Bynner, J. and Joshi, H. (2002) 'Equality and opportunity in education: evidence from the 1958 and 1970 birth cohort studies'. *Oxford Review of Education*.

Bynner, J. and Parsons, S. (1997a) 'Getting on with qualifications'. In J. Bynner, E. Ferri and P. Shepherd (eds), *Twenty-something in the 90s: Getting on, getting by; getting nowhere*. Aldershot: Ashgate Publishing Ltd.

Bynner, J. and Parsons, S. (1997b) *It Doesn't Get any Better: The impact of poor basic skills on the lives of 37 year olds*. London: Basic Skills Agency.

Bynner, J. and Parsons, S. (2000a) 'Impact of poor numeracy on employment and career progression'. In C. Tikly and A. Wolf (eds), *The Maths We Need Now: Demands, deficits and remedies*. London: Institute of Education.

Bynner, J. and Parsons, S. (2000b) 'Marginalisation and value shifts under the changing economic circumstances surrounding the transition to work: a comparison of cohorts born in 1958 and 1970'. *Journal of Youth Studies*, 3, 237–49.

Bynner, J. and Parsons, S. (2001) 'Qualifications, basic skills and accelerating social exclusion'. *Journal of Education and Work*, 14, 279–91.

Bynner, J. and Parsons, S. (2002) 'Social exclusion and the transition from school to work: the case of young people not in education, employment or training (NEET).' *Journal of Vocational Behaviour*, 60, 289–309.

Bynner, J. and Roberts, K. (eds) (1991) *Youth and Work: Transition to employment in England and Germany*. London: Anglo German Foundation.

Bynner, J., Ferri, E. and Shepherd, P. (eds) (1997) *Twenty-something in the 90s: Getting on, getting by; getting nowhere*. Aldershot: Ashgate.

Bynner, J., Goldstein, H. and Alberman, E. (1998) 'Neville Butler and the British Cohort Studies', *Paediatric and Perinatal Epidemiology*, 12, suppl., 1, 1–14

Bynner, J., Joshi, H. and Tsatsas, M. (2000) *Obstacles and Opportunities on the Route to Adulthood: Evidence from rural and urban Britain*. London: Smith Institute.

Bynner, J., Elias, P., McKnight, A., Pan, H. and Pierre, G. (2002) *Young People in Transition: Changing pathways to employment and independence*. York: Joseph Rowntree Foundation.

Calnan, M., Douglas, J.W.B. and Goldstein, H. (1978) 'Tonsillectomy and circumcision – comparison of two cohorts'. *International Journal of Epidemiology*, 7, 79–85.

CBI (Confederation of British Industry) (1989) *Towards a Skills Revolution: Interim report of the vocational education and training task force*. London: Confederation of British Industry.

Chamberlain, R., Chamberlain, G., Howlett, B.C. and Claireaux, A. (1975) *British Births: Vol. 1: The First Week of Life*. London: Heinemann.

Chamberlain, G., Philipp, E., Howlett, B.C. and Masters, K. (1978) *British Births: Vol. 2: Obstetric Care*. London: Heinemann.

Chennells, L. and Van Reenen, J. (1999) *Has technology hurt less skilled workers? An econometric survey of the effects of technical change on the structure of pay and jobs*. Working Paper no. W99/27. London: Institute for Fiscal Studies.

Chilvers, C., Pike, M.C., Forman, D., Fogelman, K. and Wadsworth, M.E.J. (1984) 'Apparent doubling of frequency of undescended testis in England and Wales in 1962–81'. *Lancet*, ii, 330–2.

Chinn, S. and Rona, R. (1994) 'Trends in weight-for-height and triceps skinfold thickness for English and Scottish children, 1972–1982 and 1982–1990'. *Paediatric and Perinatal Epidemiology*, 8, 90–106.

Clark, T. and Goodman, A. (2001) 'Living standards under Labour'. In T. Clark and A. Dilnot (eds), *Election Briefing 2001*, Commentary no. 84, London: Institute for Fiscal Studies.

Clark, T., Myck, M. and Smith, Z. (2001) 'Fiscal reforms affecting households, 1997–2001'. In T. Clark and A. Dilnot (eds), *Election Briefing 2001*, Commentary no. 84, London: Institute for Fiscal Studies.

Cherlin, A.J., Furstenberg, F.F., Chase-Lansdale, P.L., Kiernan, K., Robins, P.K., Morrison, D.R. and Teitler, J.O. (1991) 'Longitudinal studies of effects of divorce on children in Great Britain and the United States'. *Science*, 252, 1386–9.

Coleman, D. (2000) 'Population and family'. In A.H. Halsey and J. Webb (eds), *Twentieth Century British Social Trends*. London: Macmillan.

Coleman, J.S. (1988) 'Social capital as the basis of human capital'. *American Journal of Sociology 94/supplement*, S95–S120.

Coleman, J. and Schofield, J. (2001) *Key Data on Adolescence*. Brighton: Trust for the Study of Adolescence.

Coles, B. and Macdonald, R. (1990) 'The new vocationalism to the culture of enterprise'. In C. Wallace and M. Cross (eds), *Youth in Transition*. London: Falmer Press.

Colhoun, H. and Prescott-Clarke, P. (1996) *Health Survey for England 1994*. London: HMSO.

Davey Smith, G., Greenwood, R., Gunnell, D., Sweetnam, P., Yarnell, J. and Elwood, P. (2001) 'Leg length, insulin resistance, and coronary heart disease risk: the Caerphilly study'. *Journal of Epidemiology and Community Health*, 55, 867–72.

Davie, R., Butler, N. and Goldstein, H. (1972) *From Birth to Seven*. London: Longman in association with the National Children's Bureau.

Davies, H., Joshi, H., and Peronaci, R. (1998) 'Dual and zero-earner couples in Britain: longitudinal evidence on polarization and persistence.' Discussion Paper in Economics 8/98, Birkbeck College, London.

Department of Employment (1986) *Working Together, Education and Training*. CMND 9135. London: HMSO.

Department of Employment (1988) *Employment for the 1990s*. CMND 9823. London: HMSO.

Department of Education and Science (1981) *New Training Initiative*. CMND 9135. London: HMSO.

Department of Transport, Local Government and the Regions (2001) *Housing in England 1999–2000*. London: HMSO

De Stavola, B.L., Hardy, R., Kuh, D., dos Santos Silva, I., Wadsworth, M.E.J. and Swerdlow, A.J. (2000) 'Birth weight, childhood growth and risk of breast cancer in a British cohort'. *British Journal of Cancer*, 83, 964–8.

DETR (Department of the Environment, Transport and the Regions) (1997) *Housing Research Summary: Housing in England 1995/6*, no. 69. London: DETR

DHSS (Department of Health and Social Security) (1974) *Report of the Committee on One Parent Families*. (The Finer Report). 2 vols. London: HMSO.

Dickens, R. (2001) 'The national minimum wage'. In R. Dickens, P. Gregg, and J. Wadsworth (eds), *The State of Working Britain – update 2001*. London: Centre for Economic Performance, LSE/York Publishing Services.

Dilnot, A. and Emmerson, C. (2000) 'The economic environment'. In A.H. Halsey and J. Webb (eds), *Twentieth Century British Social Trends*. London: Macmillan.

Di Salvo, P. (1996) *Who's at home at 33?* NCDS User Support Group Working Paper 42.

Disney, R., Goodman, A. and Gosling, A. (1998) *Public Pay in Britain in the 1990s*. Commentary no. 7. London: Institute for Fiscal Studies.

Dolton, P. (1993) 'The economics of youth training in Britain'. *Economic Journal*, 103, 1261–78.

Dolton, P. and O'Neill, D. (1996) 'Unemployment duration and the restart effect: some experimental evidence' *Economic Journal*, 106, 387–400.

Dolton, P. and Taylor, R. (1999) *Retrospective Data and Recall Bias: The case of work experience*. Discussion paper 99–03. Newcastle upon Tyne: University of Newcastle upon Tyne.

Douglas, J.W.B. (1964) *The Home and the School*. London: Macgibbon and Kee.

Douglas, J.W.B. (1975) 'Early hospital admissions and later disturbances of behaviour and learning'. *Developmental Medicine and Child Neurology*, 17, 456–80.

Douglas, J.W.B. and Blomfield, J.M. (1958) *Children Under Five*. London: Allen and Unwin Ltd.

Douglas, J.W.B., Ross, J.M. and Simpson, H.R. (1968) *All our Future*. London: Peter Davies Ltd.

DTLR (Department of Transport, Local Government and the Regions) (2001) *Housing in England 1999–00*. London: HMSO

Elliott, B.J. and Richards, M.P.M. (1991) 'Children and divorce: educational performance and behaviour before and after parental separation'. *International Journal of Law and the Family*, 5, 258–76.

Ely, M., Richards, M.P.M., Wadsworth, M.E.J. and Elliott, B.J. (1999a) 'Secular changes in the association of parental divorce and children's educational attainment: evidence from three British birth cohorts'. *Journal of Social Policy*, 28, 3, 437–55.

Ely, M., Hardy, R.J., Longford, N.T. and Wadsworth, M.E.J. (1999b) 'Gender differences in the relationship between alcohol consumption and drink problems'. *Alcohol and Alcoholism*, 34, 894–902.

Erikson, R. and Goldthorpe, J. (1993) *The Constant Flux*. Oxford: Oxford University Press.

Ermisch, J. and Francesconi, M. (2000) 'Patterns of family and household formation'. In R. Berthoud and J. Gershuny (eds), *Seven Years in the Lives of British Families*. Bristol: The Policy Press.

Essen, J. (1979) 'Living in one-parent families: attainment at school.' *Child Care, Health and Development*, 3, 301–18.

Essen, J. and Wedge, P. (1978) *Continuities of Disadvantage*. London: Heinemann.

Essen, J. and Wedge, P. (1982) *Continuities in Childhood Disadvantage*. London, Heinemann Educational.

Essen, J., Fogelman, K. and Head, J. (1978) 'Childhood housing experience and school attainment'. *Child: care health and development*, 4, 41–58.

Etzioni, A. (1993) *The Parenting Deficit*. London: Demos.

Evans, K. and Furlong, A. (1996) 'Metaphors of youth transitions: niches, pathways, trajectories or navigations'. In J. Bynner, L. Chisholm and A. Furlong (eds), *Youth, Citizenship and Social Change*. Aldershot: Ashgate.

Evans, K. and Heinz, W.R. (1994) *Becoming Adults in the 1990s*. London: Anglo German Foundation.

Evans, P. (2000) 'Social exclusion and children – creating identity capital: some conceptual issues and practical solutions'. In G. Walraven, C. Parsons, D. van Reen and C. Day (eds), *Combating Social Exclusion through Education: Laissez-faire, authoritarianism or the third way*. Leuven/Appeldorn: Garant.

Farrington, D. (1996) *Understanding and Preventing Youth Crime*. York: Joseph Rowntree Foundation.

Farrington, D. (2001) 'What has been learned from self reports about criminal careers and the causes of offending'. Report to the Home Office (mimeo).

Farrington, D.P., Ohlin, L.E. and Wilson, D.J. (1990) *Understanding and Controlling Crime*. New York: Springer-Verlag.

Feinstein, L., Hammond, C., Malmberg, L., Preston, J. and Woods, L. (forthcoming) *Quantitative Estimates of the Wider Benefits of Adult Learning: Health and Civic Participation*. London: Institute of Education, University of London.

Ferri, E. (1976) *Growing up in a One Parent Family*. Windsor: National Foundation for Educational Research Publishing Company.

Ferri, E. and Robinson, H. (1976) *Coping Alone*. Windsor: National Foundation for Educational Research Publishing Company.

Ferri, E. and Smith, K. (1996) *Parenting in the 1990s*. London: Family Policy Studies Centre.

Ferri, E. and Smith, K. (1996) *Step-Parenting in the 1990s*. London: Family Policy Studies Centre.

Fevre, R. (2001) 'Socialising social capital: identity, the transition to work and economic development'. In S. Baron, J. Field and T. Schuller (eds), *Social Capital*. Oxford: Oxford University Press.

Fitzpatrick, R. and Chandola, T. (2000) 'Health'. In A.H. Halsey and J. Webb (eds), *Twentieth Century British Social Trends*. London: Macmillan.

Fletcher, C.M., Peto, R., Tinker, C. and Speizer, F.E. (1976) *The Natural History of Chronic Bronchitis and Emphysema*. Oxford: Oxford University Press.

Fogelman, K. (ed.) (1983) *Growing up in Great Britain: Collected papers from the National Child Development Study*. London: Macmillan.

Fombonne, E. (1993) 'Depressive disorders: time trends and possible explanatory mechanisms'. In M. Rutter and D. Smith (eds), *Psychosocial Disorders in Young People*. Chichester: John Wiley, 544–615.

Forsen, T., Eriksson, J., Tuomilheto, J., Teramo, K., Osmond, C. and Barker, D.J.P.

(1997) 'Mother's weight in pregnancy and coronary heart disease in a cohort of Finnish men: follow-up study'. *British Medical Journal*, 315, 387–40.

Forth, J., Lissenburgh, S., Callender, C. and Millward, N. (1997) *Family Friendly Working Arrangements in Britain, 1996*. Sudbury: Department for Education and Employment Research Report RR16.

Furlong, A. and Cartmel, F. (1996) *Young People and Social Change: Individualization and risk in late modernity*. Buckingham: Open University Press.

Galinda-Rueda, F. (2002) 'Constructing work event histories: description of the data work on NCDS and BCS'. Mimeo. London: LSE.

Gallie, D. (1988) *Employment in Britain*. Oxford: Oxford University Press.

Gershuny, J. and Pahl, R. (1994) *Lifetime Employment in a New Context*. Paper presented to the Conference on Challenges of Unemployment in a Regional Europe (CURE), Ameland, Netherlands. Ljouwert: Fyske Akademy.

Giddens, A. (1984) *The Constitution of Society*. London: Polity Press.

Giddens, A. (1991) *Modernity and Self-Identity: Self and society in the late modern age*. Cambridge: Polity Press.

Glass, D.V. (1964) 'Introduction'. In J.W.B. Douglas (ed.), *The Home and the School*. London: Macgibbon and Kee.

Glenister, D. (1996) 'Exercise and mental health: a review'. *Journal of the Royal Society of Health*, 116, 7–13.

Golding, J. (1989) 'Illegitimate births: do they suffer in the long term?'. In S. Doxiadis and S. Stewart (eds), *Early Influences Shaping the Individual*. New York: Plenum Press.

Goodman, A., Johnson, P. and Webb, S. (1997) *Inequality in the UK*. Oxford: Oxford University Press.

Gosling, A. and Machin, S. (1995) 'Trade unions and the dispersion of earnings in British establishments, 1980–1990'. *Oxford Bulletin of Economics and Statistics*, 57, 167–84.

Gosling, A., Machin, S. and Meghir, C. (2000) 'The changing distribution of male wages in the UK', *Review of Economic Studies*, 67, 4, 635–66.

Graham, H. (1987) 'Women's smoking and family health'. *Social Science and Medicine*, 25, 47–56.

Graham, H. (1989) 'Women and smoking in the United Kingdom: the implications for health promotion'. *Health Promotion*, 3, 371–82.

Graham, H. and Wardle, J. (1999) 'Social patterning of individual health behaviours: the case of cigarette smoking'. In M. Marmot and R.G. Wilkinson (eds), *Social Determinants of Health*. Oxford: Oxford University Press, 240–55.

Graham, H., West, R., Tunstall Pedoe, H. and Vesey, C. (1984) 'An evaluation of the intervention against smoking in the multiple risk factor intervention trial'. *Preventive Medicine*, 13, 501–9.

Graham, J. and Bowling, B. (1995) *Young People and Crime.* London: Home Office.

Grant, G., Nolan, M. and Ellis, N. (1990) 'A reappraisal of the Malaise Inventory'. *Social Psychiatry and Psychiatry. Epidemiology*, 25, 170–8.

Gregg, P. and Wadsworth, J. (1995) 'More work in fewer households?' In J. Hills (ed.), *New Inequalities.* Cambridge: Cambridge University Press.

Gregg, P. and Wadsworth, J. (1996) 'More work in fewer households?' In J. Hills (ed.), *New Inequalities. The changing distribution of income and wealth in the United Kingdom.* Cambridge: Cambridge University Press.

Gregg, P. and Wadsworth, J. (2000) *Two Sides to Every Story: Measuring worklessness and polarisation at household level.* Working Paper no. 1076. London: Centre for Economic Performance.

Gregg, P., Harkness, S. and Machin, S. (1999) *Child Development and Family Income.* York: YPS.

Griffin, C. (1985) *Typical Girls: Young women from school to the full-time job market.* London: Routledge and Kegan Paul.

Hakim, C. (1996) *Key Issues in Women's Work.* London: Athlone.

Halsey, A.H. (2000) 'Twentieth century British social trends'. In A.H. Halsey and J. Webb (eds), *Twentieth Century British Social Trends.* London: Macmillan.

Halsey, A.H. and Webb, J. (eds) (2000) *Twentieth Century British Social Trends.* London: Macmillan.

Hardy, R., Wadsworth, M. and Kuh, D. (2000) 'The influence of childhood weight and socioeconomic status on change in adult body mass index in a British national birth cohort'. *International Journal of Obesity*, 24, 725–34.

Harkness, S. (1991) 'Working 9 to 5'. In P. Gregg and J. Wadsworth (eds), *The State of Working Britain.* Manchester: Manchester University Press.

Harkness, S. (1996) 'The gender earnings gap: evidence from the UK'. *Fiscal Studies*, 17, 2, 1–36.

Haskey, J. (1992) 'Pre-marital cohabitation and the probabilities of subsequent divorce: analyses using new data from the General Household Survey.' *Population Trends*, 68, OPCS/HMSO.

Haskey, J. (1994) *Stepfamilies and Stepchildren in Great Britain.* Population Trends 76. OPCS/HMSO Group Working Paper 42.

Hobcraft, J. (1998) *Intergenerational and Life Course Transmissions of Social Exclusion: Influences of childhood poverty, family disruption and contact with the police.* CASE paper 15. London: Centre for the Analysis of Social Exclusion, London School of Economics.

Hobsbawm, E. (1995) *Age of Extremes.* London: Abacus.

Holmans, A. (2000) 'Housing'. In A.H. Halsey and J. Webb (eds), *Twentieth Century British Social Trends.* London: Macmillan.

Home Office (2001) *Prison Statistics England and Wales 2000*, Cm 5250. London: Stationery Office.

Hood, R. and Roddam, A. (2000) 'Crime, sentencing and punishment'. In A.H. Halsey and J. Webb (eds), *Twentieth Century British Social Trends*. London: Macmillan.

Hope, S., Power, C. and Rodgers, B. (1999) 'Does financial hardship account for elevated psychological distress in lone mother?' *Social Science and Medicine*, 49, 1637–49.

Hotopf, M.A.H., Mayou, R., Wadsworth, M. and Wessely, S. (1999) 'Psychosocial and developmental antecedents of chest pain in young adults'. *Psychosomatic Medicine*, 61, 861–7.

Hotopf, M., Wilson Jones, C., Mayou, R., Wadsworth, M.E.J. and Wessely, S. (2000) 'Childhood predictors of adult medically unexplained hospitalizations: results from a national birth cohort'. *British Journal of Psychiatry*, 176, 273–80.

Hutton, J.L., Pharoah, P.O., Cooke, R.W. and Stevenson, R.C. (1997) 'Differential effects of preterm birth and small gestational age on cognitive and motor development'. *Archives of Disease in Childhood (Fetal and Neonatal Edition)*, 76, F75–F81.

Hutton, W. (1995) *The State We Are In*. London: Jonathan Cape.

Huxley, R., Neil, A. and Collins, R. (2002) 'Unravelling the "fetal origins" hypothesis: is there really an inverse association between birth weight and blood pressure?' *Lancet*, 360, 659–65.

Inglehart, R. (1990) *Culture Shift in Advanced Society*. Princeton: Princeton University Press.

Jarvis, M., West, R., Tunstall-Pedoe, H. and Vesey, C. (1984) 'An evaluation of the intervention against smoking in the multiple risk factor intervention trial. *Preventive Medicine*, 13, 501–9.

Jarvis, M.J. and Wardle, J. (1999) 'Social patterning of individual health behaviours: the case of cigarette smoking'. In M. Marmot and R.G. Wilkinson (eds), *Social Determinants of Health*. Oxford: Oxford University Press, 240–55.

Johnes, G. and Taylor, J. (1992) 'Labour'. In M.J. Artis (ed.), *The UK Economy: A manual of applied economics*. London: Weidenfeld and Nicholson.

Johnson, P. and Webb, S. (1993) 'Explaining the growth in UK income inequality: 1979–1988'. *The Economic Journal*, 103, 417, 429–35.

Joint Committee (1948) *Maternity in Great Britain*. Oxford: Oxford University Press.

Jones, G. (1995) *Leaving Home*. Buckingham: Open University Press.

Jones, P., Rodgers, B., Murray, R. and Marmot, M. (1994) 'Child developmental risk factors for adult schizophrenia in the British 1946 birth cohort'. *Lancet*, 344, 1398–402.

Joshi, H. (1990) 'Obstacles and opportunities for lone parents as breadwinners in

Great Britain'. In E. Duskin (ed.), *Lone Parent Families: The economic challenge*. Paris: OECD, 127–50.

Joshi, H. and Hinde, P.R.A. (1993) 'Employment after childbearing in post-war Britain: cohort-study evidence on contrasts within and across generations'. *European Sociological Review*, 9, 203–27.

Joshi, H. and Paci, P. (1997) 'Life in the labour market'. In J. Bynner, E. Ferri and P. Shepherd (eds), *Twenty-Something in the 1990s: Getting on, getting by; getting nowhere*. Aldershot: Ashgate.

Joshi, H. and Paci, P. (1998) *Unequal Pay for Men and Women: Evidence from the British Birth Cohort Studies*. London: MIT Press.

Joshi, H., Dale, A., Ward, A. and Davies, H. (1995) *Dependence and Independence in the Finances of Women Aged 33*. London: Family Policy Studies Centre.

Joshi, H., Macran, S. and Dex, S. (1996) 'Employment after childbearing and women's subsequent labour force participation: evidence from the British 1958 birth cohort'. *Journal of Population Economics*, 9, 325–48.

Kiernan, K. (1995) *Transition to Parenthood: Young mothers, young fathers – associated factors and later life experiences*. London School of Economics, STICKERD Welfare State Programme, WSP/113.

Kiernan, K. (1997a) *The Legacy of Parental Divorce: Social, economic and demographic experiences in adulthood*. CASE paper 1. London: Centre for Analysis of Social Exclusion, London School of Economics.

Kiernan, K.E. (1997b) 'Who divorces?' Paper presented to ESRC Dissemination Conference on Population and Household Change Programme, London.

Kiernan, K.E. (1992) 'The impact of family disruption in childhood on transitions made in young adult life.' *Population Studies*, 46, 2, 213–34

Kiernan, K. and Diamond, I. (1983) 'The age at which childbearing starts – a longitudinal study.' *Population Studies,* 37, 363–80.

Kiernan, K.E. and Estaugh, V. (1993) 'Cohabitation: extra-marital childbearing and social policy'. *Occasional Paper 17*. London: Family Policy Studies Centre.

Kiernan, K., Land, H. and Lewis, J. (1998) *Lone Motherhood in Twentieth Century Britain*. Oxford: Clarendon Press.

King, J. (1997) *Family Spending 1996–97*. London: The Stationery Office.

Kuh, D.J.L. and Ben Shlomo, Y. (eds) (1997) *A Life Course Approach to Chronic Disease Epidemiology: Tracing the origins of ill-health from early to adult life*. Oxford: Oxford University Press.

Kuh, D.J.L. and Wadsworth, M. (1991) 'Childhood influences on adult male earnings in a longitudinal study'. *British Journal of Sociology*, 42, 537–55.

Kuh, D.J.L. and Wadsworth, M.E.J. (1993) 'Physical health status at 36 years in a British national birth cohort'. *Social Science and Medicine*, 37, 905–16.

Kuh, D.J.L., Power, C. and Rodgers, B. (1991) 'Secular trends in social class and sex differences in adult height'. *International Journal of Epidemiology*, 20, 1001–9.

Kuh, D.J.L., Wadsworth, M.E.J. and Yusuf, E.J. (1994) 'Burden of disability in a post war birth cohort'. *Journal of Epidemiology and Community Health*, 48, 262–69.

Kuh, D.J.L., Head, J., Hardy, R. and Wadsworth, M. (1997) 'The influence of education and family background on women's earnings in midlife: evidence from a British birth cohort study'. *British Journal of Sociology of Education*, 18, 385–405.

Kuh, D.J.L., Hardy, R. and Wadsworth, M. (2000) 'Social and behavioural influences on the uptake of hormone replacement therapy among younger women'. *British Journal of Obstetrics and Gynaecology*, 107, 731–9.

Kumar, V. (1993) *Poverty and Inequality in the UK: The effects on children*. London: National Children's Bureau.

Lambert, L., Essen, J. and Head, J. (1977) 'Variations in behaviour ratings of children who have been in care'. *Journal of Child Psychology and Psychiatry*, 18, 4, 335–46.

Langenberg, C., Hardy, R., Kuh, D., Brunner, E. and Wadsworth, M.E.J. (in press) 'Central and total obesity in middle aged men and women in relation to lifetime socioeconomic status: evidence from a national birth cohort'. *Journal of Epidemiology and Public Health*.

Larroque, B., Bertrais, S., Czernichow, P. and Leger, J. (2001) 'School difficulties in 20-year-olds who were born small for gestational age at term in a regional cohort study'. *Pediatrics*, 108, 111–15.

Lindelow, M., Hardy, R. and Rodgers, B. (1997) 'Development of a scale to measure symptoms of anxiety and depression in the general population: the Psychiatric Symptom Frequency (PSF) Scale'. *Journal of Epidemiology and Public Health*, 51, 549–57.

Lundgren, E.M., Cnattingius, S., Jonsson, B. and Tuvemo, T. (2001) 'Intellectual and psychological performance in males born small for gestational age with and without catch-up growth'. *Pediatric Research*, 50, 91–6.

Lupton, D. (1995) *The Imperative of Health: Public health and the regulated body*. London: Sage.

McAllister, F. and Clarke, L. (1998) *Choosing Childlessness*. London: Family Policy Studies Centre.

Macdonald, R. (ed.) (1997) *Youth, the Underclass and Social Exclusion*. London: Routledge.

Machin, S. (1996) 'Wage inequality in the UK'. *Oxford Review of Economic Policy*, 12, 1, 47–64.

Machin, S. and Manning, A. (1994) 'Minimum wages, wage dispersion and employment: evidence from the UK wages councils'. *Industrial Relations Labor Review*, 47, 319–29.

McNeill, A.D., Jarvis, M.J., Stapleton, J.A., Russell, M.A.H., Eiser, J.R., Gammage, P. and Gray, E.M. (1988) 'Prospective study of factors predicting uptake of smoking in adolescents'. *Journal of Epidemiology and Community Health*, 43, 72–8.

Macran, S., Joshi, H.E. and Dex, S. (1996) 'Employment after childbearing: a survival analysis'. *Work, Employment and Society*, 10, 2, 273–96.

Makepeace, G.H., Paci, P., Joshi, H. and Dolton, P.J. (1999) 'How unequally has equal pay progressed since the 1970s?: A study of two British cohorts'. *Journal of Human Resources*, 34, 534–56.

Mann, S.L., Wadsworth, M.E.J. and Colley, J.R.T. (1992) 'Accumulation of factors influencing respiratory illness in members of a national birth cohort and their offspring'. *Journal of Epidemiology and Community Health*, 46, 286–92.

Man-Yee Kan (2001) 'Gender asymmetry in the division of domestic labour'. Paper presented at BHPS 2001 Conference, ISER, University of Essex.

Marks, D.F., Murray, M., Evans, B. and Willig, C. (2000) *Health Psychology: Theory, research and practice.* London: Sage.

Marmot, M. and Wilkinson R.G. (1999) (eds) *Social Determinants of Health.* Oxford: Oxford University Press.

Martyn, C.N. (1997) 'Infection in childhood and neurological diseases in adult life'. In M.G. Marmot and M.E.J. Wadsworth (eds), *Fetal and Early Childhood Environment: Long-term health implications.* London: The Royal Society of Medicine Press.

Marwick, A. (1982) *British Society since 1940.* London: Pelican.

Maughan, B. and Lindelow, M. (1997) 'Secular change in psychosocial risks: the case of teenage motherhood'. *Psychological Medicine*, 27, 1129–44.

Maughan, B. and Taylor, A. (2001) 'Adolescent psychological problems, partnership transitions and adult mental health: an investigation of selection effects'. *Psychological Medicine*, 31, 291–305.

Maughan, B., Collishaw, S. and Pickles, A. (1999) 'Mild mental retardation: psychosocial functioning in adulthood'. *Psychological Medicine*, 29, 351–66.

Montgomery, S.M. and Ekbom, A. (2002) 'Smoking during pregnancy and diabetes mellitus in a British longitudinal birth cohort'. *British Medical Journal*, 324, 26–7.

Montgomery, S.M. and Schoon, I. (1997) 'Health and health behaviour'. In J. Bynner, E. Ferri and P. Shepherd (eds), *Twenty-Something in the 1990s: Getting on, getting by; getting nowhere.* Aldershot: Ashgate.

Montgomery, S.M., Bartley, M.J., Cook, D. G. and Wadsworth, M.E.J. (1996) 'Health and social precursors of unemployment in young men in Great Britain'. *Journal of Epidemiology and Community Health*, 50, 415–22.

Montgomery, S.M., Bartley, M.J. and Wilkinson, R.G. (1997) 'Family conflict and slow growth'. *Archives of Disease in Childhood*, 77, 326–30.

Montgomery, S.M., Bartley, M.J., Cook, D.G. and Wadsworth, M.E.J. (1998) 'Unemployment, cigarette smoking, alcohol consumption and body weight in young men'. *European Journal of Public Health*, 8, 21–7.

Montgomery, S.M., Pounder, R.E. and Wakefield, A.J. (1999) 'Smoking in adults and passive smoking in children are associated with acute appendicitis'. *The Lancet*, 352, 379.

Mooney, C. (1990) 'Cost and availability of healthy food choices in a London health district'. *Journal of Human Nutrition and Dietetics*, 3, 111–20.

Nakagomi, T., Itaya, H., Tominaga, T., Yamaki, M., Hisamatsu, S. and Nakagomi, O. (1994) 'Is atopy increasing?' *The Lancet*, 343, 121–2.

Nauck, B. (2001) 'Social capital and intergenerational transmission of cultural capital within a regional context'. In J. Bynner and R.K. Silbereisen (eds), *Adversity and Challenge in the New Germany and England*. Basingstoke: Macmillan.

Neeleman, J., Wessely, S. and Wadsworth M. (1998) 'Predictors of suicide, accidental death and premature natural death in a general-population birth cohort'. *Lancet*, 351, 93–7.

NIH Consensus Developmental Panel (1996) 'Physical activity and cardiovascular health'. *Journal of the American Medical Association*, 276, 241–6.

Norris, P. (2001) *Making Democracy Work: Social capital and civic engagement in 47 societies*, Paper for the European Science Foundation EURESCO conference on Social Capital: Interdisciplinary Perspectives, University of Exeter, 15–20 September 2000.

O'Brien, M. (1992) 'Changing conceptions of fatherhood.' In U. Bjornberg (ed.), *European Parents in the 1990s: Contradictions and comparisons*. New Brunswick and London. Transaction.

OECD (2001) *The well-being of Nations: the role of human and social capital.* Paris: OECD.

Office of Population Censuses and Surveys (1995) *Infant Mortality. OPCS Monitor DH3 95/3*. London: HMSO.

ONS (Office of National Statistics) (1998) *Living in Britain*. London, HMSO.

ONS (Office of National Statistics) (2000) *Social Trends Pocketbook*. London: ONS.

ONS (Office of National Statistics) (2001) *Social Trends no. 31*. London: ONS.

ONS (Office of National Statistics) (2002a) *Social Trends no. 32*. London: ONS.

ONS (Office of National Statistics) (2002b) *Population Trends no. 107*. London: ONS.

Organisation for Economic Co-operation and Development (OECD) (2001) *OECD Health Data 2001: A comparative analysis of 30 OECD countries*. Toronto: Federal Publications Inc.

Osborn, A.E. and Milbank, J.E. (1987) *The Effects of Early Education*. A report from the Child Health and Education Study of children in Britain born 5–11 April 1970. Oxford: Clarendon Press

Osborn, A.F. (1990) 'Resilient children: A longitudinal study of high achieving socially disadvantaged children'. *Early Child Development and Care*, 62, 23–47.

Osborn, A.F. and Morris, A.C. (1979) 'The rationale for a composite index of social class and its evaluation'. *British Journal of Sociology*, 30, 39–60.

Osborn, A.F., Butler N.R. and Morris, A.C. (1984) *The Social Life of Britain's Five Year Olds. A report of the Child Health and Education Study.* London: Routledge and Kegan Paul.

Paneth, N. and Susser, M. (1995) 'Early origin of coronary heart disease (the "Barker hypothesis"): hypotheses, no matter how intriguing, need rigorous attempts at refutation'. *British Medical Journal*, 310, 411–12.

Parsons, S. and Bynner, J. (1998) *Influences on Adult Basic Skills.* London: Basic Skills Agency.

Paykel, E.S., Hayhurst, H., Abbott, R. and Wadsworth, M.E.J. (2001) 'Stability and change in milder psychiatric disorder over seven years in a birth cohort'. *Psychological Medicine*, 31, 1373–84.

Paz, I., Laor, A., Gale, R., Harlap, S., Stevenson, D.K. and Seidman, D.S. (2001) 'Term infants with fetal growth restriction are not at increased risk for low intelligence scores at age 17 years'. *Journal of Pediatrics*, 138, 87–91.

Peach, C., Rogers, A., Chance, J. and Daley, P. (2000) 'Immigration and ethnicity'. In A.H. Halsey and J. Webb (eds), *Twentieth Century British Social Trends.* London: Macmillan.

Pearson, R. and Peckham, C. (1977) 'Handicapped children in secondary schools from the National Child Development Study (cohort)'. *Public Health*, 91, 296–304.

Peckham, C.S., Stark, O., Simonite, V. and Wolff, O. (1982) 'The prevalence of obesity in British children born in 1946 and 1958'. *British Medical Journal*, 286, 1237–42.

Pelz, M. (1992) 'Living with children: desire and reality'. In U. Bjornberg (ed.), *European Parents in the 1990s: Contradictions and comparisons.* New Brunswick and London. Transaction.

Piachaud, D. (1988) 'Poverty in Britain 1899 to 1983'. *Journal of Social Policy*, 17, 335–49.

Pilling, D. (1990) *Escape from Disadvantage.* London: Falmer Press, in association with National Children's Bureau.

Pitts, M. (1996) *The Psychology of Preventive Health.* London: Routledge.

Plowden Report (1967) *Children and their Primary Schools.* London: HMSO.

Power, C.M. (1995) 'Health related behaviour'. In B. Botting (ed.), *The Health of our Children: The Registrar General's decennial supplement for England and Wales.* London: HMSO.

Power, C. and Bartley, M. (1993) 'Health and health service use'. In E. Ferri (ed.), *Life at 33.* London: ESRC, City University, National Children's Bureau.

Power, C. and Hertzman, C. (1997) 'Social and biological pathways linking early life and adult disease'. In M.G. Marmot and M.E.J. Wadsworth (eds), *Fetal and Early Childhood Environment: Long-term health implications*. British Medical Bulletin, 53, 198–209. London: Royal Society of Medicine Press Ltd.

Power, C. and Li, L. (2000) 'Cohort study of birthweight, mortality and disability'. *British Medical Journal*, 320, 840–1.

Power, C., Manor, O. and Fox, J. (1991) *Health and Class: The early years*. London: Chapman and Hall.

Prentice, A.M. and Jebb, S.A. (1995) 'Obesity in Britain: gluttony or sloth?' *British Medical Journal*, 311, 437–9.

Pringle, M.K., Butler, N.R. and Davie, R. (1966) *Eleven Thousand Seven Year Olds*. London: Longman.

Prynne, C.J., Paul, A.A., Price, G.M., Day, K.C., Hilder, W.S. and Wadsworth, M.E.J. (1999) 'Food and nutrient intake of a national sample of 4-year-old children in 1950: comparison with the 1990s'. *Public Health Nutrition*, 2, 537–47.

Prynne, C.J., Paul, A.A., Mishra, G.D., Hardy, R.J., Bolton-Smith, C. and Wadsworth, M.E.J. (2002) 'Socio-demographic inequalities in the diet of young children in the 1946 British birth cohort'. *Public Health Nutrition*, 5.

Putnam, R.D. (1995) 'Tuning in, tuning out: the strange disappearance of social capital in America'. *Political Science and Politics*, December, 664–83.

Putnam, R.D. (2000) *Bowling Alone: The collapse and revival of American community*. New York: Simon and Schuster.

Rake, K. (ed.) (2000) *Women's Incomes over the Lifetime*. Report to the Women's Unit. Contributing authors: Davies, H., Joshi, H., Rake, K. and Alami, R. London: The Stationery Office.

Ravelli, A., van der Muelen, J., Michels, R.P.J., Osmond, C., Barker, D.J.P., Hales, C.N. and Blecker, O.P. (1998) 'Glucose tolerance in adults after prenatal exposure to the Dutch famine'. *Lancet*, 351, 173–7.

Richards, M., Kuh, D., Hardy, R. and Wadsworth, M.E.J. (1999) 'Lifetime cognitive function and timing of the natural menopause'. *Neurology*, 53, 308–14.

Richards, M., Hardy, R., Kuh, D. and Wadsworth, M.E.J. (2001) 'Birth weight and cognitive function in the British 1946 birth cohort: longitudinal population based study'. *British Medical Journal*, 322, 199–203.

Richards, M., Maughan, B., Hardy, R., Hall, I., Strydom, A. and Wadsworth, M.E.J. (2001) 'Long-term affective disorder in people with mild learning disability.' *British Journal of Psychiatry*, 179, 523–7.

Richards, M., Hardy, R., Kuh, D. and Wadsworth, M.E.J. (2002) 'Birthweight, postnatal growth and cognitive function in a national UK birth cohort'. *International Journal of Epidemiology*, 31, 342–8.

Roberts, K. and Parsell, G. (1989) 'Recent changes in the pathways from school to work.' In Hurrelmann, K. and Engel, U. (eds), *The Social World of Adolescents*. New York: de Gruyter.

Roberts, K., Clark, S. and Wallace, C. (1994) 'Flexibility and individualization: a comparison of transitions into employment in England and Germany'. *Sociology*, 31–4.

Robins, L. and Rutter, M. (eds) (1990) *Straight and Devious Pathways from Childhood to Adulthood*. Cambridge: Cambridge University Press.

Rodgers, B. (1978) 'Feeding in infancy and later ability and attainment'. *Developmental Medicine and Child Neurology*, 20, 421–6.

Rodgers, B. (1994) 'Pathways between parental divorce and adult depression'. *Journal of Child Psychology and Psychiatry*, 35, 1289–308.

Room, G. (1998) *Social Exclusion, Solidarity and the Challenge of Globalisation*. Bath Social Policy Papers, 27. Bath: University of Bath.

Rose, G. (1992) *The Strategy of Preventive Medicine*. Oxford: Oxford University Press.

Rowntree (2001) 'Monitoring poverty and social exclusion'. *Findings* (December). York: Joseph Rowntree Foundation.

Rutter, M. (1991) 'Childhood experiences and adult psychosocial functioning'. In G.R. Bock and J. Whelan (eds), *The Childhood Environment and Adult Disease*. Chichester: Wiley.

Schooling, M. and Wadsworth, M.E.J. (forthcoming) 'The social context of health behaviour'.

Schoon, I. (2001) 'Overcoming disadvantage: a life-span approach to the study of risk and protective factors'. *Proceedings of the 42nd Congress of the German Psychological Society*.

Schoon, I., Bynner, J., Joshi, H., Parsons, S., Wiggins, R.D. and Sacker, A. (2002) 'The influence of context, timing and duration of risk experiences for the passage from childhood to mid adulthood'. *Child Development*, 73, 1486–1504.

Scott, J. (1999) 'Family change: revolution or backlash in attitudes'. In S. McRae (ed.), *Changing Britain: Families and households in the 1990s*. Oxford: Oxford University Press, 68–99.

Shaheen, S.O., Sterne, J.A.C., Montgomery, S.M. and Azima, H. (1999) 'Body Mass Index, asthma and wheeze in young adults'. *Thorax*, 54, 396–402.

Simmons, J. (2002) *Crime in England and Wales 2001/2002*. London: Home Office.

Smith, K. and Joshi, H. (2002) The Millennium Cohort Study. *Population Trends*, 107, 30–4.

Social Exclusion Unit (1999a) *Teenage Pregnancy*. CM4342. London: The Stationery Office

Social Exclusion Unit (1999b) *Bridging the Gap: New opportunities for 16–18 year-olds not in education employment or training*. London: The Stationery Office.

Social Exclusion Unit (2000a) *National Strategy for Neighbourhood Renewal: A framework for consultation*. London: Cabinet Office.

Social Exclusion Unit (2000b) *Report of Policy Action Team 12 on Young People.* London: The Stationery Office.

Social Exclusion Unit (2000c) *Report of Policy Action Team 8: Anti-social behaviour.* London: The Stationery Office.

Social Exclusion Unit (2000d) *Minority Ethnic Issues in Social Exclusion and Neighbourhood Renewal.* London: The Cabinet Office.

Social Exclusion Unit (2001) *A New Commitment to Neighbourhood Renewal: National strategy action plan.* London: The Cabinet Office.

Stacey, M., Batstone, E., Bell, C. and Murcott, A. (1975) *Power, Persistence and Change.* London: Routledge and Kegan Paul.

Stansfeld, S.A. and Marmot, M.G. (eds) (2002) *Stress and the Heart.* London: British Medical Journal Books.

Steedman, J. (1980) *Progress in Secondary Schools.* London: National Children's Bureau.

Stephen, A.M. and Gieber, G.M. (1994) 'Trends in individual fat consumption in the UK 1900–1985'. *British Journal of Nutrition,* 71, 775–88.

Stewart-Brown, S., Haslum, M.N. and Butler, N.R. (1983) 'Evidence for increasing prevalence of diabetes mellitus in childhood'. *British Medical Journal,* 286, 1855–7.

Strachan, D.P., Cox, B.D., Erzinclioglu, S.W., Walters, D.E. and Whichelow, M.J. (1991) 'Ventilatory function and winter fresh fruit consumption in a random sample of British adults'. *Thorax,* 46, 624–9.

Tager, I.B., Weiss, S.T., Munoz, A., Rosner, B. and Speizer, F.E. (1983) 'Longitudinal study of the effects of maternal smoking on pulmonary function in children'. *New England Journal of Medicine,* 309, 699–703.

Tanner, J.M., Hayashi, T., Preece, M.A. and Cameron, N. (1982) 'Increase in length of leg relative to trunk in Japanese children and adults from 1957 to 1977: comparison with British and with Japanese Americans'. *Annals of Human Biology,* 9, 411–23.

Taylor, B., Wadsworth, J., Wadsworth, M.E.J. and Peckham, C.S. (1984) 'Changes in the reported prevalence of childhood eczema since the 1939–45 war'. *Lancet,* ii, 1255–7.

Thomson, D. (1981) *England in the Twentieth Century.* London: Pelican.

Thurman, C.W. and Witheridge, J.R. (eds) (1994) *The Brewer's Society Statistical Handbook.* London: The Brewer's Society.

Tibbenham, A. (1977) 'Housing and truancy'. *New Society,* 39, 501–2.

Todd, G.F. (1975) *Changes in Smoking Patterns in the UK.* London: Tobacco Research Council.

Twomey, B. (2002) 'Women and the labour market, results from the spring 2001 LFS'. *Labour Market Trends,* March 2002, 110, 3, 109–27.

Udjus, L.G. (1964) *Anthropometrical Changes in Norwegian Men in the 20th Century.* Oslo: Universitetsforlaget.

Utting, D. (1995) *Family and Parenthood: Supporting families, preventing breakdown.* York: Joseph Rowntree Foundation.

van Os, J. and Jones, P.B. (1999) 'Early risk factors and adult person–environment relationships in affective disorder'. *Psychological Medicine*, 29, 1055–67.

Wadsworth, M.E.J. (1979) *Roots of Delinquency: Infancy, adolescence and crime.* Oxford: Martin Robertson; New York: Barnes and Noble.

Wadsworth, M.E.J. (1986) 'Serious illness in childhood and its association with later life achievements'. In R.G. Wilkinson (ed.), *Class and Health: Research and longitudinal data.* London: Tavistock.

Wadsworth, M.E.J. (1991) *The Imprint of Time: Childhood, history and adult life.* Oxford: Oxford University Press.

Wadsworth, M.E.J. (1996) 'Social and historical influences on parent-child relationships in midlife.' In C.D. Ryff and M.M. Seltzer (eds), *The Parental Experience in Midlife.* Chicago: University of Chicago Press.

Wadsworth, M.E.J. (1997) 'Changing social factors and their long-term implications for health'. In M. G. Marmot and M.E.J. Wadsworth (eds), *Fetal and Early Childhood Environment: Long-term health implications.* London: Royal Society of Medicine Press.

Wadsworth, M.E.J. (1999) 'Early life'. In M.G. Marmot and R.G. Wilkinson (eds), *Social Determinants of Health.* Oxford: Oxford University Press.

Wadsworth, M.E.J. (2002) 'Longitudinal research design.' In A. Jamieson and C. Victor (eds), *Researching Ageing and Later Life.* London: Open University Press.

Wadsworth, M.E.J. and Freeman, S.R. (1983) 'Generation differences in beliefs: a cohort study of stability and change in religious beliefs'. *British Journal of Sociology*, 34, 416–37.

Wadsworth, M.E.J. and Maclean, M. (1986) 'Parents' divorce and children's life chances'. *Children and Youth Services Review*, 8, 145–59.

Wadsworth, M.E.J., Cripps, H.A., Midwinter, R.A. and Colley, J.R.T. (1985) 'Blood pressure at age 36 years and social and familial factors, cigarette smoking and body mass in a national birth cohort'. *British Medical Journal*, 291, 1534–8.

Wadsworth, J., Burnell, I., Taylor, B. and Butler, N.R. (1985) 'The influence of family type on children's behaviour and development at five years'. *Journal of Child Psychology and Psychiatry*, 26, 245–54.

Wadsworth, M.E.J., Maclean, M., Kuh, D. and Rodgers, B. (1990) 'Children of divorced parents: a summary and review of findings from a national long-term follow-up study'. *Family Practice*, 7, 104–9.

Wadsworth, M.E.J., Mann, S.L. and Jones, E. (1993) 'Generation differences in in-patient care of children aged 1 to 5 years'. *Journal of Epidemiology and Community Health*, 47, 149–52.

Wadsworth, M.E.J., Montgomery, S.M., Cook, D.G. and Bartley, M.J. (1999) 'The persisting effect of unemployment in early working life on health and social well-being'. *Social Science and Medicine*, 48, 1491–9.

Wadsworth, M.E.J., Hardy, R.J., Paul, A.A., Marshall, S.F. and Cole, T.J. (2002) 'Leg and trunk length at 43 years in relation to childhood health, diet and family circumstances; evidence from the 1946 national birth cohort'. *International Journal of Epidemiology*, 31, 383–90.

Wald, N. and Nicolaides-Bouman, A. (1991) UK *Smoking Statistics*. Oxford: Oxford University Press.

Wald, N., Kiryluk, S., Darby, S., Doll, R., Pike, M. and Peto, R. (1988) *UK Smoking Statistics*. Oxford: Oxford University Press.

Walker, A. (1980) 'The handicapped school leaver and the transition to work'. *British Journal of Guidance and Counselling*, 8, 2, 212–23.

Ward, C., Dale, A. and Joshi, H. (1996) 'Combining employment with childcare: an escape from dependence?' *Journal of Social Policy*, 25, 2, 223–247.

Wedge, P.J. and Petzing, J. (1970) 'Housing for children'. *Housing Review*, 19, 165–6.

Wedge, P.J. and Prosser, H. (1973) *Born to Fail?* London: Arrow Books.

West, D.J. and Farrington, D.P. (1973) *Who Becomes Delinquent?* London: Heinemann.

West, D.J. and Farrington, D.P. (1977) *The Delinquent Way of Life*. London: Heinemann.

Widdowson, E.M. (1951) 'Mental contentment and physical growth'. *Lancet*, i, 1316–18.

Wilkinson, R. (1996) *The Afflictions of Inequality*. London: Routledge.

Williams, G.P. and Brake, G.T. (1980) *Drink in Britain 1900 to 1979*. London: Edsall.

Youth Survey (2000) *Research Conducted for the Youth Justice Board*. Mori. London: Youth Justice Board.